Citation Studies

A Performance Evaluation
Technique of LIS Scientists

Citation Studies

A Performance Evaluation Technique of LIS Scientists

Jyoti Gupta

Ess Ess Publications
New Delhi

Citation Studies
A Performance Evaluation Technique of LIS Scientists

ISBN: 978-81-7000-752-4

First Published 2015

Published by:
Ess Ess Publications
4831/24, Ansari Road,
Darya Ganj,
New Delhi-110 002.
INDIA
Phones: 23260807, 41563444
Fax: 41563334
E-mail: info@essessreference.com
www.essessreference.com

Cover Design by *Patch Creative Unit*

Printed and bound in India at Salasar Imaging Systems.

CONTENTS

ACKNOWLEDGEMENTS

I start by thanking the God Almighty.

It is a privilege to express my profound sense of gratitude to Prof.V. P. Khare, my venerable mentor for his incommensurable benevolence, fortitudinous and futuristic outlook, without which it would not have been possible for me to envisage and accomplish this task. He gave me a free-hand and provided timely suggestions and advice. I have learnt a lot from him during this work and shall always be grateful to him.

Sincere gratitude is the only thing I can offer to Dr. Vishal Vyas, who, with his keen sense of accuracy helped me to interpret the quasi statistical issues involved in this research. I extend my sincere thanks to Mr. Suresh Kumar who in spite of his busy schedule helped me with his constant support.

I am indebted to my respected teachers and mentors Prof. M.T.M. Khan, Dr. Sunil Kumar, Dr. Joginder Singh Burman and Dr.A.P.Singh . I also owe a debt of gratitude to the Librarians of Bundelkhand University, Jhansi, Jiwaji University, Gwalior and Dr. Harisingh Gour University, Sagar.

Besides those named, there are many people who have directly or indirectly helped me in getting this book to where it is. The librarians of various libraries, I have consulted, friends, colleagues, well the list is endless.

My heartfelt thanks for their encouragement and co-operation.

Words cannot express my indebthness to my parents, Guruji, brother, sister and all family members whose blessings made this book possible.

— Jyoti Gupta

PREFACE

Citation analysis is an established method of clustering documents and following paths between related documents. Citation analysis not only helps to find out highly cited authors, journals, books, trends of research etc., but also provides some relief to librarians and information centers for managing their budget. Thus, citation analysis is not only a study but has become a regular stream today. In the age of knowledge explosion, the process of selecting the appropriate and relevant literature becomes both critical and difficult. This book will be an indispensable tool in understanding the theoretical aspects and practical applications of bibliometric techniques for designing and information retrieval system, databases and collection development.

This book consists of eleven chapters. The first chapter 'Evolution of Library &Information Science' is a brief description of library & information science and chapter second, 'Growth of Doctoral Research in India' emphasizes on the research aspect in library & information science in India. Chapter on 'Citation Analysis and Citation Indexes' describes all possible aspects of citation, citation analysis, citation indexes, co-citations, bibliometric, bibliographic coupling, self-citation, impact factor, etc. Chapter 'Growth of Citation Study' covers several studies related to different areas of citation, bibliometrics and scientometrics. 'Citation

Analysis in Selected Universities' is based on the analysis and interpretation of selected universities. 'Ranking of Journals' deals with finding out core journals of the subject of LIS. Chapter 'Application of Bradford Law' tends to find out the core journals in selected universities and *Chi-Square Test for Goodness* is applied for further examination of the suitability of data. The bibliographies section is arranged according to API format in an alphanumerical system in order to avoid repetition.

It is hoped that this book shall go a long way in helping the reards grasp the subject in a much better way.

- Author

List of Abbreviations

DK	Denmark
PAK	Pakisthan
U.S.A.	United State of America
U.K.	United Kingdom
FRG	Federal Republic of Germany
E.Germany	East Germany
LIS	Library & Information Science
FID	International Federation of Documentation
ICT	Information and Communication Technology
UNISIST	United Nations International Scientific Information System
ICSU	International Council for Science
IFLA	International Federation of Library Associations and Institutions
INIS	International Nuclear Information System
AGRIS	International System for Agricultural Science and Technology
DEVSIS	Development of Science Information Systems
MEDLARS	Medical Literature Analysis and Retrieval System
NISCAIR	National Institute of Science Communication and Information Resources

SENDOC	Small Industry Extension Training Institute
DESIDOC	Défense Scientific Information & Documentation Centre
BLAISE	British Library Automated Information Service.
SDC	Staff Development Centre
SSDC,India	Social Science Documentation Centre, India
OCLC,USA	Online Computer Library Center
VINITI,USSR	Vsesoyuznyy Institut Nauchnoyi Tekhnicheskoy Informatsii All-Union Institute of Scientific and Technical Information
MARC	Machine Readable Cataloguing
UGC	University Grants Commission
ICSSR	Indian Council of Social Science Research
NCST	National Commission on Science and Technology
RRLF	Raja Ram Mohan Roy Library Foundation
DESIDOC	Defence Scientific Information and Documentation Centre
JRF	Junior Research Fellowship
IT	Information Technology
AIS	Associateship in Information Science
M.Phil.	Master of Philosophy
Ph.D.	Doctor of Philosophy
PGDLAN	Post Graduate Diploma in Library Automation & Networking
B.Lib.Sc. or B.LIS.	Bachelor of Library and Information Science
M Lib.Sc or M.LIS	Master of Library and Information Science
D. Litt.	Doctor of Letters

D.R.T.C.	Documentation Research & Training Centre
INSDOC	Indian National Scientific Documentation Centre
NASSDOC	National Social Science Documentation Centre
NISIET	National Institute of Small Industry Extension Training
AIU	Association of Indian Universities
C.L.I.Sc.	Certificate in Library and Information Science
MIM	Master in Information Management
NKC	National Knowledge Commission
NCL	National Commission of Libraries
CAS	Current Awareness Services
SDI	Selective Dissemination of Information
CDC	Committee in Library and Information Science
I.G.N.O.U.	Indira Gandhi National Open University
L.L.D.	Degree Doctor of Law
IF	Impact Factor
ISI	Institute for Scientific Information
CC	Current Content
SCI	Science Citation Index
ICRS	Index Chemicus Registry System
SSCI	Social Sciences Citation Index
JCR	Journal Citation reports
A&HCI	Arts & Humanities
OATS	Original Article Tera Sheet Services
WLW	Workshop on Wiswesser Line Notation
TIP	Technical Information Project
DIF	Discipline Impact Factor
GNP	Gross National Product

U.P.	Uttar Pradesh
M.P	Madhya Pradesh
SSCI	Social Science Citation Index
USPTO	United States Patent and Trademark Office
STEM	Science, Technology, Engineering, and Mathematics
NBD	Negative Binomial Distribution
ERIH	European Reference Index for the Humanities
JIAEE	The Journal of International Agricultural and Extension Education
NICED	National Institute of Cholera and Enteric Diseases
ICDDR, B	International Centre for Diarrhoeal Disease Research in Bangladesh
WoS	Web of Science
CSIC	Institute of Constructional Science Eduardo Torroja
OLEDs	Organic Light-Emitting Diodes
RGR	Relative Growth Rate
DT	Doubling Time
OM	Operations Management
MDS	Multi-Dimensional Scaling
ACA	Author Co-Citation Analysis
CAP	Complete Author Pair
IS	Information Science
OA	Open Access
ECIS	European Conference on IS
LLBA	Language andLinguistics Behavior Abstracts
UCSB	University of California at Santa Barbara
PESR	Pakistan Economic and Social Review

PDR	Pakistan Development Review
WAJE	West African Journal of Education
TIM	Technology Innovation Management
IMEC, Leuven Belgium	Interuniversity Centre for Micro-Electronics
NEERI	National Environmental Engineering Research Institute
MEDLINE	Medical Literature Analysis and Retrieval System Online
Excerpta	The Full Set of the Excerpta Medica Abstract
Medica	Journals contains forty-one printed current awareness journals, each devoted to a specific biomedical topic
ASLIB	Association of Special Libraries and. Information Bureaux
IASLIC	Indian association of Special Libraries and Information Centres
ILA	Indian Laser Association
Cum.	Cumulation
Fig.	Figure
NISSAT	National Information System for Science and Technology
ALA	American Library Association
UNESCO	United Nations Educational,Scientific and Cultural Organization
IBM	International Business Machine
IFLA	International Federation of Library Associations
IAALD	International Association of Agricultural Information Specialists
INFLIBNET	Information and Library Network

IEEE	Institute of Electrical and Electronics Engineers
IATUL	International Association of Technological University Libraries
AALD	Australian American Leadership Dialogue
ICSSR	Indian Council of Social Science Research
INSPEC	INSPEC is a major indexing database of scientific and technical literature, published by the Institution of Engineering and Technology (IET),
SLA	Special Library Association
INCAE	Instituto Centroamericano de Administracion de Empresas -Central American Institute of Business Administration -Nicaragua
DELNET	Developing Library Network
INICA	Insecticidas Internacionales

1

Evolution of Library & Information Science

1.1. INTRODUCTION

There are several developments taking place in Library & information science field and the librarians, should be aware of them and understand their significance and implications for their routine work[1]. In fact it is one of the most rapidly expanding disciplines and it is essentials for the librarians and library professionals to put in special efforts to be effective in their work and useful to the community they serve.

1.2. LIBRARY EARLY CONCEPT

At one time, a library was regarded as a store house and books were meant for preservation, the librarian was supposed to be a custodian, who did not encourage the use of books. The readers were expected to use the library on their own[2].At the most, if a reader asked for a book, then so called librarian would pass on the book and leave him alone. As for as possible a librarian kept out of 72 the way of the readers. Libraries tended to be passive and archival institution. Perhaps, there was not enough incentive for them to become dynamic[3].

1.3. LIBRARY SCIENCE

Modern scholars establish that library science is a perfect Science in its own right like other sciences. It has some fundamental principles which a modern science normally possesses. A science is considered as human knowledge reduced to a system or a study of natural laws and principles and forming a definite branch of human knowledge. Also it is defined as a systematized body of knowledge derived from observations, study and experimentation or a branch of knowledge especially concerned with establishing and systematizing facts, principles and methods.

On the basis of the above statement 'Librarianship' can also treated as a 'science'. To support this proposition the following definition is given. "Library Science is that branch of learning which has to do with recognition, collection, organization, preservation and utilization of graphical and printed records". In other words, it is the knowledge and skill concerned with administration of libraries and their contents; library economy and bibliography.

Among the modern library scientists, Melvil Dewey is regarded as the father of library science because he developed the concept of library science branch into a systematized and organized branch of human knowledge. In 1873 he formulated he Decimal scheme of library classification and in1887 he established the first school of library science.

The other eminent scientists who did pioneering work for the cause of Library Science were H.E. Bliss. WCR Sayers, E.E. Richardson, C.C. Jewett, C.A. Cutter. H. A. Sharp. Margarete Mann, E.A. Savage, J.C. Brown, S.R. Ranganthan, B.C. Vickery and many others. They formulated different schemes of classification and cataloguing codes based in the internationally accepted and recognized logical principles and thus they made everlasting contributions in transforming librarianship into a perfect science in its own right.

Like other vocational subjects, Library Science has different levels of education such as certificate, diploma, bachelor degree, Master degree M.Phil., Ph.D., D.Litt. Thus the standard of education in the field of Library Science is no less than in any other science. In addition to the conventional courses of reading, new topics such as reference services, information automation have been included in the courses of studies of library science education.

Beside the problems highlighted above there are many other problems which are equally frustrating. These relate to scattering of information in journals not related to the subject field in journals having not the remotest relation with them. All these problems make the library scientists to formulate the concept of documentation.

1.4. CONCEPT OF DOCUMENTATION

The word 'Documentation' has been derived from the word 'document'. In the restricted sense, as used by the historian, documentation is citation of written evidence in support of a statement, while according to liberal sense documentation covers all actions related to documents from identification to dissemination.

Paul Otlet, one of the founders of the International Institute of Bibliography, in Brussels, was perhaps the first person to use the term documentation to denote the specific activity of gathering, processing, storing retrieving and circulating document as early as in 1905. Later in 1934, he brought out his Traite de documentation, the first work in this new field and in 1937, the name of his Institute was changed to International Federation of Documentation (FID).

The term documentation is in use for quite some time now. In the seventies of the present century, it may be safely said, every educated person had some notion about the activities that go on under this label or even might have used some kind of documentation services either in pursuit of educational and research attainment or for taking decisions in carrying out governmental, legal, industrial, commercial and scientific activities. However, if a precise definition is asked for, even a documentation worker may fail to provide one.

It is certain that no two workers will define documentation in the same way. This is because there is no precise definition which would be acceptable to all. In fact the absence of such definition has resulted in the proliferation of definitions. The concept of documentation has also been changing over the years.

According to Ralph R. Show "documentation is any process connected with identification, recording, organization, storage, and recall, conversion into more useful forma, synthesis and dissemination of intellectual content of print or any other recorded materials". This indeed is a broad definition of the term documentation. The term documentation acquired a new dimension when ASLIB adopted the following definition in 1945 the Journal of Documentation, recording, or in other words, documentation means collecting organizing and providing micro thought to the scientists and research scholars. S.C.Bradford defined it as the "process by which is put before the creative specialist the existing literature bearing on his subject of investigation". J.H.Shera who defined documentation as the group of techniques necessary for the ordered presentation, organization and communication of recorded specialized knowledge in order to give maximum accessibility and utility to the information contained. S.R. Ranganathan clearly defined the scope of documentation when he defined it as Pinpointed, exhaustive and expeditious services of nascent micro thought to specialists. Thus according to him documentation lays stress on[4].

- Nascent thought, rather than on old thoughts,
- Micro document rather than on macro documents and
- Specialist reader rather than on generalist reader.

He also emphasized the need for pin-pointed, exhaustive and expeditious service as is required by the researchers and the specialists.

1.5. INFORMATION SCIENCE

The nature and scope of library professional has been increasing with the changing needs of information users. As such different nomenclatures were given from to time to time to denote the concept. The methodology and techniques for organization of though also changed with the technological advancements. The methods of selection, organization, analysis and dissemination of information are ever changing in order to improve the existing ones.

The search for an identify for information science continues unabated. Even though there are no two opinions regarding the importance of information to human society, both the concept of information and the science remain tangled in loosely defined terms, controversies, multitudinous opinions. In other words the profession lacks consensus in respect of its nature and scope. Despite the fact that the term 'Information Science' has come to stay with us in theory, practice and preaching it remains elusive. Educational institutions, throughout the world, offer educational programmes in information science and award degree in professionals style themselves as information scientists, still there is no definite answer to the questions what is information science?

Information science is not a discipline an independent of librarianship, but enlargement and improvement of library science which took place to ever increasing social needs of information and computer applications in information handling. As D.J.Fosket rightly said the "Information Science" is the discipline that is emerging from cross fertilization of ideas involving the ancient art of new media of communication Transfer of organized thought.

According to Russian scientist Mikhailow and others. It is in a way a continuation of bibliography and library science but the experience inherited by 'Information' from these branches of science is being subjected to complete reappraisal and appears in a new quality.

Almost simultaneously with the American developments a parallel situation was developing in the Soviet Union and other East European countries, due to the discrepancies of view existing in arriving at a uniform definition of information science. The term documentation was not very popular, so several scientists suggested alternative names such as documentastics, Documentlogy, Epistemology, Information and Documentation science, Informlogy, Social Epistemology and so on. Likewise the professionals working in Information Science field have been various designated as Information Scientists, Information Brokers, Technological Gatekeepers, Kingpins, Document lists and so on. The Russian scientists coined a new term informatics which was defined as the process, methods and laws related to the recording and analytical synthetically processing of scientific information but not the scientific information as such which is the attribute of a respective science of the discipline.

Having established itself in Russia, East Germany and several East European countries the term informatics is now finding favour in the english speaking countries also.

In order to provide need base information services

to their readers the librarians were adopting the mathematical and statistical applications to the Library and Information Science literature. This leads the emergence of Librametry.

Emergence of Librametry: In most cases the observation relating to library work and services ultimately involved large numbers. Handling of these numbers or observations become an important managerial activity. For effective handling the laws of statistical calculus started being applied to such studied. In the course of time this application needed a new name also. In the meantime S.R. Ranganathan coined the term 'Librametry' in 1948, at the ASLIB conference held at Hamington spa.

1.6. LIBRARY & INFORMATION SCIENCE IN INDIA

1.6.1. Pre-Independence Period

The history of library education in India began in 1911 in Baroda State. When W.A. Borden (1853-1931), an American disciple of Melvil Dewey, for the first time started a short term training programme in library science at Baroda The establishment of a library school in Braoda State was due to the efforts of His Highness the Maharaja Sayajrao III, Gaekwar of Baroda (1862-1939). He was an enlightened ruler, educationalist and library promoter. He invited "Williamn Alanson Borden (1853-1931), a leading American librarian, who had been a pupil assistant of Charles cutter at the Boston Athenaeum and a lectures associate of Melvil Dewey at Columbia University's School of Library Economy". Borden was responsible for organizing a free public library system in Baroda, Baroda State. He envisioned the system in needs of trained personnel. He taught the first class in the Baroda Central Library[5].

The "report on Public Instruction" for the year 1910-1911 claimed about the first class the "nowhere in

India has there been up to now a single library class attached to any of the libraries where young men and women could be trained in the most up-to-date requirements of Library Economy.

Four years later in 1915, another American student of Dewey, Don Dickinson (1876-1960), the then librarian of Punjab University, Lahore (now in Pakistan) started a three-month apprentice training programme for working librarians. Before independence, only five universities (Andhra, Banaras, Bombay, Calcutta and Madras) were offering the diploma course in library science.

1.6.2. Post-Independence Period

Following independence, a number of library schools were established in various states. Some are administered by university, or through their affiliated colleges in some states. Delhi was the first to create a separate department of library science; it established the Institute of Library Science in 1958, but it closed down in 1964. Delhi was also the first library school to be under the administrative control of a university. The directory of Library and Information School in India "contains information of about 93 schools and other institutions in India, offering training in Library and Information Science at various levels". There were sixty-six schools that offer a bachelor's degree in Library and Information Science thirty eight of which offer a master's degree in Library and Information Science and four of which offer a Matter of Philosophy degree in Library and Information Science. There were nineteen schools that offer a doctoral program in library in Library and Information Science. There were also three school offering correspondence courses for a bachelor's in Library and Information Science and other school are emerging for this purpose. After that seventy-eight universities offered bachelor's of Library and Information Science program. Forty universities offered this program through forty four institutes. Five universities offered master's of philosophy program, and forty universities have provision for a doctorate degree.

After independence, new colleges, universities, educational institutions and learned societies were emerging and the need for professionally qualified personnel to manage their libraries was realized. As a result, the number of library science schools started to increase. Library associations which exist at various places started providing training courses.

Dr. S.R. Ranganathan started a certificate course at Madras Library Association in 1929 which was taken over by the University of Madras, and in 1937 the course was converted into Postgraduate (PG) Diploma in Library Science. This was the first diploma programme in Library Science in India. University of Delhi was the first university to establish a full-fledged Department of Library Science just before independence in 1946, and started admitting students to the PG Diploma in 1947. In 1951, the diploma was changed to Master in Library Science (M.Lib.Sc). Later, between1956 to 1959, six new LIS departments were established (Mangla,1998,) at Aligarh Muslim University, M.S.University of Baroda, Nagpur University, Osmania University, Pune University and Vikram University. Since 1960s, the number of LIS departments established has continued to increase. During this period, several institutions played important role for the development of LIS education. University of Madras started her first PG Diploma in library science. University of Delhi contributed many first such as the starting of Master in Library Science in 1951; which in 1972, on account of a major course revision was renamed Master in Library and Information Science (MLIS). The department name was also changed to Department of Library & Information Science. The course on "Computer Applications in Libraries" was introduced for the first time in the MLIS programme in 1972. The M.Phil. programme started in 1978. The first Ph.D. was awarded to D B

Krishna Rao in 1957, under the guidance of Dr. Ranganathan. At that time it was the only university in the whole of the British Commonwealth conducting Ph.D. programme in LIS.

1.7. CONTRIBUTION OF DR. S. R. RANGANATHAN (1892-1972)

Ranganathan was one of the greatest Librarians of his time. He has been acknowledged as Father of Library Science and master architect of Library Movement in India. He was a pragmatic nationalist, a project strategist, master of details, an analytical thinker and a master library legislator. He created new ideas and techniques giving new dimensions to library science. He initiated library science education programmes on modern lines, research activities, profusely contributed to the development of this new subject and also stimulated a good number of young librarians to the growth of library science literature.

In 1930s, there existed no facilities in India for advance training in librarianship. So, the authorities of the Madras University decided to send Ranganathan to England for acquainting himself with modern library methods.

He made an intensive study of the organisation and administration of the various sections in different types of libraries in England. There he noticed the gap between the various practices followed in the libraries and the teaching of out moved subjects at the school of librarianship. This prepared the ground for his future work to lay foundation for a sound and systematic practice of library work be fitting to the contemporary needs of the Madras University Library. He returned home in July 1925 with an Honours Diploma in Librarianship and started the organization of the Madras University Library with great zeal.

He was not only noted the deficiencies in the working of the contemporary classification, cataloguing and administrative methods used in libraries, but also engaged his mind in thinking of improvement and their reorientation. He concentrated on improving the library, developing new methodology and techniques and a systematic theory and practice of library science.

As Ranganathan entered the library profession, he was always anxiously searching for the over-all basic principles that underlie all activities in the library. He adopted the Newtonian approach of what? Why? And How? In formulating the universal laws. Which governed the library activities, i.e. the acquisition of reading materials their organisation and service to the readers. He proceeded in a systematic manner on the basis of observation and experimentation. The data collected by him during his visit to hundreds of libraries in England were analysed, classified, correlated and through an inductive generalization empirical principles were formulated with the help of intuition to explain the observed facts. The scientific approach to library problems was explained through a "Spiral of Scientific Method". Proving "Library Science" as science. The five fundamental laws underlying this newly established science enunciated by Ranganathan in 1929 are given below:

1. Books are for use;
2. Every Reader his/her books;
3. Every book its reader;
4. Save the time of the reader;
5. Library is a growing organism;

These were first published in his famous book: "Five Laws of Library Science". One of his close associated and co-workless at madras university:

Five Laws of Library Science provided a frame work to explain and evaluate all library operations and to guide every area of the librarian's work. On the basis of these laws a prediction of likely development become possible. What so was for considered as a bundle of practices could be explained as a part of coherent system? "Ranganathan established that the subject of pursuit of the librarian is amenable for cultivation by the scientific method and, therefore, it is a science".

Five laws of library science were universally accepted as the library philosophy in India and abroad. "At numerous occasions librarians from different cultures are heard quating Ranganathan's "Laws of Library Science white resolving numerous problems". According to Siva Raman, publication of Five Laws of Library Science may be taken as a mark of "Renaissance in Library Science". He opined that this book is the progenitor of all other books on library science by Ranganathan and his associates, and it is a fact. Sayers the teacher of Ranganathan wrote about Five Laws of Library Science "a work of great simplicity which conceals depth and yet reveals what may be called spiritual intensely practical springs of his activity".

The President of India said that Five Laws of Library Science enunciated by Ranganathan have made great impact on the development of library thought in the world, elevating the study of library problems to the level of science. The arguments in detail in support of Library Science as a subject of scientific study have also been discussed by Ranganathan in his book "Preface to Library Science".

Although these statements might seem self-evident today, they certainly were not to librarians in the early part of this century. After all, the democratic library tradition we currently enjoy had arisen in America and England only in the latter part of the nineteenth century. Previously, many libraries restricted their services to paying subscribers from the moneyed classes. Often libraries served primarily a custodial function. The libraries of India, as a colony and a developing country, were hardly among the most progressive. In Ranganathan's day, they were usually associated only with universities and other academic institutions. There was no public library system as such. But even given a well-established public library system, the tendency toward bureaucratic entrenchment must always be guarded against. The five laws help ensure that libraries are service-oriented. For Ranganathan and UK followers, the five laws were a first step toward putting library work on a scientific basis. These laws provided general principles from which all library practices could be deduced. Thus, the first law books are for use leads naturally to a library system in which libraries are centrally located, open long hours, hospitably furnished and staffed by trained, service oriented, and adequately compensated workers. (Of course, the term "books" here stands for all information items.) The second law every reader his book dictates that libraries serve all readers, regardless of social class, sex, age, or any other factor. The third law every book its reader stipulates that a book exists for every reader, and that books should be well described in the catalogue, displayed in an attractive manner, and made readily available to readers. This law leads naturally to such practices as open access rather than closed stacks, a coherent shelf arrangement, an adequate catalogue, and a reference service. The fourth law save the time of the reader emphasizes efficient service, which implies an expeditious book-charging system and easy-to-understand guides to the stacks. This law has a corollary-save the time of the staffs which requires the use of those techniques and technology that enable the staff to perform most efficiently. The fifth law a library is a growing organism recognizes that growth will undoubtedly occur and must be planned for systematically. From the physical facilities to administrative practices, the library must be open-ended, always ready to expand.

Besides encouraging formulation of the five laws, Ranganathan's visit to England stimulated another important line of thought. The more he learned about the orthodox Anglo-American Library Classification systems, the more convinced he became that they were seriously flawed. Library classification is the systematic arrangement of documents by subject. As such, it may determine the arrangement of books on library shelves or of documents in an information retrieval system. However, in many libraries, particularly in Europe, classification determines only the order of the catalogue cards describing information items, rather than the physical arrangement of the items themselves. Ranganathan's objection to the prevailing classification systems, such as Dewey Decimal Classification and Library of Congress Classification, was that they tried to enumerate all possible subjects and provide preconceived pigeonholes to accommodate all documents[6]. But this enumerative approach made little allowance for the addition of new topics. Thus, these systems couldn't easily accommodate the explosion of knowledge occurring in the twentieth century. Of course, any new enumerative scheme that simply contemporary topic would itself be quickly outmoded. Rather, what Ranganathan sought was an entirely novel, more flexible, approach.

As so often happens in scientific discovery, this vague notion was fully conceptualized only with the help of an unlikely catalyst. For Isaac Newton, according to legend, the catalyst was a falling apple. For Fredrich Kekule, discoverer of the benzene ring, it was a snake with its tail in its mouth that appeared to him in a dream. For Ranganathan, it was a toy erector set at Self ridge's, the London department store. There he saw a salesperson create an entirely new toy with each new combination of metal strips, nuts, and bolts. The experience made Ranganathan realize that UK classification scheme should likewise consist of elements that could be freely combined to meet the needs of each specific subject. But this eureka experience in 1924 would require many years' gestation before it came to fruition. Not until 1933 did Ranganathan publish his first major work on the new classification system,

The Colon Classification since then has undergone several revisions. Its basic principles, however, require the *analysis* of a subject to determine its various aspects, called facets, and the *synthesis* of a class number (Call Number) from the numbers assigned in published schedules to different facets. Thus, Colon Classification is known as an *Analytico-Synthetic* Classification system. According to Bernard I. Palmer the major distinction between enumerative and analytico-synthetic classification is that "Enumerative Classification lists composite subjects, built up from a number of basic ideas. Facet classification lists the basic terms and leaves terms to the classifier." This frees the deviser of the classification scheme from the burden of specifying all conceivable subjects. By stringing together the appropriate facets, the classifier using Colon Classification can precisely specify new subjects as they arise. Therefore, in Colon Classification, a subject category with a ready-made class number never preexists without a document to occupy it. Actually, this feature, known as "literary warrant," is not unique to Colon Classification. Colon Classification shares this characteristic with the Library of Congress Classification system. Also, certain aspects of facet analysis and synthesis had been anticipated to some degree in Dewey Decimal Classifications and even more so in other classification systems, such as Universal Decimal Classification. Furthermore, as Phyllis Richmond, Baxter School of Information and Library Science, Case Western Reserve University, Cleveland, Ohio, pointed out the ideas of W.C. Berwick Sayers, Henry Evelyn Bliss, and Ernest Richardson further strengthened the foundation for facet theory of Library Classification.,

But Ranganathan was the first to fully explicate facet theory, and his work has had a major impact on modern classification schemes. In 1934, just as year after *The Colon Classification* came out Ranganathan is another important work entitled "The Classified Catalogue Code" This book grew out of Ranganathan's strong objection to the commonly used dictionary type catalogue. In the dictionary catalogue, subjects, authors, and titles are merely listed in alphabetic order. Ranganathan mentioned, however, that a catalogue should consist of two components. One part should be classified by subject, reflecting the Library's Classification system, with class number entries. The other should be a dictionary catalogue, including author, title, series, and similar identifiers, as well as alphabetized subject entries. The function of a catalogue is to itemize works so they can be found by author, title, series, and so forth. It must also allow readers to review the selection of works on a given subject. Traditionally, as a practical matter, the alphabetical catalogue was considered easiest for the ordinary reader to use. But Ranganathan thought that, although most readers are unfamiliar with classified systems, the alphabetized dictionary catalogue could be used to guide readers to the correct location in the classified catalogue. Once in the classified system, the reader would be exposed to the depth and breadth of material on the subject of interest. This would help to pinpoint the most relevant material.

To determine subject headings in alphabetical part of Classified Catalogue, Ranganathan devised an ingeniously simple method called *Chain Indexing* This method simply uses each facet of a subject, together with its immediately preceding facets, as an index entry. Thus, all important aspects of the subject, from the most general to the most specific, are automatically covered. Chain indexing can be adapted to other classification systems as well. The British National Bibliography used it in conjunction with its version of the Dewey Decimal Classification, from 1950 until 1971, when the Preserved Context Indexing System (PRECIS) substituted it. Although Ranganathan's works on classification and cataloguing are his most recognized contributions, but he published over 50 books and 1,000 papers on all aspects of library science. In addition, he founded and edited three periodicals: *Abgila,* the Indian Library Association *Annals, Bulletin,* and *Granthalaya* (the Hindi component of the journal); the *Annals of Library Science;* and *Library Science with a Slant to Documentation.* He also involved himself in every aspect of library work in India. In the course of his career, he was a member or chairman of more than 25 committees which addressed such issues as library, education of librarians, and library legislation.

In 1935, he published the first edition of his influential book, *Library Administration,* in which he broke down library work into approximately 1,000 component jobs. By precisely identifying many different library functions, he was able to simplify and streamline library routine. He also wrote extensively on the physical layout and furnishings of libraries. S.R. Ranganathan worked tirelessly to professionalize library education in India. One of his first achievements, in 1929, was to found a library school that was later incorporated into the University of Madras. He also instituted a Master of Library Science degree in 1948 and a doctoral program in 1950, both at the University of Delhi. These were the first higher degree programs in library science offered in India, and probably in any of the Commonwealth countries, Ranganathan greatly influenced the curricula and textbooks for such courses. In fact, a student of Ranganathan's, Asha Kaula, has stated, "In India, the advanced professional education is nothing but an interpretation of Dr. Ranganathan's ideas". Ranganathan's crowning accomplishment in library education was to found the Documentation Research and Training Centre at Bangalore, under the auspices of the Indian Statistical Institute. The centre is devoted solely to research and advanced training in documentation and information science. Ever since his return from England, Ranganathan had hoped to establish a Western-style network of public libraries throughout India. His first step toward achieving this end was to form the Madras Library Association in 1928, to promote development of public libraries in the state of Madras. He also drafted specific legislation to extend the public library system beyond the state of Madras into other areas of India. In 1950, he published an influential work detailing plans for a system of national, state, university, public, and school libraries for the entire country. As he told Pauline Atherton Cochrane, School of Information Studies, Syracuse University, New York, this plan was brought forward at the request of Indian government leaders whom Ranganathan helped during the struggle for independence from the U K. He brought these men books while they were in prison. Later, when they assumed responsible positions in the new Indian government, they came to him for advice on developing the nation's library system. Ranganathan held several important offices in India during his long career. He served as president of the Indian Library Association from 1944 to 1953 and as president of the Madras Library Association from 1958 to 1967. He also served as vice president of the Governing Council of the Indian Standards Institute from 1965 to 1972.

Dr. Ranganathan's Contributions to Library Science can be categorized as

1. Contribution to Library Classification.
2. Contribution to Library Cataloguing.
3. Contribution to Library Administration.
4. Contribution to Library Organization.
5. Contribution for the Development of Academic Libraries.

6. Contribution for the Development of Special Libraries and Documentation.
7. Contribution to Standardization.
8. Contribution to Library Science Education.
9. Contribution to the Development of Library Science Research and Literature.

1.8. ROLE OF UNIVERSITY GRANTS COMMISSION

Dr. C. D. Deshmukh[7] the first chairman of the University Grants was an excellent administrator, a scholar, lover of books and had the vision to sense the vital role of library service in higher education. In 1951 he appointed a Library Committee under the Chairmanship of Dr. S. R. Ranganathan to look into the conditions of academic libraries. This was the first attempt by any Library Committee in India to systematically survey academic libraries on a national basis. The conclusion of the committee in its final report, submitted in 1959, was that the plight of libraries was far from happy. Libraries were ill equipped and inadequate. The Committee's recommendations include open access for readers; more professional staff; encouragement of inter library loan; purchase of reproduction equipment for copying books, journals and microforms; quality collections development and reference service; better library buildings and hiring of full-time teaching faculty in library schools. The Committee also recommended that the qualification of professional librarians be equal to those of the teaching faculty and strongly emphasized that librarians should be recognized as equals of the teaching faculty in status and play scales. Another recommendation was to open more library schools and train more professional librarians[8].

The Library Committee on the advice of the University Grants Commission prepared a set of standards for library buildings and furniture, book selection ordering of books and qualifications of professional librarians for different ranks, and their pay scales. It was a monumental document, and the University Grants Commission accepted all proposed standards and recommendations of the Committee. The acceptance of (theses) recommendations have cleared a great obstacle in the way of library development. It was now easier for those University Libraries whose authorities were resultant to initiate a programme of reform or development to point out the norms accepted by the University Grants Commission and their willingness to help.

1.9. INFORMATION EXPLOSION

Katz reports that the invention of printing in the mid-15th century, the wide distribution of books by the 16th century, the growth of literacy among the middle classes in the 17th and 18th centuries, and the 19th century's mass education movement increased both the amount and the demand for information. The rapid development of information technology, electronic media and especially the Internet, has contributed immensely to the information explosion. Information and communication technology (ICT) has played a pivotal role for the emergence of information explosion. The ability to create and share information and knowledge is literally at our finger tips. The information explosion in a way is a never ending circle[9].

Information embodied in documents is a great national and international resource. Scientific and technological knowledge has been expanding at a terrific speed. The headings in professional journals "Information Explosion"; "The Flood of Literature"; "The Rising Information Tide" and "How to Cope with Literature" are some of the phrases that partly identify this problem.

In order to appreciate the role of the library in the dissemination of information it is better first to know what we term as information explosion. The nascent information is usually communicated through the medium of the periodicals and the research reports. Several attempts have been made to estimate the number of periodicals being published in science and technology.

The impact of this explosion of micro-documents has been estimated. A scientist can read technical literature at the rate of 200 to 300 words per minute. The following statements taken from various websites and articles assert this reality:

- As much new information will be available in the next decade as has been discovered in the whole human history.
- It is estimated that it would take seven centuries to read a year's chemical literature.
- There are 550 billion web-connected documents.
- Fifty thousand new book titles appear annually, with 1.5 million books now in print from 20,000 different publishers.
- People could read 24 hours per day, 365 days per year and never catch up with what is written.
- Almost 800mb of new recorded information is produced per person each year. It would take about 30 feet of books to store the equivalent of 800mb of information on paper.

Around 1,000 books (beside journals) are published internationally every day and that the total of all printed knowledge doubles every five years. More information is estimated to have been produced in the last 30 years than in the previous 5,000. The size of the internet, the world wide web in particular, often illustrates the information at the disposal of library users today.

Clearly the problem is out of hand and has been for a long time; as for the scientist is concreted, the end of century could not bring a worse situation.

By studying the attributes of the information explosion, it is easily realized:

1. That a scheme for classification and the methodology for its development were in adequate to meet the state of universe of ideas a few decades back[10].
2. Today, a methodology for the development of scheme for classification is likely to become inadequate and obsolete at a much faster rate.
3. Methods should be developed to overcome such a quick obsolescence of the design methodology.

The explosion of information has also led to its storage and retrieval through international agencies like UNISIST, ICSU, IFLA, and international information system and services like INIS, AGRIS, DEVSIS, INSPEC, MEDLARS, and SPINES; and through national agencies like NISCAIR, SENDOC, DESIDOC, NISSAT, SSDC (India); BLAISE, INFOLINE, EURONET (U.K.) : LOCKHEED, SDC, OCLC, (USA), and VINITI (USSR).

Similarly, indexing and abstracting services like MARC, INDEX MEDICUS, etc. have flourished. Every agency or research institution is equipped with a library serving as an information bureau.

1.10. FACTORS FOR THE GROWTH OF LIBRARY SCIENCE

The following are factors for the growth of libraries:

- Political and social stability of the society.
- High standard of living.
- High rate of literacy.
- Local and national traditions.
- Encouragement from the local, state and national governments.
- Influence of leading individuals.
- Well established book trade.

- Existence of large chunks of urban population.

From the above, it should be clear that social, political and economic conditions play an important role in the growth and development of libraries.

1.11. THE PRESENT STATUS

Over a period of time, LIS has grown and developed into a full-fledged discipline; courses are being imparted by university departments, institutions, library associations and specialized institutions. About 123 universities in India are engaged in imparting LIS education. The number of universities (including distance education) offering LIS programmes is as follows: 91 universities are offering bachelor's degree, 73 are offering master's degree, 25 universities are offering M.Phil. degree, and 95 are offering Ph.D. degree. In addition, NISCAIR (formerly INSDOC), New Delhi and DRTC, Bangalore are offering a two-year Associateship in Information Science, which is recognized by some universities as equivalent to Master's degree. India maintains its Third World leadership in library research in library education and literature. The University Grants Commission (UGC) and Indian Council of Social Science Research (ICSSR) are promoting LIS research programmes by awarding scholarships to doctoral students. The National Commission on Science and Technology (NCST), New Delhi, Raja Ram Mohan Roy Library Foundation (RRLF), Calcutta, and ICSSR are also providing research grants for non-doctoral research. The Defence Scientific Information and Documentation Centre (DESIDOC), Delhi, provides Junior Research Fellowship (JRF) in LIS.

The LIS education aims at providing trained manpower to manage different types of libraries, information and documentation centres which, over a period of time have undergone changes in terms of needs, functions, types and range of services offered, as well as tools and techniques being used when offering the services. Application of information and communication technologies has revolutionized the whole concept of libraries, the system of information storage and retrieval and ways to access the information. Therefore, the objectives of LIS education also need to be redefined. The students need to be more practical oriented and should be equipped with intensive and extensive knowledge on the use of IT in libraries. Application of technology has opened up new vistas and thus, all LIS schools should think seriously in terms of the changing context. Students need to be given adequate knowledge of computers (including hardware), computer and communication technologies, networks and networking, operating systems, Internet concepts, database management systems, with adequate practical exposure to handle these technological devices.

1.12. COURSES AVAILABLE IN LIBRARY& INFORMATION SCIENCE EDUCATION

The LIS education in India is offered at various levels such as certificate, diploma, and degree, Associateship in Information Science (AIS), M.Phil. and Ph.D. These programmes are offered on regular basis as well as through correspondence courses or distance education. Details about the types of courses are as follows[11].

1. Certificate Course : Certificate courses are mainly conducted by library associations; however, some departments in universities and affiliated colleges are also conducting this course. The duration of the course varies from few months to one academic year. The courses aim to train the students for semi-professional or junior level jobs after high school or senior secondary education. The certificate holders may be useful in the following fields:

i. ICT Application in Libraries

ii. IT enabled Services

iii. Librarianship

iv. Library & Information Science

2. Undergraduate Diploma Course : The Diploma courses are conducted at two levels that are undergraduate and postgraduate levels. Undergraduate courses are conducted by women polytechnics as a two-year course after higher secondary or intermediate. It prepares students to be junior librarian and hold library assistant positions.

3. Postgraduate (PG) : Diploma Course PG courses in some selected LIS areas of specialization are offered at the university level as a one-year course after the Bachelor of Library and Information Science programme.

- PGDLAN (Post Graduate Diploma in Library Automation & Networking)
- Diploma in Library Automation
- Diploma in Library Science /Information Science.

4. B.Lib.Sc. or B.LIS.

5. M.Lib.Sc. or M.LIS.

6. M.Phil.

7. Ph.D. (Doctorate in Philosophy)

8. D. Litt.

Associateship Courses

To provide advanced training in documentation and reprography, D.R.T.C. and INSDOC have started 'Associateship' courses. The Associateship award is considered equivalent to M.L.I.S. degree. National Social Science Documentation Centre (NASSDOC), New Delhi, once proposed to start Associateship Course from 1988 but later on the proposal was dropped.

Refresher Courses

In service training courses, known as refresher courses, short courses, workshops, demonstrations etc., on various library aspects like computer application, machine assisted indexing techniques, information management, preservation of materials, etc., are now being conducted. The promoters are library associations teaching departments/institutes, libraries and information centre, etc. University Grants Commission (U. G .C.), New Delhi also provides funds for this to the university departments. National Institute of Small Industry Extension Training (NISIET), Hyderabad conducts short terms intensive training programmes in specialized field of librarianship not only for Indian Students but also for students from other developing countries. NASSDOC had also decided to take up short term programmes at regular level. The first such Programme was conducted on "Management Information System in Library and Documentation Centres" from 11-18 May1987 at New Delhi There is ,however, need to seriously consider varying opinions expressed by scholars about such courses-To quote one" " The most important positive aspect is, that it updates the knowledge and competencies of practicing professionals..... The most negative aspect is the relative shallowness of offerings (mostly because of time constraints) and relative lack of commitment or pressure for learning by participants.

Accreditation of Courses

There is no accreditation agency in India like American Library Association, Committee on Accreditation in United States to ensure reasonable standards and quality of output. The Report of the Committee on National Policy on Library and Information System has stressed the need for such a body.

So far departments of LIS in the universities have broadly adopted the scheme of papers recommended by UGC Review Committee on Library Science in Indian Universities. But its other recommendations regarding staff requirement, physical facilities required, and maintenance of department libraries have not been faithfully followed. The Review Committee considered a minimum staff of one reader and two lecturers for BLIS course. Few universities, who have introduced these courses, have provided full strength of recommended staff. The situation is indifferent in case of other recommendations.

Regarding composition of 'Accreditation Committees', some professionals have suggested that it should consist of representatives from UGC, Association of Indian Universities (AIU), and Library Associations. But how far it will succeed in enforcing standards and quality of output in our educational system is a question mark and will require serious consideration. It is better not to have an agency rather than to have a redundant one.

1.13 LIST OF UNIVERSITIES PROVIDING LIS COURSE THROUGH REGULAR/DISTANCE MODE

The details of the latest status of Library and Information Science courses (Regular and Distance) in Indian Universities are given below:[12]

S. No.	University	Place	State	BLIS	MLIS	M. Phil.	Ph. D.
1	*Alagappa Uni.	Karaikudi	Tamil Nadu	Y	Y	Y	Y
2	Aligarh Muslim Uni.	Aligarh	UP	Y	Y	-	Y
3	Amravati Uni.	Amravati	Maharashtra	Y	Y	-	Y
4	Andhra Uni., Waltair	Visakha patnam	Andhra Pradesh	Y	Y	-	Y
6	**Annamalai Uni.**	Annamalainagar	Tamil Nadu	-	-	-	Y
7	**Annamalai Uni.	Annamalainagar	Tamilnadu	Y	Y	Y	Y
8	***Awadesh Pratap Singh Uni.**	Rewa	Madhya Pradesh	Y	Y	-	Y
10	Babasaheb Bhimrao Ambedkar Uni.	Lucknow	Uttar Pradesh	2yr. Course	Y	-	Y
11	Banaras Hindu Uni.	Varanasi	Uttar Pradesh	Y	-	D.Litt.	Y
12	Bangalore Uni.	Bangalore	Karnataka	Y	Y	-	Y
13	*Barkatullah Uni.	Bhopal	Madhya Pradesh	Y	Y	-	Y
14	Berhampur Uni.	Berhampur	Orissa	-	-	-	Y

S. No.	University	Place	State	BLIS	MLIS	M. Phil.	Ph. D.
15	**Berhampur Uni.	Berhampore	Orissa	Y	Y	Y	Y
16	Bhagalpur Uni.	Bhagalpur	Bihar	-	-	-	Y
17	*Bharathidasan Uni.	Tiruchirapalli	TamilNadu	Y	Y	Y	Y
18	Bharati Vidyapeeth	Pune	Maharashtra	Y	-	-	-
19	Bhavnagar Uni.	Bhavnagar	Gujarat	Y	-	-	-
20	Birla Institute of Technology	Ranchi	Jharkhand	M.Sc. Inf.Sc.	Y	-	Y
21	Bundelkhand Uni.	Jhansi	Uttar Pradesh	Y	Y	Y	Y
22	Calcutta Uni.	Kolkata	West Bengal	Y	Y	Y	Y
23	**Calicut Uni.	Calicut	Kerala	Y	Y	-	Y
24	Cochin Uni. of S & T	Ernakulum	Kerala	-	-	-	Y
25	*Dr. B.R. Ambedkar Open Uni.	Hyderabad	Andhra Pradesh	Y	Y	-	-
26	Dr. Babasaheb Ambedkar Marathwada Uni.	Aurangabad	Maharashtra	Y	Y	-	-
27	Dr. Bhimrao Ambedkar Uni.	Agra	Uttar Pradesh	Y	Y	-	Y
28	**Dr.Harisingh Gour Vishwavidyalaya	Sagar	Madhya Pradesh	Y	Y	-	Y
29	G. N. D. Uni.	Amritsar	Punjab	-	-	-	Y
30	Gandhigram Rural Institute	Gandhigram	Tamil Nadu	Y	Y	-	-
31	Gauhati University	Guwahati	Assam	Y	Y	-	Y
33	Gujarat University	Ahmedabad	Gujarat	Y	Y	-	Y
34	Gujarat Vidyapeeth	Ahmedabad	Gujarat	Y	Y	Y	Y
35	Gulbarga University	Gulbarga	Karnataka	Y	Y	Y	Y
37	**Guru Ghasidas Uni.	Bilaspur	Chhattisgarh	Y	Y	-	Y
38	Guru Nanak Dev Uni.	Amritsar	Punjab	Y	Y	-	Y
39	H. N. Gujarat Uni.	Patan	Gujarat	-	-	-	Y
40	*Hyderabad Uni.	Hyderabad	Andhra Pradesh	Y	-	-	-
41	Indian Inst.of Tech, Delhi	Delhi	New Delhi	-	-	-	Y
42	*Indira Gandhi National Open Uni.	New Delhi	New Delhi	Y	Y	Y	Y
43	Jadavpur Uni.	Kolkata	West Bengal	Y	Y	-	Y
44	Jai Narain Vyas Uni.	Jodhpur	Rajasthan	Y	-	-	-
45	Jamia Milia Islamia	New Delhi	Delhi	Y	-	-	-
46	Jammu Uni.	Jammu	Jammu & Kashmir	-	-	-	Y
47	Jawaharlal Nehru Uni.	New Delhi	New Delhi	Y	Y	Y	Y
48	Jiwaji Uni.	Gwaliar	Madhya Pradesh	Y	Y	Y	Y

S. No.	University	Place	State	BLIS	MLIS	M. Phil.	Ph. D.
49	*Kakatiya Uni.	Warangal	Andhra Pradesh	Y	-	-	-
50	Kalyani Uni.	Kalyani	West Bengal	Y	Y	-	Y
51	Karnatak Uni.	Dharwad	Karnataka	Y	Y	-	Y
52	*Karnataka State Open Uni.	Mysore	Karnataka	Y	-	-	-
53	Karnataka Uni.	Dharwad	Karnataka	-	-	-	Y
54	Kerala Uni.	Thiruvananthapuram	Kerala	Y	Y	Y	Y
56	**Kurukshetra Uni.	Kurukshetra	Haryana	Y	Y	-	Y
57	Kuvempu Uni.	Shimoga	Karnataka	Y	Y	-	Y
58	Lalit Narayan Mithila Uni.	Darbhanga	Bihar	Y	-	-	Y
59	M. C. R. P. Viswavidyalaya, Bhopal	Bhopal	Madhya Pradesh	Y	Y	-	-
60	M. D. Uni.	Ajmer	Rajasthan	Y	Y	-	Y
61	M. K. Uni.	Madurai	Tamil Nadu	-	-	-	Y
62	M. S. Uni.	Udaipur	Rajasthan	-	-	-	Y
63	M.S. Uni. of Baroda	Baroda	Gujarat	Y	Y	-	Y
64	**Madurai Kamraj Uni.	Madurai	Tamil Nadu	Y	Y	-	Y
65	Maharastra Uni., Anandavalli	Anandavalli	Maharastra	-	-	-	Y
66	**Mahatma Gandhi Gramodaya Vishwavidyalaya	Chitrakoot	Madhya Pradesh	Y	Y	-	Y
67	Mahatma Gandhi Kashi Vidyapeeth	Varanasi	Uttar Pradesh	Y	-	-	-
68	Mangalore Uni.	Mangalore	Karnataka	Y	Y	-	Y
69	Manipur Uni.	Imphal	Manipur	Y	-	-	-
70	Mohanlal Sukhadia Uni.	Udaipur	Rajasthan	Y	-	-	-
71	Nagpur Uni.	Nagpur	Maharashtra	Y	Y	Y	Y
72	North Bengal Uni.	Siliguri	West Bengal	Y	-	-	-
73	North Eastern Hill Uni.	Shillong	Meghalaya	Y	Y	-	Y
74	North Gujarat Uni.	Patan	Gujarat	Y	Y	-	-
75	North Maharashtra Uni.	Jalgaon	Maharashtra	Y	-	-	-
76	Orissa Uni. of Agri. S & T.	Bhubaneswar	Orissa	-	-	-	Y
77	Osmania Uni.	Hyderabad	Andhra Pradesh	Y	Y	Y	Y
78	Panjab Uni.	Chandigarh	Chandigarh	Y	Y	-	Y
79	Pt. Ravishankar Shukla Uni.	Raipur	Madhya Pradesh	Y	Y	-	Y
80	Punjab Agricultural Uni.	Ludhiana	Punjab	-	-	-	Y

S. No.	University	Place	State	BLIS	MLIS	M. Phil.	Ph. D.
81	Punjab Uni.	Chandigarh	Punjab	-	-	-	Y
82	Punjabi Uni.	Patiala	Punjab	Y	Y	-	Y
83	R. T. M. Nagpur Uni.	Nagpur	Maharashtra	Y	Y	-	Y
84	Rabindra Bharati Uni.	Kolkata	West Bengal	Y	-	-	Y
85	Rajasthan Agri.Uni.	Bikaner	Rajasthan	-	-	-	Y
86	Ranchi Uni.	Ranchi	Jharkhand	-	-	-	Y
87	Rani Durgavati Vishwavidyalaya	Jabalpur	Madhya Pradesh	Y	-	-	-
88	S.G.B.Amravati Uni.	Amaravati	Maharashtra	-	-	-	Y
89	S.P.M.Visvavidyalaya	Tirupati	Andhra Pradesh	-	-	-	Y
90	S.R.T.Marathwada Uni.	Nanded	Maharashtra	-	-	-	Y
91	S.V. Uni.	Tirupati	Andhra Pradesh	-	-	-	Y
92	S.K. Uni.	Anantpur	Andhra Pradesh	-	-	-	Y
93	S.N.D.T Women's Uni.	Mumbai	Maharashtra	Y	Y	-	-
94	Sambalpur Uni.	Sambalpur	Orissa	Y	Y	Y	Y
95	Sampurnanand Sanskrit Vishwavidyalaya	Varanasi	Uttar Pradesh	Y	-	-	-
96	Sardar Patel Uni.	Vallabh, Vidyanagar	Gujarat	Y	Y	Y	Y
97	Saurashtra Uni.	Rajkot	Gujarat	Y	-	-	-
98	Shivaji Uni.	Kolhapur	Maharashtra	Y	Y	Y	Y
99	South Gujarat Uni.	Surat	Gujarat	Y	Y	Y	Y
100	Sri Krishnadevaraya Uni.	Anantapur	Andhra Pradesh	Y	Y	Y	Y
101	**Sri Venkateswara Uni.	Tirupati	Andhra Pradesh	Y	Y	Y	Y
102	Swami Ramanand TeerthMarathwada Uni.	Nanded	Maharashtra	Y	Y	-	Y
103	Tilak Maharashtra Vidyapeeth	Pune	Maharashtra	Y	Y	-	-
104	Tilak Manjhi Bhagalpur Uni.	Bhagalpur	Bihar	Y	Y	-	Y
105	University of Burdwan	Bardhaman	West Bengal	Y	Y	-	Y
106	Uni. of Calicut	Kochi	Kerala	-	-	-	Y
107	Uni. of Delhi, Delhi	Delhi	Delhi	Y	Y	Y	Y
108	Uni. of Jammu	Jammu	Jammu and Kashmir	Y	Y	-	Y
109	Uni. of Kashmir	Srinagar	Jammu and Kashmir	Y	Y	Y	Y
110	Uni. of Kolkata	Kolkata	West Bengal	-	-	-	Y
111	Uni. of Lucknow	Lucknow	Uttar Pradesh	Y	Y	-	Y
112	Uni. of Madras	Chennai	Tamil Nadu	Y	Y	-	Y
113	Uni. of Mumbai	Mumbai	Maharashtra	Y	Y	-	Y

S. No.	University	Place	State	BLIS	MLIS	M. Phil.	Ph. D.
114	Uni. of Mysore	Mysore	Karnataka	Y	Y	-	Y
115	**Uni. of Patna	Patna	Bihar	Y	-	-	Y
116	Uni. of Pune	Pune	Maharashtra	Y	Y	Y	Y
117	Uni. of Rajasthan,	Jaipur	Rajasthan	Y	Y	-	Y
118	Utkal Uni.y	Bhubaneswar	Orissa	Y	Y	-	Y
119	Vardhaman Mahaveer Open Uni.	Kota	Rajasthan	Y	Y	Y	Y
120	Vidhyasagar Uni.	Vidyasagar	West Bengal	-	-	-	Y
121	Vidyasagar Uni.	Midnapore	West Bengal	Y	Y		Y
122	Vikram Uni.	Ujjain	Madhya Pradesh	Y	Y	Y	Y
123	*Yashwantrao Chavan Maharashtra Open Uni.	Pune	Maharashtra	Y	-	-	-
				91	**73**	**25**	**95**

**These universities provide LIS education through both regular and distance modes.

*These universities provide LIS education through distance modes.

1.14. CURRENT TRENDS IN LIBRARY & INFORMATION SCIENCE EDUCATION IN INDIA

Technology has become an integral part of LIS education in India. Particularly from the last decade of 20th century, the majority of LIS schools in India started offering courses on computer applications and preparing their students for the electronic information environment. There is a growth of Distance Education Programme in LIS which are being conducted by various universities of India. As we find from a report published by the Association of Indian Universities (AIU) in 1997 that 5 universities offer Certificate in Library and Information Science (C.L.I.Sc.), 5 Diploma in Library and Information Science (D.L.I.Sc.), 15 Bachelor of Library and Information Science (B.L.I.Sc.) and 13 Master's in Library and Information Science (M.L.I.Sc.) 4 M.Phil. and 12 Ph.D. in Library and Information Science through distance mode of education[13].

As far as curriculum content is concerned, LIS education today not only includes specific library based subjects like classification, cataloguing, reference service etc., but also some related areas like computer application, statistics, information science management studies and operation research. Various departments are now offering parallel courses like Master in Information Management (MIM), P G Diploma in Digital Libraries, courses in Health Sciences Librarianship etc. M.Phil. Courses in LIS are introduced in different universities either in formal or in distance mode. Some of these are self-financing courses where several working librarians are also participating.

Research Methods used in Doctoral research has gone through several changes during last fifty years or so. Researchers of present days are using variety of research methods including bibliometrics, content analysis, and experimental research comparative studies between traditional and web-based courses and methodology of design, development and delivery of web-based learning resources are the emerging area of research.

Library schools are emerging as full- fledged Departments with full time heads and full time teachers along with computer laboratories. Two years integrated Master of Library and Information Sciences is offered in some of the LIS schools. A few are having separate B.L.I.Sc and M.L.I.Sc. courses.

The establishment of National Knowledge Commission (NKC) by Govt. of India in 2005 is undoubtedly helping the library and information professionals of our country. It has recommended setting up of a National Commission of Libraries (NCL).

Faculty members are increasingly getting involved in taking courses in IT and also attending seminars and conferences on IT. Most of the faculty members are having Ph.D. in LIS those who do not have a Ph.D. are working towards it.

Students are getting greater exposure towards information technology. Some of the present days students have expertise in computer application. This definitely helps the LIS departments. In the near future a day will come when each and every student will have his/her laptop as an essential tool for his/her learning.

Side by side, when we look by the services provided by the libraries in India, we find most of the libraries are switching over from traditional type of services, (such as documentation services, reference services, inter-library loan, catalogue based services, current awareness services (CAS) and selective dissemination of Information (SDI) services) to online and e-generated library services. Application of information and communication technology has revolutionized the whole environment of Indian libraries and information centres.

1.15. REFERENCES

1. Krishan Kumar. (1999). *Library Organization.* New Delhi: Vikash Publication House.
2. Patel, Jashu. & Krishan Kumar.(2008).*Libraries and Librarianship in India.* London: Green wood Press.
3. Gul, Sumeer.,& Khan, Samina. (1999).*Growth and Development of Oriental Libraries in India.*Library Philosophy and Practice Delhi: A.P.H. Publication Corporation.
4. Kannappanava, B.U. (1991). *Citation Analysis of doctoral dissertations in Library and Information Science accepted by the universities in Karnataka.* (Doctoral dissertation. Karnataka University, Karnataka. 2001).
5. Kumar, P.S.G. (2004). *Festschrift: Library and Information Profession in India.* (Vol.1.). Delhi: B.R. Publication.
6. Kawatra, P.S. (2008).*Textbook of Information Science.* New Delhi: APH Publishing Corporation.
7. Ghai, Daljit. (2001). Citation analysis of Ph.D dissertations in Library and Information Science submitted to the Universities of Madhya Pradesh &Punjab. (Doctoral dissertation, Jiwaji University, Gwalior, 2001).
8. Satija, M.P. (1999).Doctoral Research in Library and

Information Science in India: Some Observations and Comments. *Libri, 49,* 236–242. Retrieved from www.librijournal.org/pdf/1999-4pp236-242.pdf

9. Jungwirth, B. (2002). Information overload: Threat or opportunity. *Journal of Adolescent & Adult Literacy, 45*(5), 90-91.
10. Katz, W. A. (2002). *Introduction to reference work.* New York: McGraw-Hill.
11. Chakraborty, Susmita.& Sarkhel, J. K. (2009, August 23-27). *LIS Education in India: An Appraisal* of the Parity between the Syllabus and the Market Demands. Conference on World Library and Information Congress: 75th IFLA General Conference and Council, Italy: Milan. Retrived August 23, 2010 from www.translendium.net:8080/.../url.do?... ENGLISH...://conference.ifla/
12. Dutta, Bidyarthi & Das, Anup Kumar. (2001). Higher Education in Library &Information Science in India. *LA Bulletin, 37(1),* 25-30.
13. Dasgupta, Arjun. (2009, August 23-27).*Preparing Future Librarians in India: A Vision for LIS Schools of Indian Universities in the 21st Century.* Paper at the conference on World Library and Information Congress: 75th IFLA General Conference and Council. Information Congress: 75th IFLA General Conference and Council. Italy: Milan. Retrieved August 23, 2010, from www.ifla.org/files/hq/papers/ifla75/126-dasgupta-en.pdf.

2
Growth of Doctoral Research in India

2.1. INTRODUCTION

Research is a creative activity aiming at realizing insights, whether it is Science and Technology or Arts/ Social Sciences. It arises out of curiosity or sheer necessity. It is a systematic inquiry by objective methods. Novelty is at the heart of this activity and objectivity is the basic rule. Research is universal and democratic, not individualistic, subjective. Discovery and dissemination of new ideas/ knowledge has always been the source of excitement and offers unimaginable social benefit to the society[1].The rapid advances and spectacular achievements in many fields of human endeavor in the 20th century and after are only due to the results of extensive organized activity called 'Research' The aim of any research is to solve some of the practical problems or to know the unknown. It is the only way to constantly add to the fund of reliable knowledge- knowledge which is considered as power. Human beings are inborn curious beings and power seekers. The innate curiosity to know the unknown and control the surroundings for survival and to make life comfortable in the society has led to continue research. Library and Information Science is not an exception to this phenomenon. From in-formation on clay tablets to electronic form of information is the result of such curious activity called research.

There is always a horizon in research. Every profession puts its best brains to do research. Researchers are always on the forefront of profession and impact on the new directions and dimensions. S.R. Ranganathan firmly believed that research is necessary for well-being of humanity and peaceful co-existence of nations. Investment in research yields rich dividends. Planned and highly organized research has become the order of the day. Every government dedicated to democracy and social welfare not only encourages research but also finance it adequately without undue interference regarding the results. In the information society research has acquired a new space and dimension, researchers are the creators and information professionals are the facilitators of an information society. Research results (True) always help in the growth of intellect, solving professional problems, sharing of new information and improvement of professional traits and accumulation of new knowledge. The fast changing environment fuelled by technology has caused a paradigm shift in the library and information science profession. While the traditional roles of the library and information professionals in providing access to information continues to be important, the responsibilities of this group have extended beyond providing just access to helping in utilizing information in the right context at the right time.

But now the libraries have to provide information in all forms, at all-time and at all places. To realize the end research is inevitable. Doctoral research/degrees were a very stringent program up till 1980's. A very few people opted because of the rigorous procedures and standards. Later standards and procedures started melting down with proliferation of a number of educational institutions and autonomy of these institutions.

Realistically speaking Ph.D. programs have become an extended training program in acquiring attitude and learning the tools and methodology of research. The root of LIS research in general is a century old. India in particular has half a century history starting from 1950's.

2.2. RESEARCH IN LIBRARY & INFORMATION SCIENCE

The research in LIS in the past was considered primarily to provide a theoretical foundation to professional practice. The roots of research in LIS profession appears to be not very deep. Research in library science during the twentieth century in the areas of LIS can be traced to the Library School of the University of Chicago, in mid-1920s. The visionary efforts of the Chicago School bore abundant fruit and offered leadership to the world in library science research. The pace of library research is picking up everywhere today due to social pressure, as well as, inspiration. In justifying the Ph.D. programme in our profession, it has been urged that "if librarianship aspires to become a profession, it should depend upon research to develop its knowledge base and its theoretical framework"[2].

The credit for the formal institution of the doctoral degree programme in library science in India goes undeniably to Dr. S.R. Ranganathan (1892–1972). In 1951, he started providing Library science education at the University of Delhi, surmounting many difficulties and facing personal ridicule. The University of Delhi awarded the first doctorate degree in library science in 1957 to D.B. Krishan Rao who worked on "Fact Analysis and Depth Classification of Agricultural". Dr. S.R. Ranganathan was his guide. Doctoral research remained in the wilderness when Ranganathan shook the Delhi soil off his feet in 1955. In the 1960s and 1970s some doctorates on library-related topics were earned by library professionals under the guidance and supervision of faculties belonging to the disciplines such as sociology, history, law, economics, management, and the like. Thereafter there was no looking back. Many universities started Ph.D. programs mostly with individual efforts and enthusiasm.

Mr. Munidranath Basu was first Librarian to earn a doctorate degree for his thesis "Museum Method and Process of Cleaning and Preservation/Library Preservation" in 1950 Calcutta University awarded him Ph.D.

J. S. Sharma (1924-1993), the university librarian and head of the library science department of the Panjab University, Chandigarh. The second de jure Ph.D. in library science was awarded in 1977. He was first Indian to get a doctorate from USA. He was awarded Ph. D. by Michigan University for his thesis "Mahatma Gandhi a descriptive bibliography".

2.3. QUALITY IN LIS RESEARCH

Quantity of research is easier to assess than quality. What is most easily quantified is not research per se but the number. The evidence is fragmentary, but it appears that the quantity of published re-search has been increasing. Evaluation of the quality of research is based on two sets of criteria: one has to do with the conduct of research its underlying logic and methodology, and the validity and longevity of conclusions. And the other has to do with the topic of research: does it address questions that are useful, interesting and important? Most of the methodologies are fairly new to LIS. One reason may be that the number of journals has increased faster than the number of good research articles, so that lesser quality articles are being published. Another methodological problem is the unusual preponderance of practitioners' publications. The plurality of authors is academic librarians/librarians at special libraries mostly without doctorates, majority of them rely on descriptive statistics. The reason for such increased production/involvement in research is due to pressure on practitioners to publish/ perish logic to gain promotions, either they have to publish/conduct research/guide research. Most of the studies are, a single, short-term problem, what, how, who, when and where and are limited to single library/ geographical area at a point of time. And studies are replicated many a time, very minimum cross-library comparisons. Most of studies are strictly limited to current library practices rendering them obsolete rapidly.

2.4. RELEVANCE OF RESEARCH

In developing countries like India, there could not be a dearth of research problems to be investigated, but there seems to be a lack of perception to visualize and identify valid problems for research. A cursory glance of the topics researched on will reveal that the topics chosen do not have a problem or hypothesis, but mere state of the art reports or description of the existing conditions. The popular areas are university libraries and their services, special libraries and their services, user behaviour in special libraries, academic libraries, Information systems, collection organization, library history, and case studies of different types of libraries, library resources, and LIS education, etc. Evaluation of documents selection, procurement, cataloguing, library management (both material and human resource) are least popular topic, though they are practical and relevant to present day needs, as huge amount of money is being spent on collection and HR. The basic research is the most neglected area, which has been endorsed by other doctoral surveys. There is a need to revive research in traditional areas like classification, indexing etc in the light of information technology, globalization of information services, information networks and digital/ virtual library environments. Further the curriculum development committee in library and information science (CDC), 1992 constituted by UGC has emphasized briefly the importance of research and listed some areas for research. It has demanded uncompromisingly a clear declaration from Ph.D. candidates that the 'work is based on the discovery of new facts by the candidates or new relations of facts.... and how the work tends to the general advancement of knowledge'. Research in LIS has an important role to play towards creation of new knowledge and solutions to problems faced by practicing librarians, information scientists and other library professionals. Incidentally, these activities will also enable the programmes in LIS schools. There are three ways of carrying out research activities; one is in the form of dissertation work at P.G. level (M.L.I.Sc.) (Preliminary), at M.Phil. (Middle) and another at Ph.D. level (Advanced). Though formal research was very slow in the early days (1950-80), it gradually accelerated and the output is increasing. But research reports are not easily available to scholars who are pursuing their research because many libraries do not acquire them systematically, at least the titles could be com-piled as it is published in weekly University News of the Association of Indian Universities, New Delhi. This is a major source to keep track of Ph.D. degrees awarded by Indian Universities, to avoid duplication. Many projects are on the way like Vidyanidhi.

2.5. VALUE AND EFFECTIVENESS OF LIBRARY & INFORMATION RESEARCH:

The volume and effectiveness of research in Library & Information Science has been realized because of various factors[3].

- Library & Information Science has developed as an in-depended discipline during the last century.
- Research is a remarkable phenomenon for the growth of any discipline.
- Information explosion.
- Emergence of Information technology.

- Complexities of Information management.
- Growth in Information needs and demands of clientele.
- Recognition of official position of librarians in teaching and research.
- UGC norms for career promotion.
- Salary scales.

2.6. POPULAR AREAS OF RESEARCH IN LIBRARY & INFORMATION SCIENCE:

Following are the major areas of research in Library & Information Science in Bundelkhand region

- Collection Development
- User Studies
- Public Libraries
- Quality Management
- Classification Schemes
- Organization of Knowledge
- Role of Library in Society
- Library Legislation
- Library Movement
- Library Association
- Library/Public Relationship
- Literature Study
- Library Resources and Services
- Library Services
- Acquisition Systems
- Academic Libraries
- Collection Obsolescence
- Resource Sharing
- Rural Library Network

Some of the Emerging Areas Like

- Bibliometric Studies
- Citation Study
- Scientometric Study
- Scientific Communication
- LIS Profession
- Information Technology
- Information System
- LIS Education
- E-publishing
- E-learning
- Library S/W
- Open Library S/W
- Resources Sharing
- Library Resources and Services
- IT Application in Library
- Bibliographic Databases
- Digital Library
- Digital Resources/e-journals
- Copyright Act
- Library Automation
- IT Application Attitude of Staff
- Impact of Internet on Research
- IT Impact-Library Services
- Institutional Repository
- Internet Resources on Marketing
- IT Impact-TQM
- IT Impact-Changing Scenario
- Consortia-E-journals
- Information Network
- National Disability Network

- Networking of Libraries
- Information Services
- Current Awareness Services
- OPAC Search
- Information System Design

2.7. REFERENCES

1. Satija, M.P. (2010). What ails doctoral research in Library and Information Science in India? *DESIDOC Journal of Library & Information Technology, 30(5),* p61-66.
2. Chandrasekhar, M. & Ramasesh, C.P. (2009). Library and information science research in India. Asia –Pacific Conference on Library & Information Education & Practice, 530-534.Retrieved August 23, 2011, from http://www.tulips.tsukuba.ac.jp/dspace/bitstream/2241/102596/2/PS_11.pdf
3. Kumar, P.S.G. (2004). *Festschrift: Library and Information Profession in India.* (Vol.2). Delhi: B.R. Publication.

3
Citation Analysis And Indexing

3.1. INTRODUCTION

The origin of footnotes or citation practices cannot be easily determined. But the practice seems to have been well established in scientific writing even when the early periodicals started about three centuries ago. Derek de Solla Price has found out that the earliest name of a foot—note was 'Scholia', which means "relating to scholarship", footnoting was considered to be a scholarly practice[1]. In the sphere of science this elevation is reflected in the sentiment of Newton when he candidly expressed- If I have seen anything further that is standing on the shoulders of giants, This indebtness of researchers, whether in sciences or social sciences, has found expressions in citations or bibliographic references, accompanying researcher communication.

An essential part of research papers, particularly in the science, is the list of references pointing to prior publications. As Ziman observes, "a scientific paper does not stand alone; it is embedded in the literature of the subject". Frencis Nerin and other comment, that "A reference is the acknowledgement that one document gives to another; a citation is the acknowledgement that one document receives from another". According to Martin "a citation implies a relationship between a part or the whole of the cited document and a part of the whole of the citing document". Citation analysis is that area of bibliometric which deals with the studies of this relationship.

3.2. MEANING OF CITATION

Many scientists have given their own way of the meaning of citation. According to Krauze "by reference we mean a foot note in an article which gives bibliographic information about an earlier article". By a citation we mean a footnote referring to a given article and necessarily contained an article written at a later date. It is useful to think of 'reference' as a backwards looking concept and 'citation' as a forward looking concept. A foot note is of course, both a reference and a citation. In other words both citations and references are one and the same[2].

Roland Hjerppe takes the word citation in a generic sence, "encompassing forms of written records or communications (books, Journals, papers, reports etc.)". The term 'document' will be used for brevity although in The case of articles it refers only to a part of the physical document. The physical documents themselves are too comprehensive and difficult to handle in large quantities. The primary working materials for citation analysis is therefore the document representation, uniquely identifying the physical document these document representations are usually called (bibliographic) 'references' or 'citations'.

"Citation analysis is a technique of bibliometric study of literature based upon some degree of relationship between citing and cited articles of documents".

***According* to F.W. Lancaster**, "One very important group of bibliometric studies relates to what sources authors cite. Citation analysis is concerned with such phenomena as which authors are most cited, which journal are most cited, and what linkages exist through citation (Who cites whom, which journals cite which journals, what subject areas are cited in the literature of a particular discipline, and so on)".

***According* to Martyn,** "Citation analysis has been defined as an analysis of the citations or references which form part of the scholarly apparatus of primary communication".

According to Garfield point out, "citation frequency is measure of research activity or of communication about research activity".

Broads defines the "true citations analysis as one which deals with works cited as having actually been used in preparation of, or having otherwise contributed to, the source paper".

According to Encyclopedia of Library & Information Science, "Citation is a reference to a record in a standard bibliographic form Bibliographic description: A set of data items used to uniquely identify a document, namely, author, publisher, title, edition, place of publication. It may also other elements such as pagination, footage and format. The term document may be broadly defined to cover any container of information"[3].

According to Encyclopedia Dictionary o of Library & Information Science, "Citation refers to a note of reference to a work from which a passage has been quoted or to some source as authority for a statement of proposition.

Especially in Law books refers to a quotation from or a reference to statutes decided case or other authorities".

Dhalig used citations to trace the diffusion of an idea and pointed out that some papers become sociometric stars while other are isolated. The frequency of the cited documents appearing in a number of citing articles is in some measure, an indication of its influence or impact on the subject. The technique of citation is largely statistical and is used for arranging those cited material in some kind of rank to study their relative importance.

3.3. HISTORICAL DEVELOPMENTS OF CITATION ANALYSIS

The first practical application of this concept was Shepard's citation a legal reference tool that has been in use since 1873. Shepard's citation owes its existence to the fact that American law, like English law, operates under the doctrine of Stare Decisis, Stare Decisis means all courts must follow their own precedents as well as those established by higher courts. The precedents are the decisions handed down in previous cases. To try a case under Stare Decisis, a lower base argument on previous decisions, however, the lawyers must make sure that the decisions have not been overruled, reversed or limited in some way. Shepard's citation enables the lawyer to do this with a minimum of trouble.

A legal case is always referred to by a code, which consists of the volume and page number of the documents in which the case is reported. Once a case is permanently reported, its reference code becomes fixed for the time. Thus 3C1 US-356 is a reference to the case reported in volume 301 of the United States Supreme Court Report on page 356. Statutes are also referred to in a similar manner. Thus, Ch-16 Sec. 24NJRS refers to the chapter 16, section 24 to the New Jersey Revised Statutes.

Taking advantages of this coding system Frank Shepard devised a listing, which shows every instance in which a reported decision is cited in a subsequent case. The listing also shows what statutes and journals cite the original decision. To use Shepard's citation a lawyer must first local a previous decision relating to his current case. He did this by consulting a digest, index or encyclopedia which provided him with the case number of any given decision, then looks up the case number in Shepard's citations and finds all the subsequent citing cases. From the information, he can determine whether the original decision was affirmed or modified in any way[4].

Since1920 the U S indexing system of the Library Literature has recorded a number of citation studies. But the terms 'citation analysis' did not appear till 1956. Many of them attempted to rank the importance of journals on the basis of an average number of references to journals cited and research papers.

In 1927 Gross and Gross published an articles on the college Libraries and Chemical Education. This was first user study, of any significance, based on a more systematic citation count. It just attempted to rank the journals in chemistry. The method employed was to make numerical counting of all the journals in chemistry cited in a small representative sample of research paper. The study remains important for its historical significance. Because Stevens formed the Bradford's Low of scattering by using the finding of this study.

During 1950's and 1960's a good number of studies smaller in scope but with greater refinement were reported. The Methodology was perfected to a degree of precision. But all of them had one uniform conclusion. These are supported a general hypothesis that in the field of science only few frequently used journals supplied more than half of the citations while the remaining citations were from the less frequently used journals. Again, these conclusions are in support of findings of Bradford in an indirect way.

Stevens was the first to undertake a comparative study of the materials cited in PhD's dissertations. A total of 6993 citations retrieved from a sample set of 90 theses. 50 on Science and 40 Humanities formed the scientific writing and of books in Humanities; a large number of citations are used in Humanities then in Science. Stevens did not stop this; he holdings of the libraries of the representative universities that awarded the degrees. He found that the dissertation on history cited a large number of titles which were not in the library. From these findings he derived the conclusions that the scholars in Humanities have to search and make use of materials available in libraries other than their own.

Linda Smith had devised two techniques, to identify documents likely to be closely related, bibliographic coupling and co-citation analysis. Two documents are co-cited when they are jointly cited in one or more subsequently published documents. Thus is co-citation in earlier documents become linked because they are later cited together? In bibliographic coupling later document become linked because they cite the same earlier documents. The difference is that bibliographic coupling is an association intrinsic to the documents. While citation is a linkage extrinsic to the documents, and one that is valid only so long as they continue to be bibliographic coupling and citation analysis have been reviewed by Weinberg Bellardo. Citation count and bibliographic coupling were the characteristics citation analysis technique in the 1960's co-citation analysis is of particular interest as a mean for mapping scientific specialties.

There are many published studies exploring citation analysis and its applications. Some reviews of this literature have already appeared and Hjerppe have compiled a bibliography of more than 2,000 entries indexing many studies in citation analysis. Eugene Garfield's writings are a rich source of information on this subject. Particularly his book on citation indexing, and many of his current comments columns reprinted from current contents.

However, it is acknowledge that the number of references appended to a research paper or a thesis is roughly a valid indicator of its significance. Citation given by author provide an indication of what form of material and how much of them are being used to support their findings. Scientific tradition requires that when a scientist announces his finding he should refer to earlier findings of similar nature which relate to his them. These references are supposed to identify those earlier researchers whose concepts the author has used to shape his own research. It is believed that when an item is cited the citing author finds in the cited article something relevant to the topic of his work. Therefore, there is some degree of relationship between the citing thesis and the cited article or book. The frequency of the cited document appearing in a number of citing articles is in some measure an indication of the importance of the document. According to this line of though, citation analysis is defined by Martyn as "analysis by the citations or references, or both of which form part of the scholarly apparatus of primary communications".

The technique is largely used for putting items of references in some kind of rank or order, whether they are journals or authors cited. The technique is used for arranging the cited materials in some kind of rank to study their relative degree of importance. The item ranked may be journals or references in journal articles. The type of ordering may be linear as in the case of periodicals ranking, or it may be multidimensional as in the generation of citation network as in science citation Index, or it may be a simple investigation of the structure of literature as attempted in the present study, Whatever The type of analysis performed the interpretation of the result throw light on identifying the nature of the relationship between the citing and the cited documents.

Use of new techniques in citation analysis had been possible by the availability of new tools. Early citation studies frequently were based on lists of reference found in articles appearing in a small number of journals. Citation has been transcribed and manipulated by hand;

because of tediousness of this process most studies were necessarily quite limited in scope. The availability of computer has significantly improved this situation in two ways; through the production of printed indexes which contain citation data from thousands of documents, and through the analysis of citation data available in machine readable form.

In recent years, citation analysis has emerged as a useful technique for studying the trends in scientific research. Citation analysis uses bibliographic references and their count to identify what a material is related to a particular topic and is worth reading. For the purpose of the present study the citation analysis means that the analysis of bibliographical references and citations which form part of a thesis. And it is understood that a citation in a thesis, as a communication artifact establishes a relationship between the two documents, the thesis which cites and article or book which is cited.

3.4. NEED OF CITATION ANALYSIS STUDY

Citation analysis is one branch of bibliometrics where the unit of analysis is a document that is being as a bibliographic cited as a bibliographic reference or a foot note in a citing document. Here the analysis does not end with the study of the distribution or scattering of references; it extends to the study of the literature of a subject which grows exponentially with time.

Citation analysis now considered as an active area of bibliometric research. Rising subscription rates, limited allocation of budget and the space problem for current holding has resulted in a number of users' studies. Limited financial resources have forces the librarian to determine collection development policies which will make maximum use of money and space available which meeting the varied needs of the users.

Kriz Harry has observed that the "traditionally, academic librarians have tried to maintain periodicals subscription in spite of shortage of funds. Thus one read from time to time of libraries that have suspended book buying". The rising trends in a price of published materials are a well-known phenomenon to all who are concerned with collection and development of library and information centre resources. The continued rise in price of journals has been a major obstacle and this has been posing serious acquisition problems to libraries and information centers, especially in universities and research libraries. This trend has forced librarians to cancel certain titles in order to keep up with increasing casts, as well as purchasing new titles and making room for the current volumes.

Eugene Garfield observed that the "citation analysis has become one of the popular methods employed in the identification of core journal in a particular subject field or for a particular scientific community in a geographical area. It is a technique of listing of references appended to articles in significant periodicals and counting the frequencies with which periodicals are cited. This method emphasizes that journals most profusely cited can be taken to be the most derisible ones in a library collection, for they are likely to be frequently used by scientists. Citation analysis provides a number of interesting and useful insights into the network of journals that functions as the primary formal communication medium of science.

3.5. REASONS FOR AN AUTHOR TO BE CITED

According to D'Etreas the doctrine of Stare Decisis provides the logic for Shepard's citation, so did the "reference tradition" provide the rationale for citation indexes for science? A citation represents relationship between cited and citing document. Although there may be a number of reasons as to why a citing author has not cited certain other works. It may be due to the fact that the author was not aware of the document or he could not obtain it or could not read the language in which it was published. The nature of relationship between cited and citing author is difficult to characterize, however, Moravicsik, for the first time, developed into the nature of citations process in the literature of physics and classified citations into following four categories:

(i) Conceptual/operational;

(ii) Organic or perfunctory;

(iii) Evolutionary of juxtaposition; and

(iv) Conformal or negational.

Eugene Garfield enumerated following fifteen reasons for citations:

1. Paying homage to pioneers;
2. Giving credit for related work;
3. Identifying methodology, equipment etc. ;
4. Providing background reading;
5. Correcting one's own work;
6. Correcting the work of others;
7. Criticizing previous work;
8. Sustaining claims;
9. Alerting researchers to forthcoming work;
10. Providing leads to poorly disseminate, poorly indexed or un-cited work;
11. Authenticating data and classes of fact-physical constants, etc;
12. Identifying original publications in which an idea or concept was discussed ;
13. Identifying the original publications describing an economic concept or term as, e.g., HodgKin's disease, Pareto's law, Friedal-craft reaction;
14. Disputing priority claims of others;
15. Disclaiming work or ideas of others.

Weinstock Isolates there are following reason for applying citation:

1. Showing respect to pioneers or explore;
2. Appreciating efforts for concerned work;
3. Acquainting with measures, methods and equipments etc;
4. Furnishing reading related to the background;
5. Rectifying one's own work;
6. Rectifying the errors in other's work;
7. Critically assessing the previous work;
8. making claims strongly;
9. Inspiring research makers for the near future work;
10. Stream lining the uncited and poorly indexed work;
11. Making the data and categories of real physical contents authentic and valid;
12. Identifying the original published material through which a dimensional idea was held;
13. Finding out original publications containing a description of eponymic concept or term as e.g. Hodgkin's disease, Friedal-Crafts Reaction, Ohm's Law etc.;
14. Renouncing other's work and thought ;
15. Rejecting other claims;
16. Self-Citation;
17. To prevent reviewer's attacks on the up-to date ness or otherwise of the paper;

Charles Oppenheim Sisan Renn highlights seven reason for citation to some highly cited old papers:

1. Historical background;
2. Description of other relevant work;
3. Supplying information or data other than for comparison;
4. Supplying information or data for comparison;
5. Use of theoretical equation;

6. Use of methodologies;
7. Theory or method not applicable or not the best one.

3.6. CITATION INDEXING

Citation indexing is a relatively new method of organizing the contents of a collection of documents in a way that overcomes many of the shortcomings of the more traditional indexing methods. The primary of citation indexing is that it identifies relationships between documents that are often overlooked in a subject index. An important secondary advantage is that the compilation of citation indexes is especially well suited in the use of man-machine indexing method that do not require indexers who are subject specialists. This helps to make citation more current than most subject indexes. Furthermore citations, which are bibliographic descriptions of documents, are not vulnerable to scientific and technological obsolescence as are the terms used in subject indexes.

Citation indexing is based on the simple concept than an author's references to previously recorded information identify much of the earlier work that is pertinent to the subject of his present document. These references are commonly called citations and a citation index is a structured list of all the citations in a given collection of documents. Such lists are usually arranged so that the cited document is followed by the citing document. In the early 1950s, the availability of this build in system for linking scientific articles began to receive attention as the possible foundation of an indexing system for the scientific literature.

Shepard's Citation Index : This is the origin of such citation index. It has been used since 1873 by the Legal Profession. Shepard's Citation Index owns its existence to the fact that american law like english law operates under the doctrine of Stare Decisis. It provides listing of individual american court cases, each case being are publications that referred to the case, other court decisions that have affected the case, and any other referred that may be of value.

Lederberg : It was not until 1958, however, that the scientific community exhibited any specific interest in Garfield's idea, in that year, Professor Joshua Leaderberg of Stanford University wrote Garfield to inquire if any further work had been done on citation indexing. When informed of the financial problems involved in starting such a project. Leduerberg suggested that Garfield should apply for a grant from the government.

William C. Adair : In 1953, the Welch Project conducted a symposium, news of which was reported in a Colorado newspaper. This article read by William C. Adair, who was former vice president of the firm that produced Shepard's citations. Adair wrote to the Welch Project and suggested that they consider the method employed by Shepard's as a possible indexing techniques. After examining Shepard's citations, Garfield realized that the "citation" principle could provide a mean of indexing review paper, which could be extended to the scientific literature in general.

After Welch Project ended, Garfield began graduate work in Library Science at Columbia University. During this period he continued correspondence with Adair and began writing a detailed article on citation indexing for scientific literature in general. A detailed article on citation indexing for scientific literature, the article was completed in 1954 and was edited and referred by Professor Bentley Glass, who was then chairman of the John Hopkins department of genetics and on editorial board of Science.

While his own article was awaiting publication, Garfield, who by then was an associate editor of American Documentation, suggested that Adair write a shorter article which would explain, in general terms, the operation of Shepard's citations The Adair article appeared in American Documentation in June 1955; Garfield article appeared in Science in July of 1955.

Garfield : This statement had considerable import on Eugene Garfield, one of the Welch project investors. Garfield realized that nearly every sentence in a review article is supported by a citation to a previous work. Thus, a review article could really be considered as a series of indexing statement. The problem then becomes one of transforming these statements into a consistent format that would be useful as an index.

Welch Medical Library Indexing Project : In 1952, Dr. Chauncey Leakey was chairman of committee of consultants for the study of Indexes of medical literature. This committee was supervision the John Hopkins Welch Medical Library Indexing Project, which was sponsored by the armed forces medical library. Dr. Leakey suggested that project workers should examine review articles in connection with their investigation of the problems with subject indexes to medical literature.

Genetics Citation Indexing : In 1961, the National Institute of Health initiated a cooperative program with Garfield's Institute for Scientific Information (ISI) to prepare a citation index for the field of Genetics. This joint programme also considered the various aspects of citation indexing and for creation of a systematical citation index for Science & Technology.

Some other efforts were also made to produce citation indexes to utilize the principle of citation indexing for dissemination of information. A bibliography of non parametic statistics published in 1962 also contained citation index. This index indicates what items of the bibliography are cited by other items in the list. The above efforts were made on adhoc basis but Eugene Garfield made special efforts for bringing out a systematical citation index in the field of Science & technology. Thus Garfield become a unique person in the field of Science

Citation Indexing for which he established an Institute for Scientific Information (ISI) at Philadelphia, USA, wherefrom a regular started since 1963.

This Institute is now a multinational corporation that provides a wide varieties of information services to Scientists/Technologist and researches of the world. In the process, the Institution (ISI) has become a massive information center in which a comprehensive bibliographic description including indexes of more than 5 lakhs items a year for every issue more than 5,000 journals from all disciplines, are continuously being generated and entered into computer bases system that produces a lot of material for the use of users. Indexing in this operation goes on to an average depth of 25 primary descriptors of which four different types are used.

This Institution has following three distinct groups of information services:

1. The current content (CC) Group of services.
2. Science Citation Index (SCI) Group of services.
3. Index Chemicus Registry System (ICRS) group of services.

The Current Content (CC) Group of Services

It provides weekly publication as contents page covering six disciplinary areas, i.e. Life Sciences, Agricultural, Biology & Environmental Sciences, Physical & Chemical Sciences, Social & Behavioral Sciences and Engineering & Technology and Clinical practices.

In addition, the Current content services for life sciences, clinical practice, the Physical & Chemical Sciences, and the social and behavioral sciences include weekly subject indexes.

Science Citation Index (SCI) Group of Services

The interdisciplinary database was eventually used to produce the first science citation index used, which was published in 1963. The first SCI covered the literature of the calendar year of 1961. It covered 613 journals, contained 1.4 million citations, and required five volumes. Nineteen percent of the citation in the 1961 SCI data were selected by special computerized procedures as 'having to do with Genetics' and were published separately as the Genetic Citations Index. The Genetic index was also published in 1963 and was complete in one volume.

This group was expended in 1973 to include two measure services i.e. Social Sciences Citation Index (SSCI) and Journal Citation Reports (JCR) which covers citation on each of the thousands of journals. It has further extended its services in 1978 to include citation indexing of the field of Arts & Humanities (A&HCI) and non-journal material.

Index Chemicus Registry System (ICRS) Group of Services

It provides a monthly tape services to the literature of chemical compounds. It also provide weekly abstracting services (current abstracts of chemistry and index chemicus) to chemical literature, a monthly substructure index (chemical substructure index) and SDI services (Automatic New Structure -ANSA) for the literature of chemical structure.

In addition to the above services, ISI offers a number of other services viz.

a) Tear Sheet services(original article tera sheet services OATS)
b) Annually directory (who is publishing in science)
c) Search services and
d) Educational services
e) Workshop on Wiswesser Line Notation(WLW)

This institution also do contact work involving development of costumed indexing, study of literature personnel. Communication and development patterns of Science and Technology.

In addition to above, there are also some important reference tools, like Chemical Abstract & Engineering index Library and Information Science, Biological abstract and Computer Science Abstracts, Excerpta Medica Indexes. Chemical abstract contains subject index, formula index, ring index, author index and patent index etc. Chemical Abstract is publishing from American Chemical Society, Ohio, since 1907. The most of the information on micro specific subjects can be traced out through these chemical abstract services, which are entirely based for the further developmental aspects of Science Citation Index (SCI).

Engineering Index (EI)

Engineering Index is also publishing from New York, USA, since 1884. It is also a very powerful reference tools to the all disciplines of engineering sciences like Inorganic Coating, Corrosion and its related aspects in the form of subjective information, Sintered Ferrous alloys. In other words, the information can be collected through this Engineering Index to develop specially the Library and Information Science area, Bibliometric Studies i.e. Citation Analysis. Conclusively it may also be considered that this Engineering Index may play very important role to develop the concept of science, citation index through their main emerging field and micro specific concepts of the subjects.

Other Citation Indexes

In addition to SCI and Genetics Citation Indexes, there have been severed other effort at compiling citation indexes or at using principle of citation indexing information retrieval systems. Most of these have been experimental in nature, extremely narrow in their converge or published on a one-time basis[5].

Some citation indexes provide coverage of the material published in just one journal one of the earliest examples of this is the cumulative index to volumes 35 through 50 of the Journal of the American statistical Association. Another example of a citation index with single journal coverage is the one that appears in a cumulative index to volume 1 through 31 of the Annals of Mathematical Statistics.

An example of citation index that covers more than one journal but is limited to a single field is the Citation Index for Statistics and Probability which is being currently produced by Dr. J.W. Tukeey at Princeton University. This project was initiated in 1961 and is being conducted in cooperation with the National Science Foundation. In 1968, the Shepard organization itself introduced Shepard's Law Review Citations. This new publication indexes 117 law review and periodicals and shows where any legal article written since 1947 has been cited in the covered journals from 1957 on.

As a final example special indexes can be prepared on demand through system that directly connects the users with the database, as is done with the Technical Information Project (TIP) at the Massachusetts Institute of Technology. TIP uses a time sharing computer connected to remote by telephone cables. The database consists of the full bibliographies of articles from 25 recent physics journals. Thus a user can obtain a citation index to all the articles or articles from only one of the covered journals, or to the articles in a single volume of a covered journal.

3.7. FORMS OF CITATION ANALYSIS

1. Citation Analysis

The evaluation of the serial collection in interdisciplinary fields is a challenging task for the collection development librarians. The content of inter disciplinary field is broad, research methodologies vary widely, specialization in a particular subject fields is common and bibliographic control may be weak. When reference resources such as standard bibliographic and specific indexing and abstracting services are locking of a particular subject core serials and new research trends.

The primary function of the citation is to provide "a connection between two documents one which cities and other which is cited. There are umpteen members of reasons for giving citations. Weinstok, Liptez, Muravesik and Murugesan, Hodges Oppenheiam and Renn, Fenney, Frost and Throne have all attempted to explore the possible reasons for giving citations. They include the positive and negative reasons for inclusion However, it has to be conceded that if the reasons are positive, then it is bound to have some connection between the citing and cited papers or document. The first recorded citation analysis was a study by P.L.K. Gross and E.M Gross published in 1972, applied a simple statistical method to the grading of the scientific serials according to their related importance based on citation counting from source journals. Similar surveys were made by other workers of the periodicals for mathematics, electrical engineering, physiology, geology, medicine, chemistry, biochemistry, etc. comprehensive list for various areas of scientific knowledge were prepared in 1944 under the direction of a committee of the Association research librarians by Brown in 1956. Sengupta[6]prepared two comprehensive lists for medicine and biomedical science from the India scientists' point of view.

2. Direct Citation Counting

Citation counting is a technique that determines how many citations in a given document, author, journal etc. has received over a period of time, originally used by Gross and Gross. The rational for this is that citations are objective indicators of use and therefore an article, author, and journal that is frequently cited, is more useful or productive, as the case may be, than one that is less frequently cited. In order to offset the limitations of citation counting, some modified measures have been suggested. The 'Impact Factor' and Immediacy Index are two such measures[7]. Garfield[8]who coined the term impact factor defines it as "the ratio of the number of times a journal is cited in a given time period to the total number oftimes a journal is cited in a given time period to the total number of source items published in a journal, during specific period of -time". The impact factor is a measure of the frequency with which the average cited article in a journal has been cited in a particular year. It offset the effect of age, size, the frequency of a publication of a journal on the frequency of citation. The immediacy index is a method of showing the frequency with which a material received by the article during the year to the number of articles published. Hirst[9]has suggested the discipline impact factor (DIF), a method of determining core journals for a discipline, which is similar to impact factor, which measure that number of times a paper a journals is cited in the core literature of the given discipline.

3. Bibliometric Measurements

The bibliometric measurements are derived from the concept of citation indexing. It was based on the English legal system, which operates under the doctrine of Stare Desisi Precedent on the basis of which Garfield developed Science Citation Index, Social Science Citation Index and Art and Humanities Citation Index. Bibliometrics can be defined as the statistical exploitation of scientific publications in order to measure specific values or parameters. This analysis makes it possible to assess the activity of the producers (researcher, laboratory, institute, faculty, etc.) or distributors (periodical, publisher, etc.) of scientific information, both in quantitative and in qualitative terms.

Quantity and Quality: two approaches

In both cases, the techniques used to gather information, enumerate publications and statistical analysis strictly speaking are the same. Nevertheless, they lead to different types of processing and, consequently, produce results that have neither the same purpose nor the same use.

The simplest technique of bibliometrics is counting the total number of publications a scientist or a group' of them have published. While the publication count gives, a quantitative measure of the total volume of research output, the qualitative aspect of the published work remains to be assessed. The publication count, however, has its other limitations also. Multiple authors have shown sharp increase during past few decades owing to prevalence of collaborative research, poses problem in the process of publication count. Jones studied the correlation between the publication counts and other measures of scientific merits such as research funding, cited ness, etc. and found a reasonable correlation.

4. Co-citation Analysis

The concept of co-citation was for first time suggested independently by Small[10]and Marshaava all most simultaneous in 1973 and later developed by small. Who proposed a· new method of analyzing citations, to generate clusters of related papers? The number of times two papers are cited together in subsequent literature determines the co-citations strength of two cited papers. Two papers are co-cited if they are cited together by a third paper. The co-citation frequency is defined as the frequency with which two items of earlier literature are cited together by the later literature. Co-citation is a dynamic measure in which co-citation strength of cited papers can be studied over a period of time as they continue to be cited together in subsequent literature.

But, one of the disadvantages of co-citation technique is that it requires comprehensive citation data.

5. Bibliographic Coupling

Faro first expressed the nation of bibliographic coupling although it was Kessler in 1963 who introduced the although it was Kessler in 1963 who introduced the bibliographic coupling as a measure of the subject similarity between two documents. Two documents are bibliographically coupled when both of them cite one or more reference in common. The numbers of such common references determine the strength of bibliographic coupling. The strength of bibliographic coupling increases with the increase in number of references cited in common. The concept has since been applied to the problems of information retrieval and for mapping the graphical structure of science.

6. Bibliographic Coupling vs. Co-citation Analysis

Co-citation and bibliographic coupling is related to each other in a kind of mirror symmetry. While the co-citation is a dynamic measure, i.e. the strength of co-citation links increases as subsequent scientist cites their predecessor's work. The bibliographic coupling of two papers does not change over time and cannot to interpret in a straight forward manner.

Bibliographic coupling and cogitation analysis have their application in clustering as classification of the micro and macro structures of citing or cited documents and their mapping. While the one generate the cluster of cited papers the other generate cluster of citing papers. Both the techniques have their application and neither should be assumed to be superior as a measure of association or relatedness of documents. The choice between the two techniques is determined by the nature of the phenomenon to be investigated and the interpretation sought.

7. Co-word Analysis

The co-word analysis involves identification of keywords and their co-occurrence in an attempt to generate a map index of, papers linked by the degree of co-occurrence of the keywords. Methodology was developed by the center de sociologies De'l innovation (CSI)[11]Paris' and is independent to any particular database or a secondary service based on selective coverage. The institute has also developed a computer aided indexing technique for full text databases called LEXINET. The database is linked with 'online thesaurus, which is updated interactively each time a new document, is analyzed. The CSI has also developed a computerized programmer called "LEXIMAPPE" for co-word mapping. The technique is developed as a science policy tool and has already been used to analyze publications from research on various specialties.

8. Citation Classic

A Citation Classic is a highly cited publication as identified by the Science Citation Index (SCI) the Social Sciences Citation Index (SSCI), or the Arts & Humanities Citation Index (A&HCI).

Citation rates differ for each discipline. The number of citations indicating a classic in botany, a small field, might be lower than the number required to make a classic in a large field like biochemistry. In general, a publication cited more than 400 times should be considered a classic; but in some fields with fewer researchers, 100 citations might qualify a work.

Citation Classics authors were asked to write an abstract and a commentary about the publication, emphasizing the human side of the research - how the project was initiated, whether any obstacles were encountered, and why the work was highly cited.

Six weekly editions and one bi-weekly edition of Current Contents (CC) include Citation Classics that were selected to fit the interests of CC readers. However, some were deemed appropriate for more than one edition. Since there is a larger number of highly cited life sciences publications, that edition of CC included two classics each week[12].

9. Webometrics

Recently, a new growth area in bibliometrics has been in the emerging field of webmetrics, or cybermetrics as it is often called. Webmetrics can be defined as using of bibliometric techniques in order to study the relationship of different sites on the World Wide Web. Such techniques may also be used to map out (called "scientific mapping" in traditional bibliometric research) areas of the Web that appear to be most useful or influential, based on the number of times they are hyperlinked to other Web sites.

Research into webometrics has also revealed many shortcomings, some of which are related to its advantages.

First, the web is not quality controlled, unlike the ISI publication lists. Hence web data tends to be of lower quality, which means that webometric results are normally indicative rather than providing robust evidence[13].

Second, web data is not standardized and so it is difficult to extract all except the simplest data (e.g., link counts). In particular, it is difficult to separate out the different types of publication. For example, there does not seem to be a simple way to separate out web citations in online journal articles from those in online course reading lists. Hence webometric results (e.g., link counts, web citation counts) tend to be the total of a mix of sources with variable value[14,15].

Third, although web data can be very timely, it can be impossible to find the publication date of a web page and so webometric results typically combine new and old web pages into one data set. Finally, web data is incomplete in several senses and in arbitrary ways. Although some academic articles are freely available online, the majority probably are not. Similarly, some researchers and research groups maintain extensive and comprehensive web sites but others do not. Hence the results reflect the web, which in turn is a very partial reflection of the activities of research.

Comparing the advantages and disadvantages of webometrics, it seems that it is unlikely to replace traditional bibliometrics but can be useful for several other purposes.

First, it can be used for fast pilot studies to identify areas for follow-up systematic bibliometric analyses.

Second, it can be used to assess the extent to which researchers are successful in publicising their work online, given that this is an important activity.

Third, it can be used for relational analyses of communication in disciplinary or geographic areas of science. Finally, its methods can help the analysis of Web 2.0 and online repositories for social sciences and humanities research goals.

10. Bibliometrics Today

Mainstream bibliometrics has evolved rather than undergone revolutionary change in response to the Web and web-related developments[16]. The core citation-based impact measures are still in place, but are now supplemented by a range of complementary techniques. In addition, there is now a body of theory and case studies to draw upon so that an experienced bibliometrician can be reasonably sure of finding good ways to generate indicators from citations for any common task and also of how to interpret the results. In particular there has been an ongoing debate about the validity of using citations to measure impact, in parallel with the development of theories of citer motivations, which have recently been extensively reviewed.

Aside from the core citation analysis methods, the biggest change in bibliometrics stems from the availability of new significant sources of information about scholarly communication, such as patents, web pages, and digital library usage statistics. Of course, bibliometrics has never been exclusively interested in academic papers and has also used other data such as funding as well as qualitative indicators, such as peer review judgments.

There are perhaps three main trends in the recent history of bibliometrics, and citation analysis in particular. These are to improve the quality of results through improved metrics and careful data cleaning, to develop metrics for new tasks, and to apply bibliometrics to an increasing range of problems, particularly in descriptive relational contexts (see the knowledge domain visualization section below for examples of the latter).

1. The h-index and current bibliometric indicators
2. National research evaluation exercises
3. New bibliometric databases: Google Scholar and Scopus
4. Knowledge domain visualization

11. Bibliometric Maps

So far, the following four types of bibliometric maps have been frequently used, constructed from research journals/articles:

(a) Journal-to-journal citation maps to uncover journals having strong linkages with each other, journals that are central implying most of the other journals refer to them, etc. By juxtaposing the fields/subfields of each journal in this map, it is possible to reveal the linkages among the fields or sub-fields. These maps thus can reveal the macro-level structure of a scientific field.

(b) Co-citation maps depicting the extent to which two articles are cited together in other articles. Clustering procedures make it possible to obtain co-citation clusters which reflect the structure and content of research-front specialties.

(c) Co-word maps are based on identifying pair of keywords, which occur together in large number of documents. The framework assumes that when two words appear together in titles or abstracts or in full text for a same document it indicates possible link between two distinct centers of interest designated by these words. Links like this when repeated in large number of documents can delineate a research sub-topic or intellectual sub-domain that may not have entered the mainstream of research delineation of that field.

(d) Co-classification maps are based on the analysis of the co-occurrences of subject classification terms. The classification terms mostly represent cognitive elements, which relate to scientific topics, specialties, or fields. Using sufficiently large amount of publications data, this enormous network of linkages combines to 'abstract' structures.

3.8. CITATION ANALYSIS –USE

Citation analysis as presently practiced is largely used for putting things in order. The things ordered can be journals, papers in journal, and authors of papers in journals or organizations to which authors of journal papers are affiliated. The type of order' can be linear, as in ranking, or multidimensional, as in the generation of citation networks. Studies of obsolescence rates of journals or documents may be considered to be special cases of raking, over time. Whatever the type of analysis performed, the interpretation of the results things on the nature of relationship between the citing and cited documents. Weinstok observed that scientific tradition requires that when a reputable scientist or technologist publishes an article, he should refer to earlier articles, which relate to his theme. Citation analysis is very often fruitfully applied to derive the following benefits:

A. To Lead Reader to Further Studies in the Field

This is perhaps, the primary purpose of citations. Readers can verify the correctness of the information and thereby convince themselves.

B. For the Preparation of Bibliographies

The first use of citation indexing was made in Shepard's citations published in 1973. Eugene Garfield and others have perfected this technique of citation indexing, since the early 1960s. It is a fact that compilation of bibliographies in new fields is really difficult. In such circumstances, analysis of citation of articles may be the only way to gather information. The very fact that the citations have been verified, evaluated and recommended by authors who are expert in their own fields make them all the more acceptable for inclusion in bibliography.

C. To Study the Use Pattern of Different Types of Documents

Citation given may be of books, journals, articles, reports, standards, patents, thesis/dissertation etc. the relative use of each of these types can be ascertained based on the frequency of citations.

D. To Find Out the Relative Use of Different Language

Since English has emerged as a world language, especially in science and technology, there is a predominance of English language publication is all branches. This can easily be understood from citation analysis. In the mid-sixties, e.g., the share of English language papers in mathematics and chemistry was 50 percent. Russian occupied second position with about 20% followed by German and French.

Citation practices have also shown that the relative amount of literature in different-subjects produced, by different changes with time. So any one can easily find out the relative use of different language in a particular field or subject.

E. To Study the Use of Literature from Different Countries

From the citations, the country of their origin can be identified in all types of materials like journal articles, books, reports, etc. In many subject areas US publications were found to be used more heavily. Journals of UK occupied second position, but they come nowhere near their American counter parts in the frequency of use.

F. To Study the Scattering of Subjects

Studies about the dispersion or scattering of subjects in different sources as evidenced by citation analysis have brought out interesting results, for example, Social Sciences and arts subject show a wider scatter of publication than the science.

(i) Research publications in technology show a greater dispersion than those in sciences.

(ii) A new branch of science in interdisciplinary one, show a greater dispersion than an older branch of science.

(iii) There can be differences in scatter between sub-fields with in a subject as also among the subjects.

(iv) The rate of scatter within the same subject alters with time.

G. To Decide Obsolescence Rate of Document in Different Subjects

Citation in subsequent literature and usage pattern of libraries are considered as two indicators of the obsolescence of literature. Analysis of citations by age of cited document can show the useful life of a document. In order to measure the decay or obsolescence rate of document, the concept of 'half- life' has been borrowed from Nuclear Physics. Using this measure Burton and Kebler had suggested a range of half-lives for different subjects. The fast growing subjects would have lesser half-lives for different subject.

H. To Determine the Interdependence and Lineage of Subjects

The interdependence of basic and applied fields can be understood by citation studies. Establishment of this interdependence can be of use in the acquisition policy of special libraries or information centers. The analysis of citations of the Annual Review of Medicine for the years 1965-69 by I.N. Sengupta, has established the contribution made by journals in the field of bio-chemistry and physiology to the medical research. Further studies by him have bought to light the Acquisition Systems mutual contribution of biochemistry, physiology and microbiology.

As far as lineages of subjects are concerned, Garfield's experiments in citation indexes have very much contributed in mapping the history or many of them.

I. To Prepare Rank List of Periodicals

Ranked list of periodicals can be prepare by two methods,

a. By actual citation counting; and
b. By counting the number of entries in indexing and abstracting periodicals.

In the first method, information is collected from the references cited in source articles. By studying the average number of citations, one can develop a list of cited journals in the ranked order.

In second method, the number of items contributed by different periodicals during a specific period of time is calculated from the secondary source and the ranked list is prepared based on the productivity of journals. Such ranked lists are very often used as guidelines in the acquisition of periodicals and other materials in the library.

J. To Study the Rate of Collaborative Research

Collaborative research can be effectively measured from the number of authors in papers. Such studies can be conducted to understand global trends, national trends or trends in different subjects. Studies in this direction have indicated that collaboration varies from discipline to discipline, with in the same discipline from time to time and from country to country. However, the extent of collaboration may not be revealed from the citations.

K. For the Analysis of Scientific Journals

Citation analysis provides a number of interesting and useful insights into the networking of journals. Insights were developed from five different citation measures perfected by the Institute for Scientific Information (ISI), these are:

Citation Rate of Journal : This is the number of times a journal has been cited. It consists of all the references to the cited journals counting eve duplicate references from the same source articles as a separate citation. It can also be calculated by counting only the number of source articles that cited the journal. A third method of calculating the citation rate that is followed by ISI is by counting the number of references from the same source duplicate references to the cited journal, by treating article as only a single citation link.

Impact Factor (IF) : (IF) is an average citation rate of journal's articles. It is basically a ratio between the citation rate of the journal and its citation potential citation rate is defined as the number of times cited, whereas citation potential is defined as the number of citable items published.

The impact factor is a measure of the frequency with which the "average article" in a journal has been cited in a particular year or period. The annual JCR impact factor is a ratio between citations and recent citable items published. Thus, the impact factor of a journal is calculated by dividing the number of current year citations to the source items published in that journal during the previous two years[17].

Therefore,

$$IF = \frac{\text{The number of times a journal was cited}}{\text{The number of citable items the journal published}}$$

Self-Citing Rate : This is a measurement of the frequency with which journals cite themselves. It shows what percentage of Journal's references cited articles it published.

Self-Cited Rate : This again is a measurement of self-citation. It shows what percentage of citations received by a journal originated in articles published by the journal. These self-citation rates serve as indexes to the newness, size and isolation of the intellectual universe in which a journal operates.

Citation Cycle : The citation cycle exhibits an interlocking metabolic complex of bibliometric and scientometric parameters in a comprehensive and integrated structure (in the manner of nitrogen cycle. This cycle delineated the citation process and the recurrent construction of citation indexes the cycle begins with the selection of the source journals and the items contain in them. The numbers of source items are then connected with the authors of those items .Thus there is an integral connection of source-media, citable source items and authors of those items. These components are then connected to citations and references on their part. A source items may or may not contain references and in itself is a potential citable item. A reference is also item with an author and a medium. Thus an item in a source journal or source can have links in two directions respectively with items of references and with items of citations (members of citing pack) become source-items themselves and the cycle continues.

The citation cycle is a fact the chain of citations and references in continues in continuous order through selection of source items.

Citation Index : This is the main component of a citation index data-base (e.g. SCI, SSCI or AHCI) and is comprised of all the references (cited items) found in source index items (citing items) during the period covered. It is designed so that for any cited item (Authored or anonymous, published or unpublished) one can find at a glance who are citing it and in what publications. The citation index is accessed by an alphabetic listing of cited primary authors. One should differentiate between the Citation Index of ISI (Institute for Scientific Information) and citation index in general. Citation index or citation indexing also means the typical process of listing and indexing items through references appended to published items.

Citation Process : Citation process is the description and understanding of underlying dynamics of scientific phenomenon of recognition. It covers citation cycle, citation behavior and citation practice of authors in different disciplines and other aspects of referencing and citation distributions.

Citation Scattering : This refers to the distribution or concentration of citations (citing items) in respect of authors, journals, topics etc. of cited items. Citation scattering is one of a number of bibliometric scattering phenomena.

Cited Half-Life-Journal : The number of journal publication years going back from the current year which account for 50% of the total citations received by the cited journal in the current year[18].

Clustering : This is a technique, which, with the help of citation analysis, tries to link different groups of documents with similar citations. Clusters are formed when an article (a member of the cluster) has coupling link with a member of another member. No member of one cluster would have link with a member of another separate cluster.

Half Life : The time during which one half of all the currently active literature was published. This literature becomes 'unused', but not 'unusable'. Unlike radio-active decay it does not become 'disintegrated' but obsolescent.

- ***Corrected Half Life* :** The half-life as estimated by removing the growth element from the median citation age.
- ***Median Citation Age (or Apparent Half-life)* :** The time within which half of the citations study occurs.
- ***Immediacy Index* :** Immediacy Index is a measure to show how quickly the 'average article' of a particular journal is cited ,and is expressed by the ratio of the number of citations received in a particular year, by the source items of the journal of the same year.

  Mathematically, it can be expressed as:

  I, (I) = C/X

  Where,

  I, (I) = Immediacy index of the journal J for the year Y

  C = Number of citations received by x source items published in journals J in the Y

  X = Number of the source items published in journal in the year Y

3.9. LIMITATIONS IN APPLICATION

We have seen that many researchers have questioned the very logic of depending on citations, which are, given according to the whims and fancies of authors. They believe that any result that is obtained through such a study of citation leads to erroneous conclusions. Maurice B. Line is a strong votary of this point of view.

The common arguments leveled against citation analysis are the following:

1. Negative citation i.e. citing a paper just to repudiate it. The result is that controversial papers will get more citations than really worthwhile papers.
2. Too much of self-citation and in-house citation.
3. Practice or citing only to get the favors of the powerful or appears to others.
4. Citation given just to dress up the proper.
5. Variation of citation rate during lifetime of paper.
6. Variation of citation rate with type of paper and specialty.

It is a fact that there are extraneous considerations in giving citations. But, they do not totally undermine the value of them. As Sangupta argues, "the numbers of scientist who are capable of doing such mal-practices are not significantly high to make citation studies unworkable or misleading" Further, it is- too much to question the honesty and integrity of the majority of Scientists.

3.10. APPLICATION OF BIBLIOMETRY IN CITATION ANALYSIS

Bibliometrics is a type of research method used in library and information science. It utilizes quantitative analysis and statistics to describe patterns of publication within a given field or body of literature. Researchers may use bibliometric methods of evaluation to determine the influence of a single writer, for example, or to describe the relationship between two or more writers or works. One common way of conducting bibliometric research is to use the Social Science Citation Index, the Science Citation Index or the Arts and Humanities Citation Index to trace citations.

3.11. REFERENCES

1. Haridashan, Sudarma. (2003). *Citation analysis of doctoral dissertation submitted in social sciences at Bundelkhand*

University, Jhansi (U.P.). (Doctoral dissertation. Bundelkhand University, Jhansi. 2003).

2. Kannappanava, B.U. (1991). *Citation Analysis of doctoral dissertations in Library and Information Science accepted by the universities in Karnataka.* (Doctoral dissertation. Karnataka University, Karnataka. 2001).
3. Ghai, Daljit. (2001). *Citation analysis of Ph.d. dissertations in library and information science submitted to the Universities of Madhya Pradesh &Punjab.* (Doctoral Dissertation. Jiwaji University, Gwalior. 2001).
4. Kent, Allen, & Lancour, Haeold. (Eds.). (1972). *Encyclopedia of Library and Information Science,* (Vol 5), New York: Marcel Dekker.
5. Martyn, J. (1966). Citation Indexing. *Indexer, 5(1),* 5-15
6. Sengupta, I.N.H. (1984). A weightage formula to rerank biochemical journals. *International Library Review, 16,* 447-458.
7. Helen, E. Chandler, & Vincent De, P. Rope. (1991, October).Citation indexing: uses and limitations. *The Indexer, 17 (4),* 242-249
8. Garfield, E. (1972). Citation analysis as a tool in journal evaluation: journals can be ranked by frequency and impact of citations for Science Policy Studies. *Science, 178 (4070),* 471-479.
9. Hirst, G. (1978). Described impact factors: a method for determining core journal lists. *Journal of American Social Information Science, 29(4),* 171-72.
10. Small, H.G. (1973). Co -citation in the scientific literature: a new measure of the relationship between two documents, *Jr. Amer. Soc Inf. Sc., 24 (4),* 256-265.
11. Callon, M., Law, J. & Rip, A. (1986).eds. *Mapping the dynamics of Science and Technology.* London: McMillan.
12. Garfield, E. (1974, January). Selecting the all-time citation classics; here are the fifty most cited papers for 1961-1972. *Current Contents (CC), 6(9),* 5-8.
13. Thelwall, Mike. (2008, August). Bibliometrics to webometrics. *Journal of Information science, 34 (4),* 605-21.
14. Harries, G. et al. (2004). Hyperlinks as a data source for science mapping. *Journal of Information Science,* 30(5), 436-47.

15. Wilkinson, D., et al. (2003). Motivations for academic web site interlinking: evidence for the web as a novel source of information on informal scholarly communication. *Journal of Information Science, 29(1),* 49–56.

16. Gupta, B. M., & Bhattacharya, Sujit. (2004, January). A Bibliometric approach towards Mapping the Dynamics of Science and Technology. *DESIDOC Bulletin of Information Technology,* 24 (1), 3-8.

17. Patel Jasu. & Krishan Kumar.(2001). Libraries and librarianship in India. London: Greenwood Press.

18. Kawatra, P.S. (2008). *Textbook of information science.* New Delhi: APH Publishing Corporation.

4
Bibliometric Laws

4.1. INTRODUCTION

A distribution is defined as segregating the items according to their productivity.Many[1]bibliometric processes such as the distribution of papers in a discipline over journals, the distribution of citations over paper or over authors, the distribution of circulation transactions over library items and over library users, and the distribution of publication over authors, are claimed to be the result of a "success–breeds–success" phenomenon. It is common in bibliometric matters and in many diverse social phenomena that success seems to breed success. As stated by De Solla Price[2], "A paper which has been cited many times is more likely to cite again than one which has been little cited. An author of many papers is more likely to publish again than one who has been less prolific. A journal which has been frequently consulted for some purpose is more likely to be turned to again than one of previously infrequent use. Words become common or remain rare. A millionaire gets extra income faster and easier than a beggar". In a similar way, Ravichandra Rao[3]argues that "those documents which have been borrowed frequently are likely to be borrowed again than borrowed infrequently in an academic library in an academic year. Those users who borrow documents frequently are more likely to borrow documents again than those who seldom borrowed documents in an academic year".

In statistics, such a phenomenon is generally described by a skew or hyperbolic distribution function. De Solla Price characterizes such a distribution by a Cumulative Advantage Distribution (CAD). It is known as Yule distribution in statistics. It provides a sound conceptual basis for such empirical laws as the Lotka Distribution for Scientific Productivity, the Bradford Law for Journal Use, and the Zipf's Law for Literary Word Frequencies. It is, therefore, an underlying probability mechanism of phenomena of widespread application and versality throughout the social sciences.

It is usually observed that the top-ranked frequently co-occurring terms are relatively few in number and account for a relatively large proportion of overall co-occurrence. Om the other hand, the lower ranked, less frequent terms are increasingly many, with the largest single group constituting a long "tail" of terms that each co-occurs with the criterion terms only once. The few top-ranked terms constitute the "core" and the more numerous, lesser – to least-ranked terms constitute the "scatter". Within a given distribution, core maintains identity; scatter individualizes. Core contains redundancy; Scatter variety. The best specification of the relations between core and scatter is "zones" of productivity. All of these human choices with language take a distinctive pattern of concentrations (core) and dispersion (scatter) when plotted as statistical distributions over the whole file(or a part of it)[4].

4.2. LAWS FOR CITATION / BIBLIOMETRIC ANALYSIS

Bibliometric data are found to conform rather closely to a number of Laws and mathematical distributions. The three basic laws in the field of bibliometrics (Lotka

Bradford and Zipf) are related to the authors of papers, the articles in the journals and word count in the text of papers respectively. In all of these laws, the cumulated forms have the advantage of being more tractable mathematically. All these laws are either rank-frequency relation instead of class rank-frequency relations so favored in statistics. In fact, till date, there is no sophisticated tool in statistics for tacking rank-frequency or size-frequency data.

The three most commonly used laws in bibliometrics are:

4.2.1. Lotka's Law of scientific productivity,

4.2.2. Zipf's Law of word occurrence, and

4.2.3. Bradford's Law of Scattering of Scientific Papers

4.2.1. Lotka's Law of Scientific Productivity

Lotka's law is one of the three major laws of bibliometrics that mainly explain the literature distribution of various authors' productivity in a given field. It finds that most articles are being contributed by a few researchers, with a large proportion of researchers contributing just one publication. Therefore, Lotka summarizes the logarithmic relation between researchers and publication quantities. It states that "the number (of authors) making n contributions is about $1/n^2$ of those making one publication; and the proportion of all contributors, that make a single contribution, is about 60 percent"[5]. The general formula is $X^nY = C$, where X is the number of publications, Y the relative frequency of authors with X publications, and n and C are constants, depending on the specific field. In brief, the author who publishes two articles accounts, on average, for 1/4 of the total number of publications. The authors who publish three articles account for about 1/9 of the total number of publications, and so on. Therefore, authors who publish one article account for 60% of all the publications. That is to say, authors who publish n publications will be 1/

n^2 of the proportion of total publications. This formula is also called the Inverse Square Law.

4.2.2. Zipf's Law of Word Occurrence

Zipf's Law is often used to predict the frequency of words within a text. The Law states that in a relatively lengthy text, if you "list the words occurring within that text in order of decreasing frequency, the rank of a word on that list multiplied by its frequency will equal a constant". The equation for this relationship is: r x f = k, Wherethe rank of the word is, fits the frequency and k is the constant (Potter 1988). Zipf applied the formula to the way the authored use words as an expression of what he called the "principle of least effort". He regarded it as a natural law which governs all human activities. In any language, the words which have a high frequency of occurrence are those that coat less in usage or require less effort in communication. Zipf illustrated his law with an analysis, which had been made on the frequency of the 26,530 words used by of James Joyce's in composing Ulysses. He found that the rank order of the word in the frequency list multiplied by the frequency remained relatively static along the entries distribution. The tenth word in the list, for example, was used 26 times. The law represents only an approximation between rank and frequency, which is hyperbolic.

4.2.3. Bradford's Law of Scattering of Scientific Papers

It has been observed that most of the relevant sources for any particular subject seem to be contributes in a relatively small part of the literature, and the rest are scattered in a fixed ratio. This phenomenon has been called the "Law of Scattering and was first described by the British Librarian S. C. Bradford Samuel[6] Clement Bradford, a chemist turned librarian was interested in the problem of the scatter of papers on a scientific subject through the scientific journals. Bradford's law of scattering describes a quantitative relation between journals and the papers they publish.

Bradford's Law serves as a general guideline to librarians in determining the number of core journals in any given field. It states that journals in a single field can be divided into three parts, each containing the same number of articles: 1) a core of journals on the subject, relatively few in number, that produces approximately one-third of all the articles, 2) a second zone, containing the same number of articles as the first, but a greater number of journals, and 3) a third zone, containing the same number of articles as the second, but a still greater number of journals. The mathematical relationship of the number of journals in the core to the first zone is a constant n and to the second zone the relationship is n^2. Bradford expressed this relationship as 1: n: n^2...

In other words, if the top n journals contribute (or publish) 33.33 % of the articles in a given subject, the next n^2 journals contribute only 33.33 % of the literature and the rest of the literature (i.e.33.33 %) is scattered in n^3 least productive journals. This means that only a small number of journals will be needed to supply the nucleus of a narrow scientific subject. Beyond the nucleus or first zone, however, the number of journals required to produce the same number of papers increases geometrically.

Bradford, chief librarian at the London Science Museum, has made a statistical analysis of two geophysics bibliographies, the Current Bibliography of Applied Geophysics (1928-1931) and the Quarterly Bibliography of Lubrication (1931-1933). He made graphical representation of these data and plotted a bibliography with cumulative number of reference (R) against logarithm of the cumulative number of journals (log n). It is popularly known as "Bradford Bibliograph". The graphical form of his data points out some ambiguity in his Law of Scattering. Mathematically, his theoretical speculation and his graphical representation are not identical. His theory only corresponds to the linear portion of his bibliography but does not tally with the rising slope or drop of the bibliograph. Bradford formulated his empirical law of scatter as follows: "The aggregate number of articles in a given subject, apart from those produced by the first group of large producers (periodicals), is proportional to the logarithm of the number of producers concerned, when these are arranged in order of decreasing productivity". This may be stated differently: if periodicals contributing to a subject are ranked and then grouped in such a way that each group increases geometrically. Bradford himself provides the least complicated explanation: The whole range of periodicals thus acts as a family of successive generations of diminishing kinship, each constituent of a generation producing inversely according to its degree of remoteness.

Mathematically, Bradford's Law can be stated as: $f(x) = a + b \log x$, Where $f(x)$ is the cumulative number of references as contained in first x most productive journals, a and b are constants. Law of scatter says that $n^1: n^2: n^3 = 1: \alpha : \alpha^2$... where á is a constant[7]. He tested the journals containing references to these fields in their descending order of productivity and then divided the articles into three approximately equal zones or groups[8]. He termed the first one as the nuclear zone, which is highly productive; the second zone as moderately productive zone; and the third he described as peripheral zone or low productive zone.

Bradford has discovered regularity in calculating the number of titles in each of the three zones. On the basis of the observations, Bradford concluded that the ratio of the titles of journals in successive zones followed a common pattern. Bradford's verbal formulation stated that "if scientific journals are arranged in order of their decreasing productivity of articles on a given subject, they may be divided into a nucleus of periodicals more particularly devoted to the subject, and several 'group' or 'zones' containing the same number of articles as the nucleus, where the number of periodicals in the nucleus and Succeeding zones will be 1: n: n^2, 'n' is a multiplier".

Based on Bradford's observations, Brookes[9] suggested the following linear relation to describe the scattering phenomenon as:

$$F(x) = a + b \log x$$

Where F(x) is the cumulative number of reference contained in the first x most productive journals; a and b are constants. This is the most widely used formulation of Bradford's law.

Vickery extended the verbal formulation to show that it can be applied to any number of zones of equal yield. Leimkuhler issued a simple function for Bradford' distribution, which was named after him:

$$R(x) = a \log (1+br)$$

Where R(r) is the cumulative number of article contributed by journals ranked 1 through r, and a and bare parameters.

Similarly, Brookes derivation for journal productivity takes the form $R(r) = a \log (b/r)$ Further, Wilkinson noticed that the formulae provided by Leimkuhler and Brookes did not really describe the same phenomenon.

Starting from the late 1960s, several mathematical formulations, models, and syntheses of previous statements related to Bradford's law have been put forth, but very little agreement exists about which model is the best.

Brooke's expression of the Bradford distribution has however gained wide acceptance.

4.2.3.1. Theoretical Aspects of Bradford's Law

Bradford's law of scattering describe a quantitative relationship between journals and the papers they publish. It explains that, only a small number of core journals will be need to supply the nucleus of papers on a given topic which accounts for a substantial percentage (1/3) of the articles, to be followed by a second larger group of journals that accounts for another third, while a much larger group of journals picked up the last third.

There are two most widely recognized formulations of the Bradford's law: the verbal formulation which is derived from the verbal statement of Bradford's conclusion, and the graphical formulation, which is an empirical expression derived from the graphical survey of a distribution of periodicals.

If scientific periodicals are arranged in order to decreasing productivity of articles on a given subjects, they may be divided into nucleus of periodicals more particularly devoted to the subjects and several group or zones containing the same number of articles as the nucleus, when the number of periodicals of the nucleus and the succeeding zones will as 1: á: á^2.... The constants á is the property of the collection of periodicals called the Bradford multiplier. This statement is called the verbal formulation of Bradford's law.

Bradford did not give a mathematical model for his law. Models were suggested later by Brookes, Vickery and Leimkuhler. Several authors, while explaining the scattering of articles in journals, have formulated many different models of Bradford's law.

Leimkuhler developed a model based on Bradford's verbal formulation as:

$$R(r) = a \log (1+br) \qquad \text{... (1)}$$

r = 1, 2, 3.........

While explaining Leimkuhler's law, Egghe (1985) shows that

$$a = y_0 / \log k \qquad \text{... (2)}$$

$$b = k-1 / r_0 \qquad \text{... (3)}$$

Here

r_0– is the number of sources in the first Bradford group.

y_0 – the number of items in every Bradford group (all these group of item being of equal sizes), and

k– The Bradford multiplier.

R (r) is the cumulative number of items produce by the sources of rank 1, 2, 3........r

a and b are constants a appearing in the law of Leimkuhler.

y_m is the number of items in the most productivity sources

In forming Bradford groups, it is shown that the number of group's p is a parameter that can be chosen freely.

Once p is determined we have also k, since in Egghe

$k = (e^{\gamma} * y_m)^{1/p}$ ... (4)

Where γ is Euler's number (e^{γ} = 1.781).

If the sources are ranked in decreasing order of productivity, then y_m is the number of items in the most productivity sources.

Then y_0 and r_0 as follows

$y_0 = y^2_m \log k$, and ... (5)

$r_0 = (k-1)\, y_m$ ... (6)

In principles, choose any whole number of p of Bradford group that one want to obtain an element in the decision what p is going to be used is offered by the practical advantage of founding a value for r_0 (the number of sources in the first Bradford group), which is a whole number. This is not really the requirement since one can always round off to the nearest. Whole number, but if the calculated r_0 is close to the whole number this reduces some initial fluctuations, when construction Bradford's group.

Once p is chosen, calculate (Egge, 1996) the value

of k can be calculated by using

$$k = (1.781^* y_m)^{1/p} = (1.781^* y_m)^{1/r} \quad \text{... (7)}$$

and

$$y_0 = A / P$$

Where A denotes the total number of articles in the bibliography; indeed we have p group, each containing y_0 items.

Let T denote the total number of journals. In Bradford group, these are $r_0\ k^{i-1}$ sources (i = 1, 2, 3....p)

$$T = r_0 + r_0 k + r_0 k^2 + ...r_0 k^{p-2} \quad \text{... (8)}$$

So,

$$r_0 = \frac{T}{1 + k + k^2 + ... k^{p-1}} = \frac{T(k-1)}{k^{p-1}} \quad \text{... (9)}$$

Since A and T are obviously known from the raw date set, r_0 and y_0 are calculated, once p is calculated by the formula (7).

According to Brookes, to the test the conformity of Bradford's law, one should meet three implicit conditions.

(i) In dividing the journals into zones, the number of articles in each zones must remain constant

(ii) The Bradford's multiplier k must be greater than one.

(iii) The Bradford multiplier must remain approximately constant.

4.2.3.2. Graphical Aspect of Bradford's Law

The graphical formulation is obtained by plotting curves in a plane whose coordinates are the cumulative number of articles (in the y-axis) and the logarithm of the cumulative number of journals of the collection (in the x-axis),where journals are cumulated from most to least productive. This curve has invariably an ascending shape, which after a certain point approaches a straight line. According to Bradford, the area described by the curving line is usually regarded as nucleus zone or core journals and considered as the most productive zone: the area covered by the linear straight line is the moderately productive zone; and the area which is often called as the Groos Droop (or 'inflection point') represents the peripheral zone or outer zone, i.e. the least productive zone where relevant references are widely scattered among a great number of periodicals. Brookes discussed the groos droop and argued that droop was an indication of the incomplete nature of the bibliography examined.

If the distribution confirms to Bradford's law, the graph is known as 'Bradford Bibliograph' and it will display the characteristics of 3 distinct regions (i) a rapid rise for the first few points. (ii) a major portion of linear relation between two variables and (iii) a 'droop' at the tail end of the distribution indicating the incompleteness of the bibliography.

$R(n) = k \log(n/s)$

R (n) = The number of relevant papers contributed by journal ranked n.

k = is a constant which determines the slope of the Bradford's curve and is related to the document collection.

s = is a constant which determines where the straight line, if extended, would intersect the horizontal axis.

Bradford's verbal formulation of the law of scattering was not mathematically equivalent to the geometrical representation described in his article. The verbal form was the result of theoretical speculation while the graphical form was obtained from empirical data derived from the bibliographies. The graphical formulation has been found to be more accurate when compared with data and also more convenient to use.

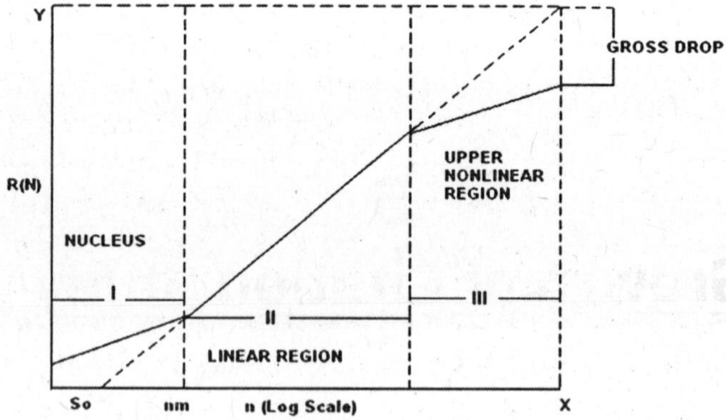

Bradford Distribution

General Form of Bradford Distribution

4.3. REFERENCES

1. More, Philip M. & Leimkular, Ferdinard F. (1979). Technical note: exact solution for the Bradford distribution and it use in modeling informational data. *Oper Res, 27 (1),* 187-98.
2. De Solla Price, Derek J. (1976). A general theory of bibliometric and other cumulative advantage process. *Journal of American Society Information Science, 27,*292-306.
3. Ravichandra Rao, I. K. (1983). *Quantitative methods in Library and Information Science.* New Delhi: Wiley Eastern.
4. White, Howard D. & Mccain, Katherine W. (1989). Bibliometrics. *Ann. Rev. Information Science Technology, 24,* 119-86.
5. Potter, William Gray. (1988, September). Of making many books there is no end: bibliometrics and libraries. *The Journal of Academic Librarianship,* 14 238a-238c (insert between 238 and 239).
6. Bradford, S.C. (1950). *Documentation.* Washington, D C: Washington Affairs Press.
7. Bradford, S.C. (1934).Sources of information on specific subjects. *Engineering, 137(3550),* 85-86.
8. Brookes, B.C. (1968). Derivation and application of Bradford-Zipf distribution. *Journal of Documentation, 24 (4),* 247-65.
9. Brookes, B.C. (1969). Bradford's law and bibliography of science. *Nature, 232 (5223)* 955.

5

Growth of Citation Study

5.1. INTRODUCTION

Growth of literature is an account of what has been published on a topic by accredited scholars/researchers. Studies of the related literature are very essential for a new research. Study of related literature implies locating, reading and evaluating report of research as well as report of casual observation and opinion that are related to the individuals planned research project.

For the good foundation of any research, review of the related literature is very important, which provides all needed ideas to the researches to make the work relevant, unique and qualitative.

The search of literature should be conducted in a systematic way to achieve optimum results. Otherwise the search may lead to wastage of labour and time and poor retrieval of relevant information. Mualy (1969) has pointed out the importance of related literature as follows, "the survey of literature is crucial aspect in the planning of the body and the time spends in such a survey, invariably is wise statements".

As research technique bibliometrics has been used to study the literature of many subject fields. The literature in this area has grown in tremendous quantities.

A survey of the trends was felt necessary to identify if anysimilar study has already been made and to get an idea of the process of application of quantitative analysis /methods.

1. Chen, J., Wang, D.N., Zhu, C.L., Guo, R.H., Liu, Y., Wang, H., Li Y. & Liu, N. (2011)[1], studied in "Analysis of highly cited papers published in Chinese Journal of Endemiology during 2000-2006". To analysis the inherent quality of highly cited papers published in Chinese Journal of Endemiology, so as to identify the direction of invitation for contributions, find high quality articles, and to improve the journal's core competitiveness. A total of 68 highly cited papers were obtained. These articles were statistically analyzed according to publication year, section type, author, and geographical distribution of units. The citation frequency of the highly cited papers ranged from 20 to 94, with an average of 31.09 times. The highly cited papers were published in 2000 at most, accounting for 25.0 % (17/68); followed by 2001, accounting for 20.6% (14/68); at least in 2006, accounting for 2.9% (2/68). Of the highly cited papers, experimental study articles was in the highest proportion of 30.9% (21/68); followed by field epidemiological investigation articles, accounting for 23.5% (16/68); editorial, review articles accounting for 10.3% (7/68) and 8.8% (6/68), respectively; short reports, case reports, meeting records etc were not highly cited papers. The number of highly cited papers in editorial, expert forums, academic contend accounted for higher proportion of total number in corresponding section types (7/19, 3/11, 3/7). Highly cited papers came from 13 provinces (municipalities), there were 10 authors contributed two or more highly cited papers, and 8 units contributed two or more highly cited papers.

2. Dingyu (2011)[2], made Quantitative study under the title "Quantitative analysis of research papers on library personalized service in China in 2000-

2010".Chinese Academic Journal Web Publication Library as a data source, with the bibliometric methods, the author Statistics and analyzes the distribution about the research Papers on Library personalized service in 2000-2010 including Published time, journals, authors, subjects and so on, to understand the development Status about the field in the past 11 years, in order to provide the reference on sustainable research.

3. Fardi, A., Kodonas, K., Gogos, C., & Economides, N. (2011)[3], made the study in "Top-cited Articles in Endodontic Journals". The purpose of this study was to identify the 100 top-cited articles published in journals dedicated to endodontology and analyze their characteristics to describe the quality and evolution of research in the field of endodontology. The top-cited articles were selected and analyzed with regard to journals, authors, institution, country of origin, publication title and year, number of citations, article type, study design, level of evidence, and field of study. The top 100 articles were cited between 87 and 554 times. These articles appeared in 4 different journals, with more than half in the Journal of Endodontics, followed by the journals Oral Surgery Oral Medicine Oral Pathology Oral Radiology and Endodontology, the International Endodontic Journal, and Endodontics & Dental Traumatology. Forty-eight articles were published between 1990 and 1999. All articles were published in English and primarily originated from the United States (n=52). The majority of articles were basic science articles (n=55), followed by clinical research studies (n=28) and nonsystematic reviews (n=17). Uncontrolled case series with level IV of evidence and narrative reviews with level V of evidence were the most frequent types of study design. The main topics covered by the top-cited articles were micro leakage and endodontic microbiology.

4. Kumar, H. Anil & Dora, Mallikarjun (2011)[4], investigatedin "Citation analysis of doctoral dissertations at IIMA: A review of the local use of journals" This study analyzed the citations of the 49 doctoral dissertations submitted at the Indian Institute of Management, Ahmadabad, during the period 2004 to 2009. The study revealed that journals were the most cited sources, and based on the pattern of citations, a local ranking list of journals has been developed. The study applied Bradford's law to identify the groups of journals differentiated by their use. Results indicated that the top 48 journals that were ranked among the 30 most used journals contributed to more than 55% of the journal citations.

5. Maharana, B., Majhi, S. & Sethi, B. B. (2011)[5], did a citation study in "Citation analysis of top research papers in chemistry with specific reference to India". The main purpose of this study was to determine India's position in publishing top research papers in chemistry as reflected in Science Direct. It also aimed to found out authorship pattern, countries with major contributions, journals with high publication rates, etc. Design/ methodology/approach: Citation analysis methods were applied to study citations of 450 research papers in chemistry taken from the listing of top 25 papers in Science Direct database. The citations covered 18 issues of the Science Direct generated alert service for the period 2004-2008. The bibliographic data were entered in Excel sheets for necessary analysis. Findings: The studies revealed that, out of 450 research papers, 36 (8 per cent) contributed by Indian researchers. In the ranking of contributing countries, India reserves third position after the USA and China. More than 86 per cent of Indian chemistry research papers were cited by others. As regards to number of citations, 25 per cent of Indian papers were cited between 10 and 25 times each. The journal Tetrahedron was found as the highest publishing journal with 71 (16 per cent) publications.

6. Nederh of, A. J. (2011)[6], did a bibliometric study

in "A bibliometric study of productivity and impact of modern language and literature research". A bibliometric evaluation was made of research performance in modern language and linguistics research. Separate analyses were made for language and linguistics and for literature components of each language in the study. The study covered both publications directed at a national or international scholarly output and publications destined for the general public. The latter accounted for 8-73% of the output, and were particularly important in literature output. Publication and citation behavior differed considerably between language and linguistics on the one hand and literature on the other hand, calling for a tailored design of monitoring studies in both fields. In publications directed at scholars, the national language did not dominate. In literature fields, the language of the object of study was most important, while in language and linguistics, the object language was not always more important than English. The study indicated that both journal articles and book output need to be included in bibliometric evaluation.

7. Walters, G.D. (2011)[7], studied under the title "The citation life cycle of articles published in 13 American Psychological Association journals: A 25-year longitudinal analysis". The annual citation counted of 1,172 articles published in 1985 by 13 American Psychological Association journals were analyzed over a 25-year period. Despite a 61% reduction in citation counts from the peak year (1989: Year 4) to the final year (2010: Year 25), many of these articles were still being cited 25 years after they had been published. When the sample was divided into four categories of impact using the total citation counts for each article-low impact (0-24 citations), moderate impact (25-99 citations), high impact (100-249 citations), and very high impact (250-1763 citations)-the yearly citation counts of low to high-impact articles peaked earlier and displayed a steeper decline than the yearly citation counts of very high-impact articles. Using 5 or more citations a years, 10 or more citations a year, and 20 or more citations a year as markers of moderate-impact, high-impact, and very high-impact articles, respectively, and using the most cited articles in a journal during the first 5 years of the follow-up period as indicators of high impact and very high impact showed promise of predicting impact over the entire 25-year period.

8. Edgar, L. D. (2010)[8], performed a citation study under the title "Citation structure: An analysis of the literature cited in the Journal of International Agricultural and Extension Education from 1997 to 2006". The Journal of International Agricultural and Extension Education (JIAEE) has been an outlet of international agricultural development and education publishing and research dissemination and publishing. The purpose of this study was to assess ten-years of JIAEE to determine literature cited. The study used a quantitative content analysis design. Analyzed in this study were 144 research articles published in JIAEE issues I and III, from 1997 through 2006. There were 2,286 cited literature works identified in the journal. The average number of citations per article was approximately 20. Cited works from premier agricultural education journals were tracked for citation frequencies, in terms of author(s) and year of publication. A total of 234 references were made to premier journals in agricultural education. Citation analysis indicates that JIAEE relies heavily on books published prior to the 1990s. Published articles also cited other journals and conference proceedings produced within the international agriculture arena. JIAEE does not exhibit compactness, indicating that it reaches past its citation boundaries and into interrelated areas of other disciplines. However, it does exhibit weak self-identity meaning it does little to build upon research previously cited in JIAEE.

9. Mahbuba, D., Rousseau, R., & Srivastava, D. (2010)[9], analyzed citations in "A scientometric analysis of health and population research in South Asia: Focus on two research organizations". In study they provided a scientometric comparison between two health and population research organizations, namely the International Centre for Diarrhoeal Disease Research in Bangladesh (ICDDR, B) and the National Institute of Cholera and Enteric Diseases (NICED) in India, during the period 1979-2008. They studied these two institutes because they conducted similar research and because of their collaboration ties. Data were collected from the Web of Science (WoS) as well as from official records of these two organizations. The analysis presents the evolution of publication activities. Special attention was given to research impact through time series of the institutional h- and R-indices, as well as to the trend in yearly citations received. Types of publications, international collaboration with other countries, top scientists and most cited articles co-authored by scientists from these institutions are highlighted. It was observed that female scientists play a minor role in these two institutes.

10. Maz-Machado, A., Torralbo-Rodríguez, M., Vallejo-Ruiz, M., &Bracho-López, R. (2010)[10], did a bibliometric analysis in "Bibliometric analysis of scholarly production from the University of Malaga in the Social Sciences Citation Index (1998-2007)". A bibliometric analysis was performed of the scholarly production of the University of Malaga published during 1998-2007 in journals indexed in the Social Sciences Citation Index (as accessed through the Web of Science). Study examined productivity and chronological distribution, national and international collaboration, scientific production by departments, and the journals in which articles were published. The results reveal a slight increase in productivity, as well as a slightly higher level of co-authorship (2.85) than the average for social sciences in

Spain, along with a good level of collaboration with national and foreign academic institutions.

11. Rojas-Sola, J. I., & De San-Antonio-Gomez, C. (2010)[11], performed a bibliometric study under the title "Bibliometric analysis of Mexican scientific publications in the category engineering, chemical from the web of science database (1997-2008)". The purpose of the study was to characterize the area of Engineering, Chemical at Mexico. So, it has been reviewed at the institutional level, through the database Web of Science (WoS), work on Engineering, Chemical conducted by researchers in Mexican institutions and published in international journals with impact factor between 1997 and 2008. It the Latin American context, where work has been published rate 6,183 article or review in 119 journals, and in Mexico were found 1,302 articles in 87 journals published mostly in English (96.08%), but in Spanish (3.69%) and French (0.23%). On the other hand, they have analyzed the Universities and Research Centers from the point of view quantitative and qualitative, through some bibliometric indicators as the Weighted Impact Factor, Relative Impact Factor and the ratio between the numbers of citations compared to the number of documents. Thus, among the most productive institutions stressed the Mexican Petroleum Institute by the number of documents and the National Autonomous University of Mexico for the ratio between quotes against documents and for the Weighted Impact Factor?

12. Strotmann, Andreas, & Zhao, Dangzhi (2010)[12], made the study in "Combining commercial citation indexes and open-access bibliographic databases to delimit highly interdisciplinary research fields for citation analysis". Field delimitation for citation analysis, the process of collecting a set of bibliographic records with cited-reference information of research articles that represent a research field, is the first step in any citation analysis study of a research field. Due to a number of limitations, the commercial citation indexes have long made it difficult to obtain a comprehensive dataset in this step. This study discussed some of the limitations imposed by these databases, and reports on a method to overcome some of these limitations that was used with great success to delimit an emerging and highly interdisciplinary biomedical research field, stem cell research. The resulting field delimitation and the citation network it induced both excellent. This multi-database method relies on using PubMed for the actual field delimitation, and on mapping between Scopus and PubMed records for obtaining comprehensive information about cited-references contained in the resulting literature. This method provides high-quality field delimitations for citation studies that can be used as benchmarks for studies of the impact of data collection biases on citation metrics, and may help improve confidence in results of scientometric studies for an increased impact of scientometrics on research policy.

13. Vieira, E.S., & Gomes, J.A.N.F. (2010)[13], studied in "Citations to scientific articles: Its distribution and dependence on the article features". The citation counts were increasingly used to assess the impact on the scientific community of publications produced by a researcher, an institution or a country. There were many institutions that use bibliometric indicators to steer research policy and for hiring or promotion decisions. Given the importance that counting citations has today, the aim of the work presented here was to show how citations were distributed within a scientific area and determine the dependence of the citation count on the article features. All articles referenced in the Web of Science in 2004 for Biology & Biochemistry, Chemistry, Mathematics and Physics were considered. They showed that the distribution of citations was well represented by a double exponential Poisson law. There was a dependence of the mean citation rate on the number of co-authors, the number of addresses and the number of references, although this dependence was a little far from the linear behavior. For the relation between the mean impact and the number of pages the dependence obtained was very low. For Biology & Biochemistry and Chemistry we found a linear behavior between the mean citation per article and impact factor and for Mathematics and Physics the results obtained were near to the linear behavior.

Aksnes,This article is not included in your organization's subscription. However, you may be able to access this article under your organization's agreement with Elsevier.

14. Dag W., & Rip, Arie (2009)[14], analyzed citation under the title "Researchers' perceptions of citations". This study looked at how citations were perceived among scientists. Based on a questionnaire survey it traces the repertoire of views and experiences about citations that could be found among Norwegian scientists that had published highly cited papers. Their views circle around three issues: the relation between the quality (or importance or significance) of a paper and its citation history; the importance of visibility and how different sorts of factors play a role in determining citation in general and high citation in particular; and the fairness (or lack of fairness) of the system. Taken together, the respondents' answers and comments offer an informal (and fragmented) sociology of citations and their role in the world of science. In the final section we discuss the relevance of our findings in respect to the increasing use of citation indicators in science policy and research evaluations.

15. Daniel, Gianfranco Di Vaioab & Weisdorfd, Waldenstromc Jacob. (2009)[15], investigatedin "Citation Success: Evidence from Economic History Journal Publications" This study analyzed determinants of citation success among authors publishing in economic history journals. Bibliometric features, like article length and number of authors, are top-ranked journals hardly affects citations. In regard to author-specific characteristics, male authors, full professors and authors working economics or history departments, and authors employed in Anglo-Saxon countries, are more likely to get cited than others. As a shortcut to citation success, it has been found that research diffusion, measured by number of presentations and people mentioned in acknowledgement, boosts the citation rate.

16. Dodson, M.V. (2009)[16], made the study in "Citation analysis: Maintenance of h-index and use of e-index". Citation analysis numbers were used as measures of faculty productivity and/or impact. However, after establishing initial citation numbers how did one conduct maintenance on their citation record? During this time of budgetary uncertainty it is more vital than ever to incorporate citation analysis into annual review packages or any departmental report that relies on such faculty data. The focus of this study was to describe the next step in this process.

17. Gao, Shi-Jian., Yu, Wang-Zhi., & Luo, Feng-Ping. (2009)[17], investigated the study in "Citation analysis of Ph D thesis at Wuhan University, China". This case study was a citation analysis of 56 PhD theses submitted in 2005 at Wuhan University (www.whu.edu.cn) in China. The authors analyzed 10,222 citations in theses in Library and Information Science, Biology, Photogrammetry and Remote Sensing, and Stomatology and reviewed and compared the characteristics of the literature cited in the four disciplines. The results revealed that in Biology and Stomatology mainly English language publications were cited whereas in the field of Library and Information Science, the cited literature came primarily from Chinese sources. In Photogrammetry and Remote Sensing, citations were almost evenly split between English and Chinese sources. An appendix with tables of the journal titles cited most frequently may be used to evaluate serial holdings and to serve as a guide for students preparing their theses.

18. Jan, Rosy. (2009)[18], measured the study in "Citation Analysis of Library Trends" Citation analysis of all the journal articles published in the Library Trends from 1994-2007 is carried out. 593 articles were published in the journal during 14 years. Highest number (52) of articles was published in 2004. The Journal contained 15662 references for the study period of which 13783 were p-citations and 1879 were e-citations. Every issue published approx. 11 articles and each article has an average of 23.2 p-references and 3.1 e-citations. It was found that 44.51% print books were consulted by the authors and 0% e-books were accessed. Authors have consulted 44.04% p-journals as against 11.82% e-journals. Figures shows that 88.14% other web references were used in the articles reference. Female contribution (52.34%) accounts more than male contribution (47.66%).

19. Kajikawa, Yuya., & Takeda, Yoshiyuki (2009)[19], made the citation study in "Citation network analysis of organic LEDs". The field of organic light-emitting diodes (OLEDs) was an emergent research domain because of both scientific interest in chemistry and condensed matter physics and industrial importance as flat panel displays. In study, they analyzed a citation network of OLED papers and used a topological clustering method to investigate the structure of research and to detect emerging research domains. They found that most papers belong to two main clusters: organics and polymers. These two clusters have distinctive differences in sub cluster structures and journals where papers were published. Supposing this discrepancy to indicate research progress, organics are in the applied research stage, while polymers were in the basic research stage.

20. Krishnamoorthy, G., Ramakrishnan. J., & Devi, S. (2009)[20], carried out a bibliometric study in the title "Bibliometric analysis of diabetes literature indexed in the MEDLINE database for the period 1995-2004" shows that maximum number of records (13244) was during 2003, followed by 12690 in 2002 and 11061 in 2001. Relative Growth Rate (RGR) was found to be decreasing year wise. The Doubling Time (DT) was found to increase every year. Ranking of the journals based on the quantum of research output on diabetes during 1995-2004 shows that USA in the largest contributor of literature on diabetes research. The research productivity of diabetes conforms to Bradford's Law of Scattering.

21. Olatokun, Wole Michael, & Makinde, Olayinka. (2009)[21], studied under the title "Citation analysis of dissertations submitted to the Department of Animal Science, University of Ibadan, Nigeria" during the period 2000-2007 were analyzed for finding possible relationships between citing, cited articles and authors. Frequency and percentage distributions (presented in charts, tables, and graphs) and measures of central tendency were used to analyses data. Findings showed that journals were the most utilized reference materials in the dissertations. Also, poultry nutrition works had the highest number of dissertations followed by agricultural biochemistry and nutrition. The lowest number of dissertations was from forage production and management and monogastric nutrition with just two dissertations each.

22. Pilkington, Alan, & Meredith, Jack. (2009)[22], conducted a study under the title "The evolution of the intellectual structure of operations management 1980–2006: A citation/ co-citation analysis" Citation analysis combined with a network analysis of co-citation data from three major operations management (OM) journals was being used to reveal the evolution of the intellectual structure of the OM field between 1980 and 2006. This spans the entire time since the beginning of research journals specific to the field. Employing a bibliometric citation/co-citation analysis to investigate the foundations of the discipline enables a robust, quantitative approach to uncovering the evolution of research in OM. The study finds that the intellectual structure of the field made statistically significant changes between the 1980s, the 1990s, and the 2000s and evolved from a pre-occupation with narrow, tactical topics toward more strategic, macrotopics, including new research methods and techniques. A factor analysis identifies the 12 top knowledge groups in the field and how they change over the decades. Illustrations of the structure of the co-citations represented the field were generated from a spring-embedded algorithm that was an improvement over the standard multi-dimensional scaling (MDS) approach to illustrating the knowledge groups.

23. Su, Yu-Min., Yang, Shu-Ching., Hsu, Ping-Yu., & Shiau, Wen-Lung. (2009)[23], analyzed co-citation under the title "Extending co-citation analysis to discover authors with multiple expertise". The author co-citation analysis (ACA) method was commonly used to group authors of reference papers. Since the traditional ACA method analyzes only first authors of reference papers, it disregarded the contributions of other coauthors and can only group each first author into one cluster. This study proposed an innovative ACA algorithm called "complete author pair (CAP) algorithm", which groups complete author sets of reference papers into clusters and thus finds authors who may have expertise in more than one area. The CAP algorithm was implemented in two citation data banks that collected paper references from two ACM journals during 2002–2005. The results showed that the CAP algorithm runs up to 90% of average precision in each citation bank when comparing against ACM CCS.

24. Zabed Ahmed, S. M., & Rahman, Md. Anisur. (2009)[24], under the title "Lotka's law and authorship distribution in nutrition research in Bangladesh" examined the validity of Lotka's law to authorship distribution A list of periodical articles on various aspects of nutrition research in Bangladesh published during 1972-2006 was compiled for analysis. Using "full productivity" of authorship, a total of 998 personal author names were identified. Lotka's law was tested using both generalized and modified forms and Kolmogorov-Smimov goodness-of-fit tests were applied. The results suggest that author productivity distribution predicted in Lotka's generalized inverse square law is not applicable to nutrition research of Bangladesh. Using least-squares excluding high productive authors and maximum likelihood methods, Lotka's law is found to be applicable to nutrition research of Bangladesh.

25. Jiao, Qun G., Onwuegbuzie, Anthony J. & Waytowich, Vicki L. (2008)[25], analyzed the study in "The relationship between citation errors and library anxiety: An empirical study of doctoral students in education". The study investigated whether levels of library anxiety predict simultaneously the citation error rate and quality of reference lists in doctoral dissertation proposals among 93 doctoral students in education. A canonical correlation analysis revealed a multivariate relationship between levels of library anxiety and both the citation error rate and quality of reference lists. This finding suggested that level of library anxiety plays an important role in students' ability to construct accurate reference lists.

26. Lopez-Illescas, Carmen., Moya-Anegon, Felix De., & Moed, Henk F. (2008)[26], analyzed in "Coverage and citation impact of on cological journals in the Web of Science and Scopus". This study reviewed a number of studies comparing Thomson Scientific's Web of Science (WoS) and Elsevier's Scopus. It collated their journal coverage in an important medical subfield: oncology. It was found that all WoS-covered on cological journals (n = 126) were indexed in Scopus, but that Scopus covers many more journals (an additional n = 106). However, the latter group tends to have much lower impact factors than WoS covered journals. Among the top 25% of sources with the highest impact factors in Scopus, 94% was indexed in the WoS, and for the bottom 25% only 6%. In short, in oncology the WoS was a genuine subset of Scopus, and tends to cover the best journals from it in terms of citation impact per paper. Although Scopus covered 90% more on cological journals compared to WoS, the average Scopus-based impact factor for journals indexed by both databases was only 2.6% higher than that based on WoS data. Results reflected fundamental differences in coverage policies: the WoS based on Eugene Garfield's concepts of covering a selective set of most frequently used (cited) journals; Scopus with broad coverage, more similar to large disciplinary literature databases. The study also found that 'classical', WoS-based impact factors strongly correlate with a new, Scopus-based metric, SCImago Journal Rank (SJR), one of a series of new indicators founded on earlier work. Citation influence for journal aggregates of scientific publications: Theory, with application to the literature of physics. Information Processing and Management, 12, 297–312] that weight citations according to the prestige of the citing journal (Spearman's rho = 0.93). Four lines of future research were proposed.

27. Nazim, Mohammad & Ahmad, Moin. (2008)[27], investigatedunder the title "A bibliometric analysis on nanotechnology research" examines the scientific output in the field of 'nanotechnology', the aim being to offer an overview of research trends in this field and characterize its most important aspects such as growth of literature, authorship pattern, most productive journals, authors, countries, etc. A total of 2675 articles for the period of 1991-2006 were collected from Web of Science (WoS), especially via the Science Citation Index. The various analyses focus on the presentation of publications, frequencies and percentages. Authorship pattern and core journals were examined using Lotka's Law and Bradford's Law of scattering respectively. The yearly analysis showed that there was a rapid growth of nanotechnology research from the beginning of 21st century. When applying Bradford's law of scattering with respect to the identification of core journals, three concentric zones were defined with the ratio of 32:149:639, which are partially in accordance with the Bradford's distribution. With respect to the author productivity through the application of Lotka's law it was observed that the values obtained were widely different from the real values.

28. Patil, S. K., & Chikate, R V. (2008)[28], analyzed the study in "Citation Analysis of Theses in Library and Information Science Submitted to University of Pune: A Pilot Study" The study observed more than 6,000 citations from 27 doctoral dissertations were analyzed. Nearly half of the citations recorded are from journal articles: 2,639 (42.2%).Three quarters of the journal articles were from LIS journals, with the remainder from 33 other subject areas. *College and Research Libraries* was the most cited journal, followed by *Scientometrics.* Most of the citations are from 55 journals out of the total number.

29. Vallmitjana, Núria, & Sabatwe, L. G. (2008)[29], applied the method in "Citation Analysis of Ph.D. Dissertation References as a tool for Collection Management in an Academic Chemistry Library" to ascertain what types of documents are the most frequently used in the research process, the most frequently consulted journals and obsolescence rate of the journals. The analysis covered 46 doctoral theses presented at the Institute Químic de Sarriá (IQS) from 1995 to 2003. The results obtained from the 4,203 citations revealed that the most frequently used documents were scientific papers, which accounted for 79 percent of the total; 33 journals met 50 percent of the informational needs; and the age of 50 percent of the citations was no older than 9 years.

30. Vallmitjana, Núria, & Sabatwe, L. G. (2008)[30], measured the study in "Web Citation Behavior in Scholarly Electronic Journals in the field of Library and Information Science" this study described a citation analysis of research articles from scholarly electronic journals published in 2000-2006. The analysis focused on the extent to which scholars were using web based sources in scholarly electronic journals. Results of the study showed that 81.49% of articles published in selected 9 electronic journals during 2000-2006 have web references. Out of 25,730 references 56.54 % of references were print journal references and 43.52% of them were web references. The majority of articles having web references were found in *ARIADANE* (93.24%) which ranks first, followed by *Cybermetrics: International Journal of Scientometrics, Informetrics, and Bibliometrics (*89.47%) and *D-LIB Magazine* (89.19%). It could be observed from the study that comparatively more number of articles (81.05%) published during the years 2000-2006 have web references.

31. Wakefield, Robin. (2008)[31], studied in "Networks of accounting research: A citation-based structural and network analysis". This study measured journal influence using the principles of knowledge capital and social networks. The structural index measure was used to evaluate knowledge capital flows in a network of 22 accounting research journals over the years 2000–2006. The influence measure was a function of both the quantity and quality of citations resulting in journal influence rankings that reflect each journal's contribution to the broad context of accounting research. Findings showed that although some journals were highly cited, they may be less influential in the accounting research community. Publishing research of high value was one key to increasing the influence of a journal in the network. Furthermore, the analysis of a well-defined journal network provides a view of the distinct contribution of individual journals. The network analysis diagram provides a visual perspective of journal relationships emphasizes the strength of relational ties and suggests that influential journals may take on different roles. The contribution of other disciplines to the top-five influential accounting research journals was also presented.

32. Frandsen, Tove Faber. (2007)[32], investigated under the title in "Journal self-citations-Analysing the JIF mechanism". This paper investigated the mechanism of the Journal Impact Factor (JIF). Although created as a journal selection tool the indicator was probably the central quantitative indicator for measuring journal quality. The focus was journal self-citations as the treatment of these in analyses and evaluations was highly disputed. The role of self-citations (both self-citing rate and self-cited rate) investigated on a larger scale in this analysis in order to achieve statistical reliable material that can further qualify that discussion. Some of the hypotheses concerning journal self-citations were supported by the results and some were not.

33. Nederhof, Anton J. (2006)[33], made the study in "Bibliometric monitoring of research performance in the Social Sciences and the Humanities: A review". This study addressed research performance monitoring of the social sciences and the humanities using citation analysis. Main differences in publication and citation behavior between the (basic) sciences and the social sciences and humanities are outlined. Limitations of the (S) SCI and A&HCI for monitoring research performance were considered. For research performance monitoring in many social sciences and humanities, the methods used in science need to be extended. A broader range of both publications (including non-ISI journals and monographs) and citation indicators (including non-ISI reference citation values) was needed. Three options for bibliometric monitoring were discussed.

34. Whitley, Edgar A., & Galliers, Robert D. (2007)[34], provides empirical evidence under the titled "An alternative perspective on citation classics: Evidence from the first 10 years of the European Conference on Information Systems." Purpose of this study an alternative perspective to the many citation classics papers that have appeared in the IS literature by presenting citation data from the first 10 years of the European Conference on IS (ECIS, 1993–2002), identifying the most frequently cited texts in this sample. They compared the ECIS citation classics with those presented by others and suggest that the ECIS data highlight the ways in which the IS field is more nuanced than previously reported.

35. Clarke, Maria Elizabeth, & Oppenheim, Charles. (2006)[35], evaluated the study under the title "Citation behavior of information science students II: Postgraduate students: this paper reported the results of a study of student citation behaviors in the Department of Information Science, Loughborough University. The research methods were citation analysis of student dissertation bibliographies from 1998 to 2003, a survey of student's attitudes to citation behavior and a test of student citation accuracy. The results of the investigation showed the majority of citations were to journals (32.6%), books (30.0%), and websites (24.0%). Websites were found to be cited more than books for the first time in 2002 and again in 2003. The number of citations to electronic formats increased over time. A highly significant difference was found in the correlation between the topic students studied and the numbers of citations to electronic journals. The overall percentage of citation errors was 24.9% and the majority of bibliographies (80%) were found to contain at least one error. Many students (56.9%) stated they did not feel confident when citing electronic materials.

36. Tsay, Ming-Yueh. (2006)[36], did a citation study in "Journal self-citation study for semiconductor literature: Synchronous and diachronous approach" The study investigated the self-citations of the most productive semiconductor journals by synchronous (self-citing rate) and diachronous (self-cited rate) approaches. Journal's productivity of 100 most productive semiconductor journals was gathered from INSPEC database, 1978-1997 through OVID. Data of citation frequency were obtained from the Science Citation Index (SCI), Journal Citation Reports (JCR) 2001 CDROM edition by the title-by-title search. The self-citing and self-cited data were drawn from the Citing Journal Listing and the Cited Journal Listing of the JCR CDROM version 1990–2001. Self-citing and self-cited rates were determined by the method suggested by the JCR. Eighty-seven journals common to INSPEC and JCR in semiconductor were selected as the object of this study and were listed for statistical tests. The results of the present study demonstrate that high self-citing journals were usually older than low self-citing journals. In contrast to the self-citing data, the journal self-cited rate was not closely related to the publication year but reflects the characteristics of various journals. Journals with a short time interval of publication were more possible with high self-citing and self-cited rates. Journals with higher self-citing rate tend to be more productive and receive more citation than journals with lower self-citing rate. The journal self-cited rate has no association with the number of articles that a journal published and the citation it received. A journal with a higher self-citing rate tends to be cited more by itself. The mean self-citing rate is 9.59% and the mean self-cited rate was 15.03%. There was a significant difference between self-citing and self-cited rates within the same set of journals.

37. Kristen, B. La Bonte. (2005)[37], under the title "Citation Analysis: A Method for Collection Development for Rapidly Developing Field". Made a citation analysis to determine if the Sciences-Engineering Library at the

University of California at Santa Barbara is meeting the needs of an interdisciplinary group of 60 faculty members at the new California Nano Systems Institute. The latest three publications of each faculty member (published within the last two years) were analyzed in two ways using the Science Citation Index: 1) the journals they were published in, and 2) the journals where cited articles were published. The results indicated that the library subscribes to 98 percent of the journals in which faculty members were published or were citing frequently.

38. Labonte, K. B. (2005)[38], studied in "Citation Analysis: A Method for Collection Development for a Rapidly Developing Field Science and Technology" carried out citation analysis to determine if the science-engineering library at the University of California at Santa Barbara (UCSB) is meeting the needs of an interdisciplinary group of 60 faculty members at the new California Nano systems Institute. The aimed of study to developing a core list of journals and identifying journals. That should be added to the collections in the sciences-engineering library at UCSB. Result from the study indicated that the library subscribed to 90 % of the journals in which faculty members were publishing or citing frequently. The study suggested that this information is useful to map the citation pattern of a new interdisciplinary field and can be used for future collection management decisions.

39. Gupta, B. M., & Bhattacharya, Sujit. (2004)[39], mapped in "A Bibliometric Approach towards Mapping the Dynamics of Science and Technology". This study highlighted the role of bibliometrics in studying the dynamics of science and technology. Tools and techniques available in bibliometrics to address and understand the complexities of scientific fields were explored. The study concludes that for wider acceptance among academicians and policy makers, bibliometric approach should ingrain itself within sociology and philosophy of science in studying the different facets of science and technology.

40. Faba-Pearez, Cristina & Biblioteconomi, V. P. de Guerrero-Bote Facultad. (2003)[40], made the study in "Sitation" distributions and Bradford's law in a closed Web space" The study looks at how well the distribution of "sitations" (in links received by Web spaces) fits either a power law (of the Lotka type) or a bibliometric distribution for printed publications (of the Bradford type). The experimental sample examined the sitations found in a closed generic environment of thematically-related Web sites – the case of Extremadura (Spain). Two sets of data, varying several parameters, were used. The sitation distributions found were coherent with those described in previous experiments of this type, including in the exponent. The plots of accumulated clusters of sitations and targets, however, did not fit the typical Bradford distribution.

41. Johry, Nutan. (2003)[41], performed a citation analysis under the title "International Social Science Journal (ISSJ): a bibliometric study" he analyzed that the information is growing very fast in all the fields of knowledge and the social sciences are no exception. The number of books and journals in social sciences are increasing day by day. Virtually any publication whether it is a journal, monograph or research report needs to be examined by looking into the quality of its content analysis. Such as examination can be done by using research tools like content analysis or bibliometrics.

42. Okiy, Rose B. (2003)[42], made the study in "A citation analysis of education dissertations at the Delta State University" in study the total of 4,012 citations in 70 postgraduate dissertations in education submitted to the Delta State University Library between 1992 and 2002 were studied. Most postgraduate students in education used more textbooks (60.3 per cent), than other forms of library materials. Four of the top ranked journals, including the most popularly used the West African

Journal of Education (WAJE) were available in the library. A total of 12 (66.7 per cent) of the 18 most popularly used journals were US publications, thus creating the need for Delta State University Library to improve on its local journal collection. Of the 18 most cited journals, six (33.3 per cent) ranked among the list of significant journals in the field of education.

43. Shokken, Ashu, & Kaushik, Sanjay K. (2003)[43], used citation analysis to determine the study in "Indian Journal of Economics: a citation analysis" The major objective of the study was to found out the authorship pattern and citations pattern of articles appeared in IJE published between January to December 2002.Tatal 37 articles were published in these issues. Overall 701citations featuring 1038 authors have been made. The result indicates that 48.46 % articles published in these issues were single authored. The majority of citations i.e. 450 were also single authored. The result revealed that journal articles were predominant with 52.78 % of total citations. The ratio of Author Self Citation to total citations was 1:46.73. The ratio of Journal self-Citation to total citations was 1:350.5.The result also highlight that 358 citations were less than 10 years old, whereas 102 citations were less than20 years but more than 10 years old. It was clear that a majority of documents cited in these issues were published not more than years ago.

44. Wohlin, Claes. (2002)[44], counted and analyzed citations in "An analysis of the most cited articles in software engineering journals". The objective of the analysis was to identify and list the articles that have influenced others the most as measured by citation count. An understanding of which research was viewed by the research community as most valuable to build upon may provide valuable insights into what research to focus on now and in the future. Based on the analysis, a list of the 20 most cited articles was presented. The intention of the analysis was twofold. First, to identify the most cited articles, and second, to invite the authors of the most cited articles in 2002 to contribute to a special section of Information and Software Technology.

45. Das, Anup Kumar, & Sen, B. K. (2001)[45], performed a citation analysis in "Indian Journal of Medial Research: An analysis of citation pattern" which was based on 781 citations appended to 43 research articles pertaining to January to June 2000 issues of volume 109 of Indian journal of Medical Research. The authorship pattern of citations showed that more than 15 percent contributions were single authored and about 85 percent were the result of teamwork. The team size of this field was bigger than those in the fields of chemistry and physics. Single authored articles amount to 15, 52 percent of the total citations and about 28% resulted through the collaboration of five or more authors of the citations 88.3% pertain to journal articles of the citing articles 38 contributed by Indian authors, 3 by foreign authors and 2 jointly by Indian and foreign authors of the total citations 9.48% were author self-citations and 7.3% were journal self-citations.

46. Gooden, Angela M. (2001)[46], analyzed citation in "Citation Analysis of Chemistry Doctoral Dissertations: An Ohio State University Case Study". A citation analysis of dissertations accepted in the Department of Chemistry at The Ohio State University between 1996-2000 was performed as a way to determine material use. The 30 dissertations studied generated a total of 3,704 citations. Types of materials cited, currency of literature, and dissertation topics were all analyzed. The current results corroborate past research by other authors. Journal articles were cited more frequently than monographs: 85.8% of the citations were journal articles and 8.4% of the citations were monographs.

47. Verma, Neerja. (2001)[47], in "Analysis of Contributions in Library Herald" analysed the 176 contributions included in 10 volumes of Library Herald (vol. 28-37) which was an official publication of Delhi Library Association and a leading journals in the field of Library and Information Science. It given information about average number of contributions in each volume of Library Herald. Studies authorship pattern, state wise and institution made in Library Herald in various fields of the subject. It also analysis 1587 citations appearing in 10 volumes of Library Herald.

48. Aidtya Kumari, H., & Rao, Shivram K. (2000)[48], stated in "The Nucleus: an international journal of Cytology and allied topics: a bolometric study". This study analysed articles published during 1992-95 in the journal to find the most frequently cited periodicals by the biological scientists in India. A list of 115 most commonly cited periodicals has been prepared. In addition to this, identifies the types of publication cited. Authorship pattern showed that single authored paper follow the double-authored articles. The study revealed that periodical articles are the major sources of information; the publications in English language were used maximum ; maximum number of citations are the publications from USA (37.79%); among cited journals the journals 'Cytolgia' occupied the first rank ; and collaborative research is favoured that of role research in the field of biological sciences.

49. Ghosh, Saptarshi. (2000)[49], did a study on "citations pattern of contributions in Library Science with A slant to documentation and information studies". This study analysed of 1374 citations from 117 contributions published in Library Science with a Slant to Documentation and Information Studies, VI. 32-36, which showed that the contributing authors were mainly working librarians as professionals than that of teaching faculty. Eugene Garfield appeared as the most productive author as the trend of contributing articles were mainly on bibliometric or citation analysis during 1995 to 1997

"Library Science with a Slant to Documentation and Information Studies" was the most cited journal followed by the "current content" Co-citations and bibliographic coupling strength has also been counted to observe the interdependence of the cited documents. It showed that the contributions most frequently refer to the journals in which they write.

50. Ramesh, L. S. R. C. V., & Nagaraju, A. V. S. S. (2000)[50], under title "Citation Analysis of the Indian Journal of Information, Library and Society" analysed the citations provided in articles of the Indian Journal of Information, Library and Society (IJILIS), during 1995-1999. The journal received 7 citations per article. About 67.5 % of articles had 1-20 citations. More citations were from the books and periodicals than the other type of materials. Tendency of authors seemed to cite indegenous work more as compared to the documents published in other countries. Out of 138 citing articles, 37 articles have no references. Dr. S.R. Ranganathan was first in the rank of authors whose valuable books have been utilized by several authors more frequently and has 32 citations. Second Rank goes to V. L. Kalyane having 25 citations followed by B. B. Shukla (12 citations); P. N. Kaula (11 citations); V. Venkatappaiah (8 citations); Grogan (7 citations); Lancaster (5 citations); B. Guha, D. K. Gupta and Krishna Kumar (4 citations each); R. L. Mittal (3 citations); and Neelameghan (2 citations). English language was dominating amongst the cited articles, and it was cent percent. Only 14% citing authors had tendency of self-citation, co-citation cases were 110, and only a couple of cases repeated. More than 90 % citations were from library and information science journals. Each Journal received on an average of 7 citations.

51. Buttlar, Lois. (1999)[51], analyzed the study in "Information sources in library and information science doctoral research". In this study citation analysis of 61 library science and information science dissertations revealed some interesting publication patterns. About 80% of the citations were to single authors, and as in analyses of periodical literature, males were cited more than females overall (about 61% to 39%). In dissertations related to school or public libraries, the male/female distribution was less disparate; for studies in academic or special libraries two thirds of the authors were male, and male authorship was 75% when only information science dissertations were analyzed. Journal articles were cited more than books, book chapters, proceedings, theses, and other formats with College & Research Libraries and Journal of the American Society for Information Science used most. Library and information science was impacted by several other disciplines, primarily education, computer science, health/medicine, psychology, communications, and business. Authors cited in dissertations represent a somewhat less parochial list in terms of citing U.S. publications than authors cited in studies analyzing journal citations; over half of all works cited were published within the last 10 years.

52. Noyons, E.C.M., Moed, H.F., & Luwel, M. (1999)[52], state the study in "Combining Mapping and Citation Analysis for Evaluative Bibliometric Purposes: A Bibliometric Study" The general aimed of the study was to demonstrate how the results both of a structural analysis, and of a research performance assessment of a research field, can be enriched by combining elements of both into one integrated analysis. In addition, a procedure was discussed to select and analyses candidate benchmark institutes to assess the position of a particular research institute, in terms of both its cognitive orientation and its scientific production and impact at the international research front. The combined method was applied in an evaluation of the research scope and performance of the Interuniversity Centre for Micro-Electronics (IMEC) in Leuven, Belgium. On the basis of the comments of an international panel of experts in micro-electronics, the method was discussed in detail. We concluded that the method provides a detailed and useful picture of the position of the institute from an international perspective. Moreover, we found that the results of each of the two parts are an added value to the other.

53. Redman, A.L., Manakyan, H., & Tanner, J. R. (1999)[53], made the study in "A Normalized Citation Analysis of Real Estate Journals". Tanner presented and analysis of the citation patterns and rankings for journals in real estate and related areas for the period 1990-1995. Journals were ranked based on the number of times they were cited in four base journals with adjustments for journal size and longevity. The results showed that Real Estate Economics was the most cited journal among real estate publications followed closely by the Journal of Real Estate Finance and Economics and the Journal of Real Estate Research. A temporal analysis revealed a shift in citations over the time period, away from the traditional economics and practitioner-oriented journals to the academic real estate journals.

54. Satija, M.P. (1999)[54], analyzed citation under the title "Doctoral Research in Library and Information Science in India: Some Observations and Comments" This article given a state-of-the-art overview of library and information science (LIS) education in India as a background to reviewing the doctoral research in the field. It traces the origin and growth of Ph.D. programmes in LIS in India and highlights the initiative and efforts of Dr S. R. Ranganathan (1892–1972). The study provided annual data on the quantitative output of LIS Ph.D. theses and ranks major Indian universities by their output. It includes lists of the major areas of research and identifies some arid areas. The author laments the irrelevance and lack of use of research results in library schools and libraries. He attributed that to a low quality of research work because of a mindless proliferation of programmes and a lack of co-operation and resources for research.

55. Deshpandey, Meera & Rajyalaxmi, D. (1997)[55], did a study on "citation study of dissertations in library and information science". A study of 65 dissertations in LIS submitted to NagpurUniversity during the period 1990-94 reveals the majority of work was in the field of literature survey and trends in various aspects of library and information science. Citation analysis has been carried out to find the types of cited source materials, authorship pattern and chronological distribution of cited references. The ranked list of 441 Journals has been also queen.

56. Schoonbaert, Drick, & Roelants, Gilbert. (1996)[56], studied in "Citation analysis for measuring the value of scientific publications: quality assessment tools or comedy of errors?" The basic concepts of citation analysis and journal impact factors were discussed in the light of quality assessment of scientific publications, individual scientists and research units. The major controversies concerning this topic were addressed: technical limitations, database selectivity, time and discipline-related biases, language and publication type biases, multiple authorship merits and citing motivations. Both positive and negative aspects are put into perspective. The authors concluded that citation analysis, even when based on journal impact factors, can be a worthwhile criterion for evaluating publication records of individual scientists or research units, as long as some of the problems discussed were sufficiently taken into account. However, this conclusion in no way implies that citation analysis may be considered as the one and only evolution criterion.

57. Verma, Maya. (1994)[57], analyzed in "citation analysis of some selected Indian journals in Economics". The study analysed 2599 journals citations from 1986-90 of, three Indian journals in Economics. Indian and Ecometricians give equal importance to journal and non-journal material. The median age of citation range was from12-15 years, Ranking list indicates that Indian scholars. In economics use more foreign literature and most of the journals subscribed by University library does not find place in ranked list.

58. Lal, Arjun. (1993)[58], made the study under the title" Most important journals from the point of view of Indian Social Sciences a bibliometrc study". The analyses 6273 references contained in four volume (33-36, 1985-88) of journal of the Indian Society of soil sciences. A ranked list of 50 most important journals represented 83.42% of the total citations out of 376 titles cited has been prepared. The study was revealed that 58% journals citations relate to only 6 journals out of 50 most cited journals. It also provided chronological and country wise distribution of all references. Use of the different kinds of documents as well as Indian and foreign has been shown.

59. Manju Munshi, Usha et al. (1993)[59], analyzedin "Research collaboration in Agricultural Sciences" Munshi tried to study research collaboration in Agricultural sciences amongst the scientists working in six Agricultural Universities of India. The result of finding revealed that only 15.36 % of the total publications constituted single author research output while 84.63 % is collaborative. Interestingly, the collaboration of 2 & 3 authors was more prevalent.

60. Sinha, S.C. & Mohd. Forgunullah. (1993)[60], made the citation study in "Citation profile of Dr. V.S. Ramachandran: a bibliometric analysis of his highly cited articles and books in area of cement and concrete chemistry". The citation pattern of the citation received by the works of the Dr. V.S. Ramachandran with special reference to his highest cited articles and books was studies. According to this study it was clear that Dr. Ramachandran was one of the highly quoted scientists in area of cement and concrete chemistry. He was more quoted for his books in comparison to his article. For studying the citation counts for 49 articles, the data was collected from the volume 1955-4,1965-69,1970-74,1975-79 and annual 'CITATION' cumulating volume for the year 1980-90 (April only) of the science citation index under Ramachandran, V. S.

61. Hurd, J. M. (1992)[61], made the study in "Interdisciplinary Research in the Sciences: Implications for Library Organization" Hecategorized journals in a sample population according to the disciplines of Physics, Biology, Chemistry, and Engineering. The categorization was done according to the Ulrich's subject classification. The article also specified the number of citations for the different formats of materials such as journals, monographs, conference proceedings, dissertation, unpublished and others which included government documents, handbooks, tables, technical reports and software. The total number of citations was 1931 taken from 57 articles. Journals formed the largest citations.

62. Hooten, Patricia A. (1991)[62], made the study in "Frequency and functional use of cited documents of information science." The aimed of this study was to examine the factors, which explain frequency and nature of use of documents in citing documents in citing documents text over a time. Articles published in the journal of the American Society for Information Science in 1972-74, were searched on Science to derive two sample groups. One group was frequently cited, the other was infrequently cited. The function uses of the sample document groups were examined by four classification taxonomies in 417 citing contexts. The patterns of frequency of use, multiple uses and functional use were examined overtime. The citation levels of documents citing the two sample groups were examined as well. When measured by functional citation taxonomies, frequently and infrequently cited documents were not used for significantly different functions. However, frequently cited documents, seemed more lighting linked (essential) than infrequently cites documents to the documents in which they were used.

63. Vaishnav, A.A., & Dharmapurikar, R. G. (1990)[63], did a citation analysis in "Citation Analysis of the Herald of Library Science", analysed citations provide in the Herald Library science. A survey of 10 volumes (1977-1986) revealed 202 citing articles and 1370 cited materials. The study aimed at reviewing the citation patterns prevalent in dispersion by form, author, geography etc. Books and periodicals were preferred, 70% were self-cited; 80% journal citation were from library science journals, 28 % of articles in Herald of Library Science had nil citations, the maximum citations per article were 63 and minimum was one.

64. Dombrowski, T. (1988)[64], analyzed the study in "Journal evaluation was using Journal Citation Reports as a collection development tool." And evaluation of journals in the fields of embryology, anatomy, and morphology showed what journals rank best within these fields using ranked lists in *Journal Citation Reports*, but there was no additional information such as a citation or a circulation study to examine what was being used locally. Nano science was difficult to evaluate according to ranked lists as very few journals were dedicated to this interdisciplinary field.

65. Wood, J. B. (1988)[65], made the study in "Growth of Scholarship: An online Bibliometric Comparison of Dissertations in the Sciences and Humanities. Wood analysed the growth of scholarship by using a bibliometric measure. The Dissertations Abstracts database was searched online to investigate pattern in this growth from year 1980 to 1884. The study covered total number of degrees granted per year in different fields of study. The growth pattern in the database demonstrates that there were 169 dissertations in between 1880-1884: 2360 dissertations between 1970 and 1974. This indicated that the post-second world war period experienced an exponential growth rate of dissertations. Comparative analysis of growth rates was also carried on. The comparison with national Research Council database indicated a persistent exponential rate phenomenon. Analysis of growth rates by fields, would found that the number of dissertations in information science, computer science and health science continuously increases.

66. Sattar, A. (1986)[66], showed the study in "Relationship between Political Alignment and Scientific Communication: A Bibliometric Study if Egyptian Science Publications". Sattar anlysed 1182 Egyptian science papers from Egyptian and Non-Egyptian sources accounting 15,222 bibliographic references. He found Egyptian Scientists mostly cited literature from third world countries, especially to neighbouring Arab and Muslim countries, were infrequent. The comparison of citation proportions revealed that citations, to a particular block, did not increase or decrease quite in accordance with the increase or decrease of political influence of that bloc. The change in the citations proportions were not consistently correspondent to the changes influence. Therefore, the hypothesis that there exists a position relationship between political alignment and citation behavior was rejected. The citation behavior of Egyptian scientists was not found independent of the sources in which they published. They were more likely to cite sources from countries and political blocs in which they published their works than they were to cite those countries or blocs in other circumstances. Collaboration was also shown to be related to the citation behavior of Egyptian scientists. They cited more sources the countries and political blocs of scientists with whom they collaborated then they did in other circumstances.

67. Banik, B. D. & Bandopadhyay, S. (1985)[67], analyzed in "Recent Growth of Periodicals on Glass and Cermics-their Rank." They identified the periodicals based on productivity of references of glass & ceramics. To reflect the growth of new periodicals and variation in rank order, a comparative study has been made with a similar survey accomplished a decade ago. The study was confined from the data available in chemical Abstracts. The result of investigation revealed that first 10 productive titles cover 40.7%, 16 titles cover 49.3 % and 66 titles cover 86.6 % references. The study also indicated the variations that occur if the data includes and when it did not include "See also" reference.

68. Maheswarappa, B. S. & Savadatti, S. G. (1985)[68], did the study in "Authorship Pattern and Collaborative Research in Plant Breeding (1934-1989)" they found 75% multi-authored papers in 1989 in comparison to 1212 % in 1934 using plant breeding abstracts. In IASLIC bulletin there were 3 out of 16 in 1984 and 4 out of 14 1988 were in total 21 multi-authored papers to 70 single authored papers for the period of 5 years (1984-1988).They also studied the length for article for each year papers of 1-3 pages were 6, 4-6 are 34, 7-9 are 30, 10-12 are 16 and 13-15 are3, 15 and above are 2.

69. Musib, S.K., & Mahapatra, M. (1985)[69], made the study in "Reviewing of Management Literature". They studied the linked the inter linked in the branched of economics. They found that the relationship is based on the co-occurrences in the citations. The subjects' analyses of the citations were analysed journals of economics. Altogether 5923 citations were analysed by their specific subjects. A rank list of cited subjects was compiled by arranging the subjects in order of their frequency of appearance. As many as 41 subjects were identified and of which 20 subjects accounted for a total of 95.4 % citations. The findings of the study were: (a) contributions of these subjects, towards the overall development of economics, ranged from 2 to 20 % and (b) only 15 significant associations/ mutual relationship were determined out of 55 combinations of their branches. O these 15, welfare economics was found to most significant. In short, the branches forming the strongest bond appeared within the top ten positions. This confirms the theory that they acted as 'Core' branches based on which the micro structure of economics is established.

70. Sellen, M. K. (1984)[70], analyzed in "Bibliometrics in Information Sciences: A Citation Analysis of Two Academic Library Journals" Sellen served references in two academic library journals, Viz. College and Research Libraries (C & RL) and journal of Academic Librarianship (JAL) for the year 1981. These two were among the top five journals read by academic librarians. The object of study was to analysed the characteristics of the references. 37 articles in C & R were published in 1981 with a total of 454 references; of these 258 were periodicals citations. Frequency of counting indicated that out of 258 citations 56 articles (25.1 %) belonged to College and Research Libraries and only 25 articles (77.5 %) belonged to JAL. 27 articles in JAL were published in 1981 with a total of 25 references. These references have 141 periodical citations (16.3 %). Interestingly, more references have, 23 citations, were from College and Research Libraries and less, 16 citations (11.34 %) were from JAL.

5.2. REFERENCES

1. Chen, J., Wang, D.N., Zhu, C.L., Guo, R.H., Liu, Y., Wang, H., Li Y.&Liu, N. (2011). Analysis of highly cited papers published in Chinese Journal of Endemiology during 2000-2006.*Chinese Journal of Endemiology, 30(2),* 224-226 ISSN: 10004955.doi:10.3760/cma.j.issn.1000-4955.2011.02.034.
2. Dingyu. (2011, May 6-8). *Quantitative analysis of research papers on library personalized service in China in 2000-2010.* (Article number 5884520, Pages 6150-6153). Proceedingsof 2nd2011 International Conference on E-Business and E-Government (ICEE2011), Shanghai.doi: 10.1109/ICEBEG.2011.5884520.
3. Fardi, A., Kodonas, K., Gogos, C., &Economides, N.(2011).

Top-cited Articles in Endodontic Journals. *Journal of Endodontic, 37(9),* 1183-90 ISSN: 00992399. doi:10.1016/ j.joen.2011.05.037.

4. Kumar, H. Anil, & Dora, Mallikarjun. (2011). Citation analysis of doctoral dissertations at IIMA: A review of the local use of journals, Library, *35(1),* 32-39. doi:10.1016/ j.lcats.2011.03.002

5. Maharana, B., Majhi, S.&Sethi, B.B. (2011, June). Citation analysis of top research papers in chemistry with specific reference to India. *Library Review, 60 (6),* 501-512. ISSN: 00242535. doi: 10.1108/00242531111147215.

6. Nederhof, A. J. (2011, June). A bibliometric study of productivity and impact of modern language and literature research. *Research Evaluation , 20(2),* 117-129, ISSN: 09582029 doi: 10.3152/095820211X12941371876508.

7. Walters, G.D. (2011, August). The citation life cycle of articles published in 13 American psychological Association journals: A 25-year longitudinal analysis. *Journal of the American Society for Information Science and Technology, 62(8),* 1629-1636.doi: 10.1002/asi.21560.

8. Edgar, L.D. (2010). Citation structure: An analysis of the literature cited in the Journal of International Agricultural and Extension Education from 1997 to 2006. *Journal of International Agricultural and Extension Education, 17(1),* 31-43. ISSN: 10770755.doi: 10.5191/jiaee.2010.17104.

9. Mahbuba, D., Rousseau, R., &Srivastava, D. (2010). A scientometric analysis of health and population research in South Asia: Focus on two research organizations. *Malaysian Journal of Library and Information Science, 15 (3),* 135-147. Retrieved from www.sciencedirect.com

10. Maz-Machado, A., Torralbo-Rodríguez, M., Vallejo-Ruiz, M., &Bracho-López, R. (2010). Bibliometric analysis of scholarly production from the University of Malaga in the Social Sciences Citation Index (1998-2007). *Revista Espanola de Documentacion Cientifica, 33(4),* 582-599. ISSN:02100614. doi: 10.3989/redc.2010.4.757. Retrieved from www.sciencedirect.com

11. Rojas-Sola, J. I., & De San-Antonio-Gomez, C.(2010, December). Bibliometric analysis of Mexican scientific publications in the category engineering, chemical from the web of science database (1997-2008). *Revista Mexicana de*

Ingeniera Qumica, 9 (3), 231-240. ISSN: 16652738. Retrieved from: http://www.accesowok.fecyt.es/

12. Strotmann, Andreas., & Zhao,Dangzhi.(2010, April). Combining commercial citation indexes and open-access bibliographic databases to delimit highly interdisciplinary research fields for citation analysis. *Journal of Informatics, 4(2),* 194-200.doi:10.1016/j.joi.2009.12.001.Retrieved from www.sciencedirect.com
13. Vieira, E.S., & Gomes, J.A.N.F. (2010). Citations to scientific articles: Its distribution and dependence on the article features. *Journal of Informatics, 4(1),* 1-13.doi:http://dx.doi.org/10.1016/j.joi.2009.06.002.Retrievedfrom http://www.sciencedirect.com
14. Aksnes,This article is not included in your organization's subscription. However, you may be able to access this article under your organization's agreement with Elsevier.
15. Dag W.,& Rip,Arie. (2009, July). Researchers perceptions of citations. *Research Policy, 38 (6),* 895-905. doi:10.1016/j.respol.2009.02.001. Retrieved from www.sciencedirect.com
16. Daniel, Gianfranco Di Vaioab & Weisdorfd, Waldenstromc Jacob. (2009). Citation success: evidence from economic history journal publications. Retrieved from http://www.econ.ku.dk
17. Dodson, M.V. (2009, October). Citation analysis: maintenance of h-index and use of e-index. *Biochemical and Biophysical Research Communications, 387(4),* 625-626. doi:10.1016/j.bbrc.2009.07.091. Retrieved from: www.sciencedirect.com
18. Gao, Shi-Jian., Yu, Wang-Zhi., & Luo, Feng-Ping. (2009). Citation analysis of Ph.D. thesis at Wuhan University, China. *Library Collections, Acquisitions & Technical Services, 33(1),* 8-16. Retrieved from http://www.sciencedirect.com
19. Jan, Rosy. (2009). Citation analysis of library trends. *Webology, 6(1),* Article 67. Retrieved from http://www.webology.ir/2009/v6n1/a67.html
20. Kajikawa,Yuya., &Takeda,Yoshiyuki. (2009, October).Citation network analysis of organic LEDs. *Technological Forecasting and Social Change, 76(8),* 1115-1123.doi:10.1016/j.techfore.2009.04.004.Retrieved from: www.sciencedirect.com
21. Krishnamoorthy, G., Ramakrishnan. J., & Devi, S., (2009). Bibliometric analysis of literature on diabetes (1995–2004).

Annals of Library and Information Studies, 56(3), 150-155.

22. Olatokun, Wole Michael, & Makinde, Olayinka. (2009). Citation analysis of dissertations submitted to the department of animal science, University of Ibadan, Nigeria. *Annals of Library and Information Studies, 56(2),* 117-128.
23. Pilkington, Alan, & Meredith, Jack. (2009). The evolution of the intellectual structure of operations management-1980–2006: a citation/co-citation analysis. *Journal of Operations Management, 27 (3),* 185-202. Retrieved from www.sciencedirect.com
24. Su, Yu-Min.,Yang, Shu-Ching., Hsu,Ping-Yu., & Shiau, Wen-Lung. (2009, April).Extending co-citation analysis to discover authors with multiple expertises. *Expert Systems with Applications, 36(3),* 4287-4295. doi:10.1016/j.eswa.2008.03.022. Retrieved from www.sciencedirect.com.
25. Zabed Ahmed, S. M., & Rahman, Md. Anisur. (2009). Lotka's law and authorship distribution in nutrition research in Bangladesh. *Annals of Library and Information Studies, 56 (2),* 95-102.
26. Jiao, Qun G., Onwuegbuzie, Anthony J. & Waytowich, Vicki L. (2008). The relationship between citation errors and library anxiety: an empirical study of doctoral students in education. *Information Processing and Management, 44(2),* 948–956. Retrieved from www.sciencedirect.com
27. Lopez-Illescas,Carmen., MOYA-ANEGON, Felix De., & MOED,Henk F. (2008, October). Coverage and citation impact of on cological journals in the Web of Science and Scopus. *Journal of Informatics,* 2(4), 304-316.doi:10.1016/j.joi.2008.08.001. Retrieved from www.sciencedirect.com.
28. Nazim, Mohammad & Ahmad, Moin. (2008) .A bibliometric analysis on nanotechnology research. *Annals of Library and Information Studies, 55(4),* 292-299.
29. Patil, S. K., & Chikate, R V. (2008). Citation analysis of theses in library and information science submitted to university of Pune: a pilot study. *Library Philosophy and Practice (e-journal).1-14ISSN 1522-0222* Retrieved from digitalcommons.unl.edu/cgi/viewcontent.cgi?article=1224.
30. Vallmitjana, Núria, & Sabatwe, L. G. (2008). Citation analysis of Ph.D. dissertation references as a tool for collection management in an academic chemistry library. *College and Research Libraries, 69(1),* 72-82.

30. Vallmitjana, Nûria, & Sabatwe, L. G. (2008).Web citation behaviour in scholarly electronic journals in the field of library and information science. *Webology,* 5(2). Retrieved from www.webology.org/2009/v6n1/a67.html

31. Wakefield, Robin. (2008, September).Networks of accounting research: A citation-based structural and network analysis. Review Vol, 228-244. doi:10.1016/j.bar.2008.03.001. Retrieved from www.sciencedirect.com.

32. Frandsen, Tove Faber. (2007). Journal self-citations-analyzing the JIF mechanism. *Journal of Informatics, 1(1),* 47–58.

33. Nederhof, Anton J. (2006). Bibliometric monitoring of research performance in the Social Sciences and the Humanities: A review. *Scientometrics, 66(1),* 81–100.

34. Whitley, Edgar A., & Galliers, Robert D. (2007). An alternative perspective on citation classics: evidence from the first 10 years of the European conference on information systems. *Information & Management, 44(5),* 441-455. Retrieved from www.sciencedirect.com

35. Clarke, Maria Elizabeth & Oppenheim, Charles. (2006). Citation behaviour of information science students II: postgraduate students. *Education for Information, 24(1),* 1-30.

36. Tsay, Ming-yueh. (2006). Journal self-citation study for semiconductor literature: synchronous and diachronous approach. *Information Processing and Management, 42(6),* 1567–1577.doi:10.1016/j.ipm.2006.03.020

37. Kristen, B. La Bonte. (2005, summer).Citation analysis: a method for collection development for rapidly developing field Science and Technology. *Librarianship, 43(1).* Retrieved from http://www.istl.org/05-summer/refereed.html

38. Labonte, K. B. (2005). Citation analysis: a method for collection development for a rapidly developing field science and technology. *Librarianship, 43(1),* 1-10.

39. Gupta, B. M., & Bhattacharya, Sujit. (2004). A bibliometric approach towards mapping the dynamics of science and technology. *DESIDOC Bulletin of Information Technology, 24 (1),* 3-8.

40. Faba-Pearez, Cristina & Biblioteconomi, V. P. Guerrero-Bote Facultad de. (2003). Situation distributions and Bradford's law in a closed, Web space. *Journal of Documentation, 59 (5),*

558-580.

41. Johry, Nutan. (2003). International social science journal: a bibliometric study. *Library Herald, 41(2).*

42. Okiy, Rose B. (2003). A citation analysis of education dissertations at the Delta State University, Abraka, Nigeria. *Collection Building, 22(4),* 158–161. Retrieved from http://www.emeraldinsight.com/10.1108/01604950310501735.

43. Shokken, Ashu, & Kaushik, Sanjay K. (2003). Indian journal of economics: a citation analysis. *Library Herald, 41(2),* 109-111.

44. Wohlin, Claes. (2002).An analysis of the most cited articles in software engineering journals. *Information and Software Technology,50(1),* 2–11 Retrieved from www.elsevier.com/locate/infsof.

45. Das, Anup Kumar, & Sen, B. K. (2001). Indian journal of medical research: an analysis of citation pattern. *ILA Bulletin, 31 (1),* 9-12

46. Gooden, Angela M. *(2001).*Citation analysis of chemistry doctoral dissertations: an Ohio state university case study. *Science and Technology Librarianship, 52 (4),* 309-314.

47. Verma, Neerja. (2001). Analysis of contributions in Library Herald. *Library Herald, 39 (1/2),* 32.49.

48. Aidtya Kumari, H., & Rao, Shivram K. (2000). The nucleus-an international journal of cytology and allied topics: a bibliometric study. *SRELS Journal of Information Management, 37(1),* 54-74.

49. Ghosh, Saptarshi. (2000).Citation pattern of contribution in library science with a slant to documentation and information studies. *SRELS Journal of Information Management, 37 (4),* 251- 65.

50. Ramesh, L. S. R. C. V., &Nagaraju, A. V. S. S. (2000).Citation analysis of the Indian journal of information, library and society. *Indian Journal of Information, Library and Society, 13 (3/4),* 171-179.

51. Buttlar, Lois. (1999).Information sources in library and information science doctoral research. This article is not included in your organization's subscription. However, you may be able to *access this article under your organization's agreement with ElsevierLibrary & Information Science Research, 21(2),* 227-245.

52. Noyons, E.C.M., Moed, H.F., & Luwel, M. (1999).Combining mapping and citation analysis for evaluative bibliometric purposes: a bibliometric study. *Journal of the American Society for Information Science, 50(2),* 115-131.

53. Redman, A.L., Manakyan, H., & Tanner, J .R. (1999). A normalized citation analysis of real estate journals. *Real Estate Economics, 27(1),* 169-182.

54. Satija, M.P. (1999). Doctoral research in library and information science in India: some observations and comments. *Libri, 49,* 236–242. Retrieved from www.librijournal.org/pdf/1999-4pp236-242.pdf

55. Deshpandy, Meera & Rajyalaxmi, D. (1997). Citation study of dissertation in library and information science. *Annals of Library Science and Documentation, 44 (2),* 41 –53.

56. Schoonbaert, Drick, & Roelants, Gilbert. (1996). Citation analysis for measuring the value of scientific publications: quality assessment tool or comedy of errors? *Tropical Medicine and International Health, 1(6),* 739-752. Retrieved from dns2.asia.edu.tw/~ysho/YSHO-English/Database/T-Z.docx

57. Verma, Maya. (1994).Citation analysis of some selected Indian journals in Economics. *Annals of Library Science and Documentation, 41 (1),* 33-39.

58. Lal, Arjun. (1993). Most important journals from the point of view of Indian social scientist: A bibliometric study. *IASLIC Bulletin, 38(3),* 123-131.

59. Munshi, U.M. et al. (1993) .Research collaboration in Agricultural Sciences. *ILA Bulletin, 28 (3-4),* 57-60.

60. Sinha, S.C. & Mohd. Forgunullah. (1993). Citation profile of Dr. Ramachandran: a bolometric analysis of his highly cited articles and books in the area of cement and concrete chemistry. *Annals of Library Science and Documentation, 40 (1),* 21-31.

61. Hurd, J. M. (1992). Interdisciplinary research in the sciences: implications for library organization. *College & Research Libraries, 53 (4),* 283-297.

62. Hooten, Patricia A. (1991). Frequency and functional use of cited documents of information science. *Journal of the American Society for Information Science,42(6),* 397-404.

63. Vaishnav, A.A., & Dharmapurikar, R. G. (1990). Citation analysis of the Herald of Library Science. *Herald of Library*

Science, 29 (3/4), 252-260.

64. Dombrowski, T. (1988). Journal evaluation using journal citation reports as a collection development tool. *Collection Management, 10 (3/4)*, 175-180.

65. Wood, J. B. (1988). Growth of Scholarship: An online bibliometric comparison of dissertations in the sciences and humanities. *Scientrometrics,* 13, 53-62.

66. Sattar, A. (1986). Relationship between political alignment and scientific communication: A bibliometric study if Egyptian science publications. *Dissertation Abstracts, 46,* 1767. (University of Illinois at Urbana Champaign). Retrieved from http://taher.freeservers.com/bibliometricIslam.htm

67. Banik, B. D. & Bandopadhyay, S. (1985). Recent growth of periodicals on glass and ceramics- their rank. *IASLIC Bulletin, 8,* 23-30.

68. Maheswarappa, B. S. & Savadatti, S. G. (1985). Authorship pattern and collaborative research in plant breeding (1934-1989). *IASLIC Bulletin, 35(3)*, 119-123.

69. Musib, S.K., & Mahapatra, M. (1985). Reviewing of management literature. *Library Quarterly, 57,* 32-60.

70. Sellen, M. K. (1984). Bibliometrics in Information Sciences: A citation analysis of two academic library journals. *College and Research Libraries, 45(2),* 129-132.

6
Citation Analysis in Selected Universities

6.1. INTRODUCTION

Citation analysis is a popular technique used by experts in drawing qualitative and quantitative results using the citations, footnotes, references, bibliographies given at the end of chapters, books, articles, theses etc.

The citations can be considered as indicators of quality or value and can be used for measuring the impact of specialist, or an article or an organization on the scientific and technical development. According to Smith, citations are un-obstructive measures, as they unlike data collected from interviews and questionnaires, do not depend on the cooperation of the respondents and do not influence the response.

For decades librarians have used citation counts to determine the adequacy of a collection of periodical the optimum size of back files, binding and retention schedules and for cost-benefit analysis in the management of subscription budgets. Policy makers and research funding agencies use similar techniques for evaluating the effectiveness of the research programmers and for identifying research projects and research teams, with potential. The sociologists continue to utilize the techniques to analyses the structure of science and to define the changing relationships within the establishments. The historians of science use it for tracing ideas from the conceptual roots, for development and innovation.

Analysis of data is the penultimate step in research process. It is the link between raw data and significant results leading to conclusions. This process of analysis has to be result-oriented. According to Richard Budd, analysis... leads eventually to summarizing procedures resulting in some sacrifice of details. Frequencies and column inches are summarized in tables as averages and percentages etc are transformed into indices or attention scores to be used as a single variable in subsequent analysis.

The investigation of the study start with the study of citation formats. Scholars have evolved some uniform system to information sources, either in the form of footnotes or references. There are number of standards for rendering of a citation, which may or not be followed by the scholars. Harwards Referencing System, Modern Language Association style sheet, Chicago University style manual, APA etc.., are some of the standards manuals. The scholars can also evolve their own method and style according to the peculiar nature of their subject, and all these standards to enable the reader or the information user to follow up the source document quoted. In this connection the investigator made a close study of the citation formats used by the scholars in each and every thesis. The analysis revealed that different formats have been followed by different scholars. It shows lack of uniformity among all the theses. It is to be emphasizing further that there is no consistency even within a single thesis. Some have omitted the place of publication and some other the year of publication. This is really a major hurdle for citation analysis study. In order to avoid these things learned institutions like universities should appoint thesis editors, dissertation secretary, thesis coordinator etc... who would being a uniform pattern throughout the text of the thesis, and the researcher should be strictly advise to use any of the standard format viz APA citation style, MLA citation style, Chicago University style etc.

The study aims at establishing the followings objectives:

1. An analysis of the recorded citations to determine the average number of citations of Library & Information Science.
2. To study the rate of collaborative authorship (Books) by analysing the citations pattern.
3. To determine the use pattern of different types of documents like books, periodicals, journal articles etc.
4. Observe the age wise distribution of citation to determine the productive year of used publications.
5. To study the distribution by place of publication to find out the country of origin of the published documents.
6. Compile a rank list of core journals in Library & Information Science.

Today many methods of research were available. Further, the methods of choosing a suitable method for research have grown into a systematic subject in itself, and it is called research methodology or research design. Choice of a method depends upon the nature, the scope, the objectives and the depth of the problem on hand. In other words, end must justify the mean.

The data required for the study of source articles is all the doctoral theses submitted to the Universities of Bundelkhand Region (U.P. and M.P.). A total of 28,249 citations from all 128 LIS dissertations submitted to the Universities of Bundelkhand Region are selected a source of data. All references in footnotes, endnotes and bibliographies of the entire 128 theses submitted to the three Universities of Bundelkhand region (U.P. and M.P). The 35 theses submitted from Bundelkhand University, Jhansi (U.P.), 28 theses submitted from Dr. Harisingh Gour University, Sagar (M.P.) and 65 theses submitted from Jiwaji University, Gwalior (M.P). The survey of the entire 128 theses of both States (U.P. and M.P.) in Bundelkhand region, resulted in 28,249 citations of three Universities of Bundelkhand region (U.P. and M.P): 6198 citations from Bundelkhand University, Jhansi (U.P.), 7284 citations Dr. Harisingh Gour University, Sagar (M.P.) and Jiwaji University, 14767 citations Gwalior (M.P.). This data forms the basis of the analysis in the present research. A list of Ph.D. theses submitted in Library & Information Science under the appropriate headings was selected and prepared. It was then cross checked with the records from Registrar office for any missing thesis. In present study, only those theses have been included being submitted till 2009.

6.2. AVERAGE CITATIONS PER THESIS IN LIBRARY & INFORMATION SCIENCE

Average Citations per Thesis: Bundelkhand University, Jhansi

Table-1 shows that 35 theses in Bundelkhand University, Jhansi have 6198 citations with an average 177.09 citations per thesis.

Table 1. Average Citations per Thesis : Bundelkhand University, Jhansi

S.No.	Name of University	No. of Theses	No. of Citations	Average No. of Citation
1.	Bundelkhand University, Jhansi	35	6198	177.09

Average Citations per Thesis: Jiwaji University, Gwalior

Table-2 shows that 65 theses in Jiwaji University, Gwalior have 14767 citations with an average 227.18 citations per thesis.

Table 2. Average Citations per Thesis: Jiwaji University, Gwalior

S.No.	Name of University	No. of Theses	No. of Citations	Average No. of Citation
1.	Jiwaji University, Gwalior	65	14767	227.18

Average Citations per Thesis: Dr. Harisingh Gour University, Sagar

Table-3 shows that 28 theses in Dr. Harisingh Gour University, Sagar have 7284 citations with an average 260.14 citations per thesis.

Table 3. Average Citations per Thesis: Dr. Harisingh Gour University, Sagar

S.No.	Name of University	No. of Theses	No. of Citations	Average No. of Citation
1.	Dr. Harisingh Gour University, Sagar	28	7284	260.14

6.3. BIBLIOGRAPHIC DISTRIBUTION IN LIBRARY & INFORMATION SCIENCE

Modern society faces many problems which follow from the ever increasing tempo of social change to those who use research libraries, and even more to those who manage them, the rate of growth of research collection has become a matter of serious concern. Although many libraries administrators must have been aware of difficulties created by a rapid growth of their collection, the observation of Stevens that no single library can possible contain all the manuscripts, books and other forms of communication which its users may need in research. If the attempt is to be made to preserve all such materials somewhere for possible use, decisions are needed concerning the titles, or at least the categories of materials which will be kept immediately available and those which may be stored apart from the main research collection or which need not be acquired if they are available in another research library in the area.

The different information sources in Library & Information Science vary in physical form as well as the type of information provided. Some of the common documents regularly consulted include journals, books, conference/seminar proceedings, reports, govt. publications, Ph.D. theses/dissertations, lectures, letters, newspapers, reference books, case study and websites etc.

A description of the coverage of the terms used in the investigation include books (edited publications, multi volume publications etc); reports cover reports of public sector, private sector autonomous bodies; conference/ Seminar proceedings; govt. publications; theses include doctoral research works as well as the dissertations of Master, M.Phil. degree; case study; website; reference books includes encyclopaedia, dictionary, biography, maps etc miscellanies/ others (letters, lectures, etc.).

Bibliographic Form Dispersion: Bundelkhand University, Jhansi

Table-4 and figure-1 contains the analysis of 10 categories of documents cited by the research scholars. Periodicals also played as vehicle of current thought and joined the fraternity of books. It is believed that presenting the research output the scholars have profusely made use of books and journals. Table-5 gives the form wise analysis. It is observed from the table that the number of citations from books and periodicals are higher than the other forms of documents such as conference proceedings, reports, reference sources, theses etc... 2566 (41.40%) of citations are from books followed by journals articles/ periodicals amounting to 2048 (33.04%). In other words books andjournals articles/periodicals together constitute 74.44 % of the total number of citations cited by the research scholars.

The next source of information for Library & Information scientists is the websites 585 (9.44 %), and conferences proceedings 378 (6.10%).Report 134 (2.16%) followed by reference sources 108 (1.74%), letters/ lectures 155 (2.50%), govt. publications 104 (1.68%), case study/survey 48 (0.77%),

There are very few citations of theses and dissertations, perhaps because they are not readily available to the research scholars. The theses and dissertations are by their very nature meant for reports the originals work in a specified field. These are usually unpublished sources of information. In the present investigation about the 72 (1.16%), of citations are in favor of theses and dissertations.

From the above factors we can observe that books and journals are the most important source of information as compared to other sources of information.

The relatively high percentage of citations to books and journals followed by low percentage of citations to other form of documents, indicate the fact that books and journals are the most preferred channel of information. This may be attributed to the following factors:

1. Reports, theses, conference proceeding, etc are not easily accessible to the research scholars as books and periodicals;
2. Books are better organized bibliographic forms than conference proceeding, thesis etc...; and
3. Searching of periodicals is not easy practice to the research scholars.

Table 4. Bibliographic Form Dispersion : Bundelkhand University, Jhansi

S. No.	Bibliographic Form	No. of Citations	Cumulation No.of Citations	% of Citations	Cumulation % of Citations
1	Books/Guides	2566	2566	41.40	41.40
2	Journal Articles	2048	4614	33.04	74.44
3	Web sites	585	5199	9.44	83.88
4	Conference Proceedings	378	5577	6.10	89.98
5	Letters/Lectures	155	5732	2.50	92.48
6	Reports	134	5866	2.16	94.64
7	Reference Sources	108	5974	1.74	96.39
8	Govt. Publications	104	6078	1.68	98.06
9	Theses	72	6150	1.16	99.23
10	Case study/Survey	48	6198	0.77	100.00
	Total	**6198**	**6198**	**100.00**	**100.00**

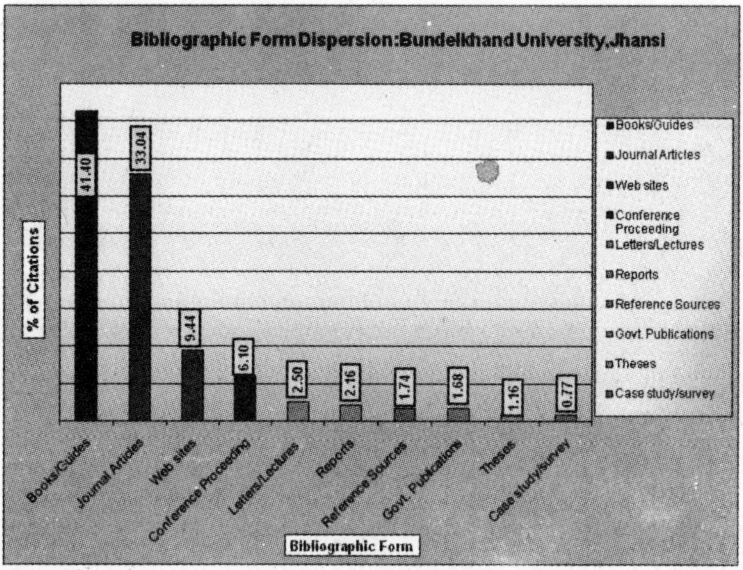

Fig. 1

Bibliographic Form Dispersion: Jiwaji University, Gwalior

Table-5 and figure-2 gives the form wise analysis. There are total of 14,767 citations in 65 theses from Jiwaji University, Gwalior. It is revealed that books, journals are the most used literature in preparation of research by scientist of Jiwaji University, Gwalior. There are books/ guides 6279 (42.52%), journal articles 4665 (31.59%), conference proceedings 879 (5.95%), reports 769 (5.21%), web sites 596 (4.04%), govt. publications 573 (3.88%), reference sources 533 (3.61%), theses 265 (1.79%), letters/lectures 153 (1.04%), case study/survey 55 (0.37%).

Table 5. Bibliographic Form Dispersion: Jiwaji University, Gwalior

S. No.	Bibliographic Form	No. of Citations	Cumulation No.of Citations	% of Citations	Cumulation % of Citations
1	Books/Guides	6279	6279	42.52	42.52
2	Journal Articles	4665	10944	31.59	74.11
3	Conference Proceedings	879	11823	5.95	80.06
4	Reports	769	12592	5.21	85.27
5	Web sites	596	13188	4.04	89.31
6	Govt. Publications	573	13761	3.88	93.19
7	Reference Sources	533	14294	3.61	96.80
8	Theses	265	14559	1.79	98.59
9	Letters/Lectures	153	14712	1.04	99.63
10	Case Study/Survey	55	14767	0.37	100.00
	Total	**14767**	**14767**	**100.00**	**100.00**

Bibliographic Form Dispersion: Dr. Harisingh Gour University, Sagar

Table-6 and figure-3 shows that there are a total of 7284 citations in 28 theses from Dr. Harisingh Gour University, Sagar. The distribution of the cited document based on ten identified bibliographic forms: books, journal articles, conference proceedings, reports, web sites, govt. publications, reference sources, theses and dissertations,

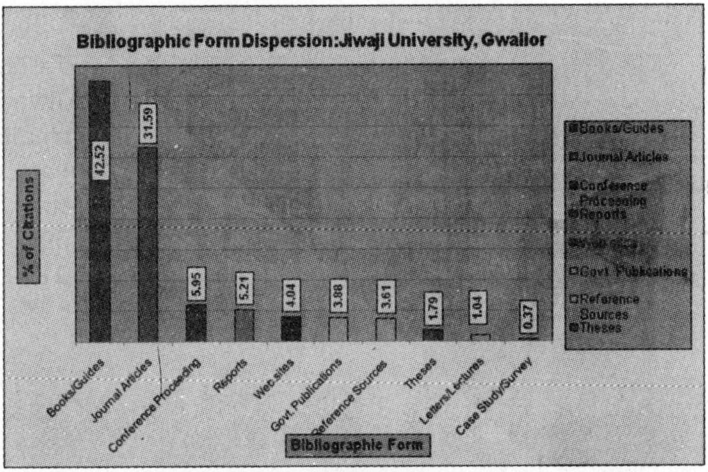

Fig. 2

conference proceedings, reports, government publications, case studies and letters/lectures.

Table 6. Bibliographic Form Dispersion : Dr. Harisingh Gour University, Sagar

S. No.	Bibliographic Form	No. of Citations	Cumulation No.of Citations	% of Citations	Cumulation % of Citations
1	Journal Articles	2953	2953	40.54	40.54
2	Books/Guides	2191	5144	30.08	70.62
3	Reports	513	5657	7.04	77.66
4	Conference Proceedings	457	6114	6.27	83.94
5	Reference Sources	411	6525	5.64	89.58
6	Theses	221	6746	3.03	92.61
7	Case Study/Survey	208	6954	2.86	95.47
8	Govt. Publications	158	7112	2.17	97.64
9	Web sites	158	7270	2.17	99.81
10	Letters/Lectures	14	7284	0.19	100.00
	Total	**7284**	**7284**	**100.00**	**100.00**

It is found that journals and books are widely used format by the researcher of Dr. Harisingh Gour University. There is more than 70% of literature in the form of journals and books.

Journal articles 2953 (40.54%) followed by books 2191(30.08%), reports 513 (7.04%), conference proceedings 457 (6.27%), reference sources 411 (5.64%), theses 221 (3.03%), case study/survey 208 (2.86%), govt. publications 158 (2.17%), web sites 158 (2.17%), letters/ lectures 14 (0.19%).

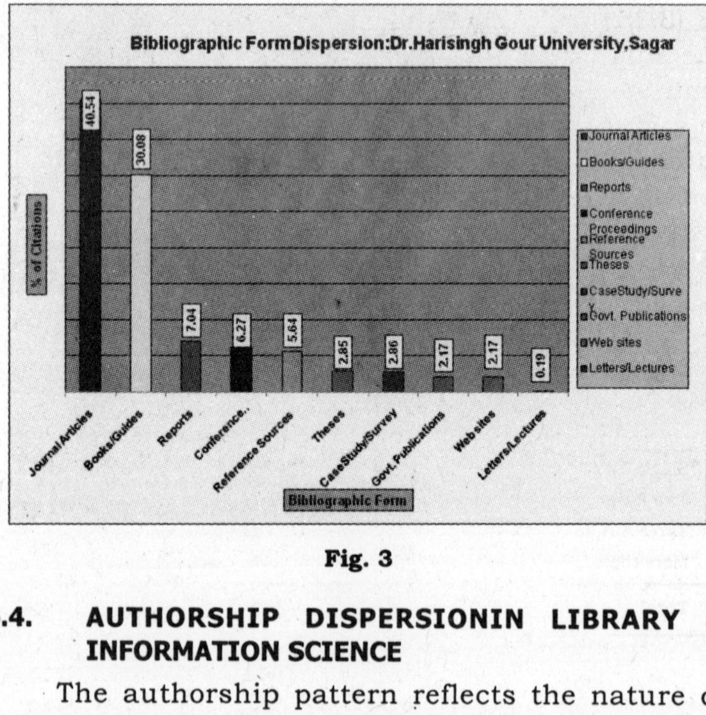

Fig. 3

6.4. AUTHORSHIP DISPERSIONIN LIBRARY & INFORMATION SCIENCE

The authorship pattern reflects the nature of productivity of writers associated with Library and Information Science. Whether the preference of solo works or collaborative works is being appreciated. The trend of authorship pattern can be gauged by analyzing the author dispersion relating to works of single authors and multiple authors. The variable selected for investigation under authors dispersion are single authors, two authors, three authors, more than three authors.

Authorship Dispersion: Bundelkhand University, Jhansi

Table-7 and figure-4 states the authorship pattern as analyzed from 2566 citations. Highlights the analysis of the authorship pattern of books as observed in this study. The analysis reveals that, 1764 (68.75%) of the books are contributed by single authors, two authors contributions account for 589 (22.95%), three authors 86 (3.35%) and more than three authors 127 (4.95%). The study shows that more and more books are being contributed under single authorship. Alternatively, it can be said that there is an increasing trend towards single authorship. It can be seen that maximum number of books are single authored and minimum number of books are three and more than three authors.

Table 7. Authorship Dispersion : Bundelkhand University, Jhansi

S. No.	Author	No. of Citations	Cumulation No. of Citations	% of Citations	Cumulation % of Citations
1	Single Author	1764	1764	68.75	68.75
2	Two Authors	589	2353	22.95	91.70
3	Three Authors	86	2439	3.35	95.05
4	More than Three Authors	127	2566	4.95	100.00
	Total	**2566**	**2566**	**100.00**	**100.00**

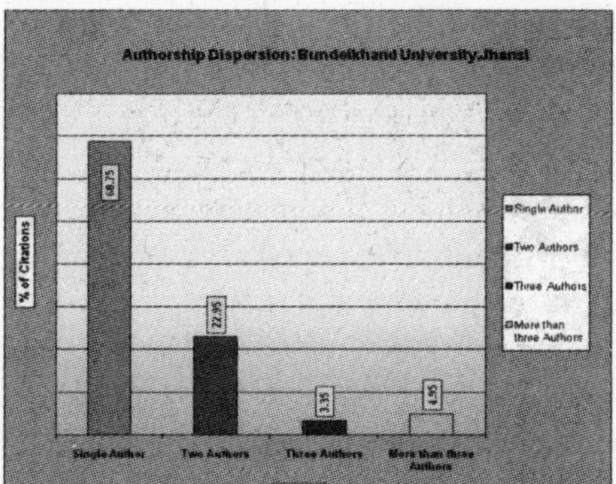

Fig. 4

Authorship Dispersion : Jiwaji University, Gwalior

Table-8 and Figure-5 highlights the authorship pattern of cited books, referred by the Library & Information Science scholars of Jiwaji University, Gwalior. Authorship study reveals that single authorship pattern secures the highest position, followed by the two authors respectively. The single authorship books which secure the highest position account for 4928 (78.48%) citations and two authorship contributions take the credit of having 1066 (16.98%) citations. Three authors books account for 100 (1.59%) and more than three authors books are 185 (2.95%). It has to be observed that single author books are frequently cited in the Library and Information Science theses and it amounts to more than 4928 (78.48%) of the total number of 6279 citations of books.

Table 8. Authorship Dispersion:Jiwaji University, Gwalior

S. No.	Author	No. of Citations	Cumulation No. of Citations	% of Citations	Cumulation % of Citations
1	Single Author	4928	4928	78.48	78.48
2	Two Authors	1066	5994	16.98	95.46
3	Three Authors	100	6094	1.59	97.05
4	More than Three Authors	185	6279	2.95	100.00
	Total	**6279**	**6279**	**100.00**	**100.00**

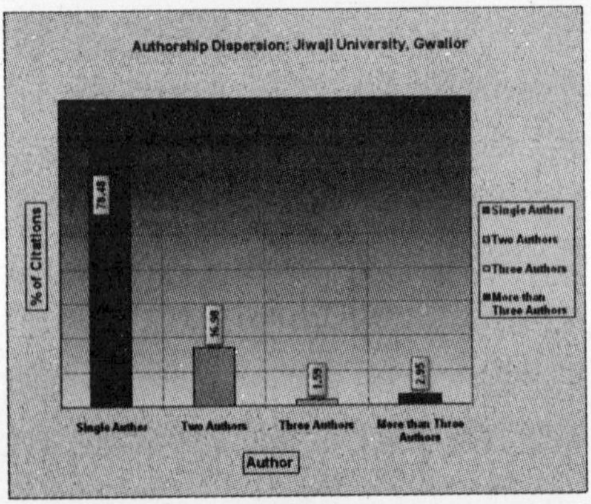

Fig. 5

Authorship Dispersion : Dr. Harisingh Gour University, Sagar

It is clear form Table-9 and figure-6,the citation analysis that majority of the publications belong to single authors, showing the fact that collaborative works are not much appreciated resulting in more of works by a lower percentage of multiple authorship. Most of the published core books are of single authors, two authors, is at second position and three authors constitute the least number of publications.

Table and figure shows that authorship dispersion of Library & Information Science in Dr. Harisingh Gour University, Sagar, single author covers 1703 (77.73%) followed by two authors 409 (18.67%), three authors 25 (1.14%) and more than three authors 54 (2.46%)in the 100% of total citations. Single author covers the more 75% of citations in out of total % citations.

Table 9. Authorship Dispersion :
Dr. Harisingh Gour University, Sagar

S. No.	Author	No. of Citations	Cumulation No. of Citations	% of Citations	Cumulation % of Citations
1	Single Author	1703	1703	77.73	77.73
2	Two Authors	409	2112	18.67	96.39
3	Three Authors	25	2137	1.14	97.54
4	More than Three Authors	54	2191	2.46	100.00
	Total	**2191**	**2191**	**100.00**	**100.00**

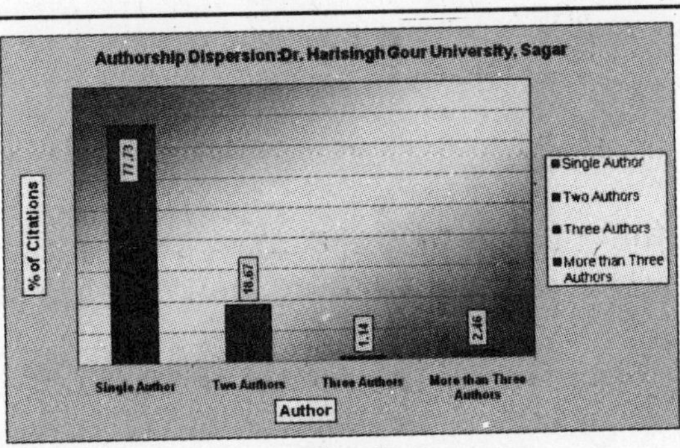

Fig. 6

6.5. DEGREE OF AUTHORSHIP COLLABORATION IN LIBRARY & INFORMATION SCIENCE

To determine the degree of collaboration in quantitative terms, the formula given by K. Subramanayam has been used.

$$C = \frac{Nm}{Nm + Ns}$$

where, C = Degree of collaboration in a discipline.

Nm = Number of multiple authored papers.

Ns = Number of single authored papers.

Degree of Authorship Collaboration : Bundelkhand University, Jhansi

Table-10 and figure-7 a show that the degree of collaboration in Library & Information Science is 0.31.This reflects the degree of prevalence of single authored publication in Library & Information Science.

Table 10. Degree of Authorship Collaboration: Bundelkhand University, Jhansi

S.No.	Author	No. of Citations	% of Citations
1	Single	1764	68.75
2	Multiple	802	31.25
	Total	2566	100.00

$$C = \frac{802}{802 + 1764} = 0.31$$

Degree of Authorship Collaboration: Jiwaji University, Gwalior

Table-11and figure-8 shows that the rate of collaboration in Library & Information Science is 0.21. This reflects the degree of prevalence of single authored publication in Library and Information Science.

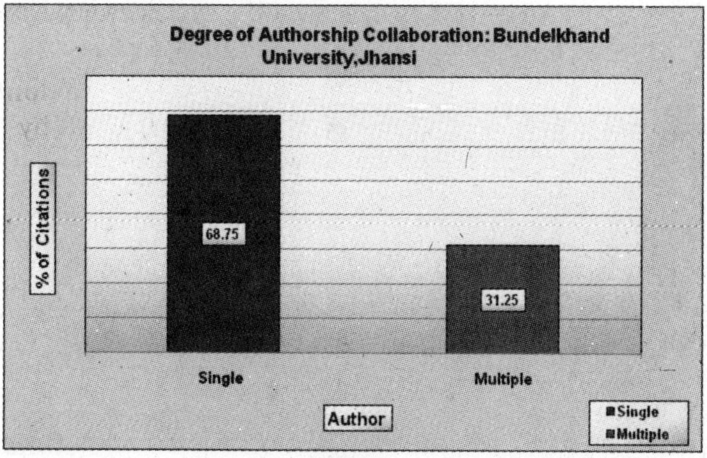

Fig. 7

Table 11. Degree of Authorship Collaboration: Jiwaji University, Gwalior

S.No.	Author	No. of Citations	% of Citations
1	Single	4928	78.48
2	Multiple	1351	21.52
	Total	6279	100.00

$$C = \frac{1351}{1351 + 4928} = 0.21$$

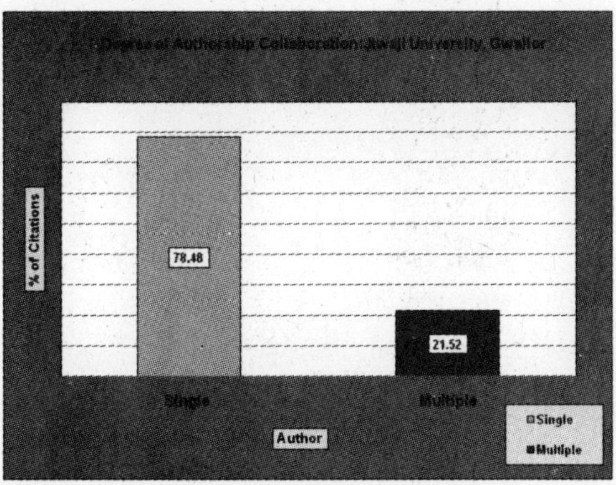

Fig. 8

Degree of Authorship Collaboration : Dr. Harisingh Gour University, Sagar

Table-12 and figure-9 shows the rate of collaboration in Library and Information Science is 0.22. This reflects the degree of prevalence of single authored publication in Library and Information Science.

Table 12. Degree of Authorship Collaboration : Dr. Harisingh Gour University, Sagar

S.No.	Author	No. of Citations	% of Citations
1	Single Author	1703	77.73
2	Multiple	488	22.27
	Total	**2191**	**100.00**

$$C = \frac{488}{488 + 1703} = 0.22$$

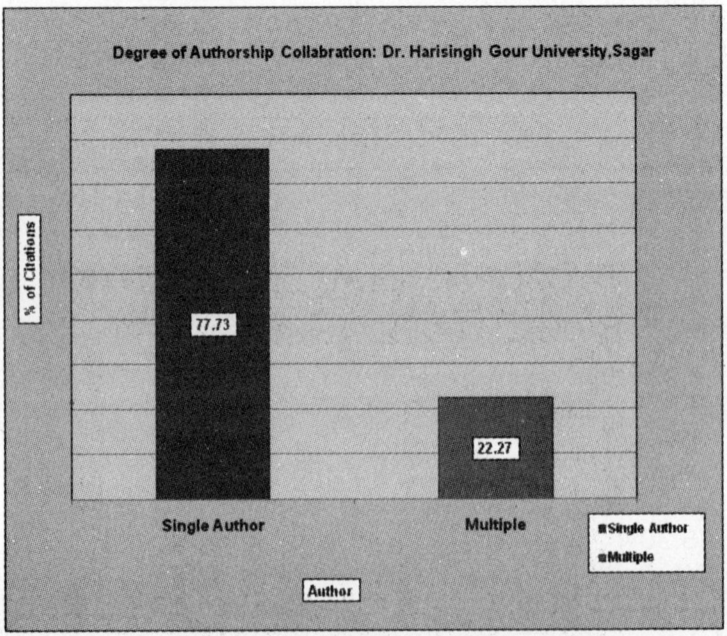

Fig. 9

6.6. TIME DISPERSION IN LIBRARY & INFORMATION SCIENCE

Here an attempt is being made to investigate time dispersion citations in Library & Information Science. The term time dispersion expresses the year of publication of the documents in use. The documents when treated into blocks of decades reveal the most productive decade and the obsolescence rate of literature. The general trend is that recent information sources are consulted but it may definitely vary depending upon the subject of research and type of study undertaken.

With the explosion of literature and multi-dimensional growth of the universe of knowledge has simultaneously stimulated the use of obsolescence of published materials. The faster the rate of recent publications higher is the obsolescence rate. It also differs from discipline to discipline. Thus, it becomes essential to study the citations to determine the documents utility depending upon the time factor.

6.6.1. Time Dispersion of Books

Time Dispersion of Books: Bundelkhand University, Jhansi

Table-13 and figure-10 gives the arability of cited documents (Books) in Bundelkhand University, Jhansi. All the 2566 citations to by 35 scholars in their research output are arranged in a decreasing chronological order in nine divisions. In which 1986-1995 is the most productive year's covered 683 (26.62%) citations followed by 1976-1985 covers 616 (24.01%) citations, 1996-2005 covers 589 (22.95%) citations and 1966-1975 covers 453 (17.65%) citations. Compare to 1956-1965 covers 136 (5.30%) citations followed by 1946-1955 covers 49 (1.91 %) citations, 1936-1945 covers 24 (0.94%) citations, 1926-1935 covers 15 (0.58%) citations are less productive years.

Table 13. Time Dispersion of Books : Bundelkhand University, Jhansi

S. No.	Year of Books	No. of Citations	Cumulation No. of Citations	% of Citations	Cumulation % of Citations
1	2006-2009	1	1	0.04	0.04
2	1996-2005	589	590	22.95	22.99
3	1986-1995	683	1273	26.62	49.61
4	1976-1985	616	1889	24.01	73.62
5	1966-1975	453	2342	17.65	91.27
6	1956-1965	136	2478	5.30	96.57
7	1946-1955	49	2527	1.91	98.48
8	1936-1945	24	2551	0.94	99.42
9	1926-1935	15	2566	0.58	100.00
	Total	**2566**	**2566**	**100.00**	**100.00**

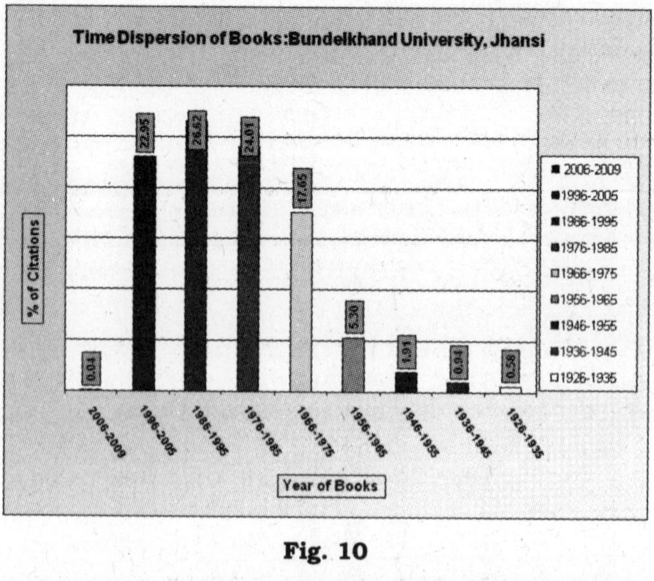

Fig. 10

Time Dispersion of Books : Jiwaji University, Gwalior:

Table-14 and figure-11 displays the age wise distribution of literature in Library & Information Science in Jiwaji University, Gwalior. As is depicted in the table and figure below the years 1986-1995 shows a higher percentage of use of published materials1729 (27.54%) than the years 1976-1985 with 1672 (26.63%) and the years 1966-1975 with 1163 (18.52 %), during 1996-2005 with 650 (10.35%), years 1946-1955 with 303 (4.83%), years 1936-1945 with 93 (1.48%),years 1926-1935 with 51 (0.81%), and 2006-2009 with 29 (0.46%) out of 6279 citations.

Table 14. Time Dispersion of Books : Jiwaji University, Gwalior

S. No.	Year of Books	No. of Citations	Cumulation No. of Citations	% of Citations	Cumulation % of Citations
1	2006-2009	29	29	0.46	0.46
2	1996-2005	650	679	10.35	10.81
3	1986-1995	1729	2408	27.54	38.35
4	1976-1985	1672	4080	26.63	64.98
5	1966-1975	1163	5243	18.52	83.50
6	1956-1965	589	5832	9.38	92.88
7	1946-1955	303	6135	4.83	97.71
8	1936-1945	93	6228	1.48	99.19
9	1926-1935	51	6279	0.81	100.00
	Total	**6279**	**6279**	**100.00**	**100.00**

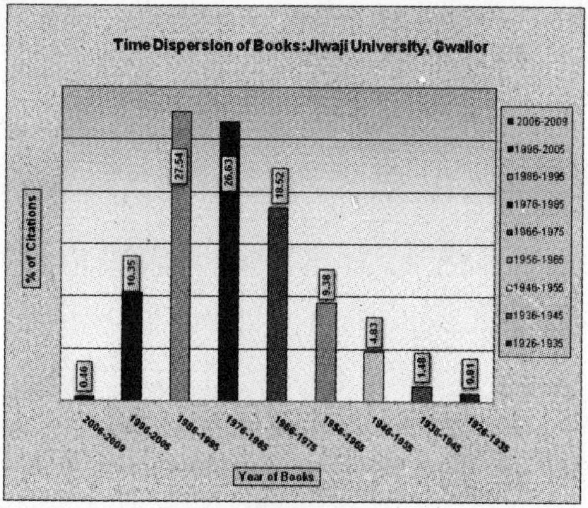

Fig. 11

Time Dispersion of Books in Dr. Harisingh Gour University, Sagar

Table-15 and figure-12 gives the result of cites documents (Books) in Dr. Harisingh Gour University, Sagar. All the 2191 citations to by 28 scholars in their research output are arranged in a decreasing chronological order. In which 1986-1995 is the most productive year's covers 749 (34.19%) citations followed by 1976-1985 covers 506 (23.09%) citations, 1996-2005 covers 461(21.04%) citations and 1966-1975 covers 265 (12.09%) citations. Compare to 1956-1965 covers 122 (5.57%) citations followed by 2006-2009 covers 32(1.46%),1946-1955 covers 29(1.32 %) citations, 1936-1945 covers 16 (0.73%) citations, 1926-1935 covers 11 (0.50%) citations are less productive years.

Table 15. Time Dispersion of Books : Dr. Harisingh Gour University, Sagar

S. No.	Year of Books	No. of Citations	Cumulation No. of Citations	% of Citations	Cumulation % of Citations
1	2006-2009	32	32	1.46	1.46
2	1996-2005	461	493	21.04	22.50
3	1986-1995	749	1242	34.19	56.69
4	1976-1985	506	1748	23.09	79.78
5	1966-1975	265	2013	12.09	91.88
6	1956-1965	122	2135	5.57	97.44
7	1946-1955	29	2164	1.32	98.77
8	1936-1945	16	2180	0.73	99.50
9	1926-1935	11	2191	0.50	100.00
	Total	**2191**	**2191**	**100.00**	**100.00**

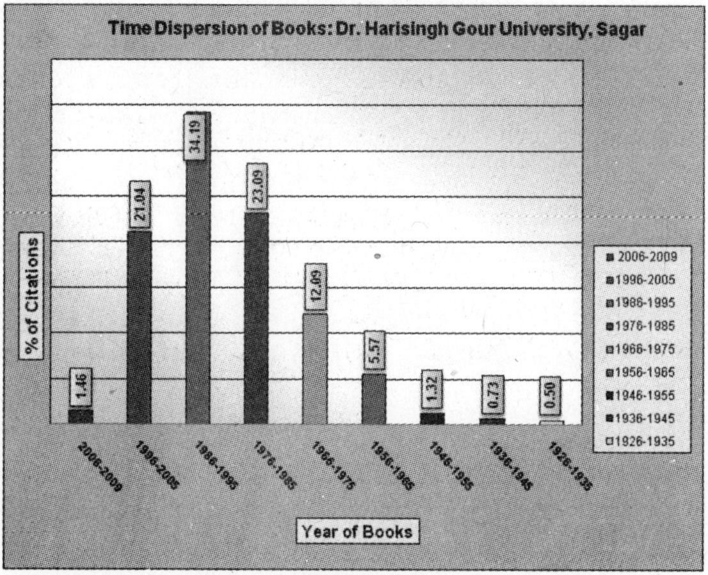

Fig. 12

6.6.2. Time Dispersion of Journals

Time Dispersion of Journals: Bundelkhand University, Jhansi

Table-16 and figure-13 examines the time dispersion of citations in Library & Information science. Total number of citations analyzed for determining the age of utility of the publications are 2048. The study covers the time span under the year blocks in decades. The analysis reveals that 652 (31.84%) citations in years 1986-1995 is the most productive decade followed by 573 (27.98%) citations in years 1976-1985 is at second position, the citations 456 (22.27%) in years 1996-2005, 219 (10.69%) citations in the years 1966-1975, 97 (4.74%) citations in the years 1956-1965,32 (1.56%) citations in the years 1946-1955, 11 (0.54%) citations in the years 1936-1945 and 5 (0.24%) citations in the years 1926-1935 and only 3 (0.15%) citations in year 2006-2009.

The maximum Journal used in Library & Information Science is published during the 1986-1995, 1976-1985 and 1996-2005.

Table 16. Time Dispersion of Journals : Bundelkhand University, Jhansi

S. No.	Year of Journals	No. of Citations	Cumulation No. of Citations	% of Citations	Cumulation % of Citations
1	2006-2009	3	3	0.15	0.15
2	1996-2005	456	459	22.27	22.41
3	1986-1995	652	1111	31.84	54.25
4	1976-1985	573	1684	27.98	82.23
5	1966-1975	219	1903	10.69	92.92
6	1956-1965	97	2000	4.74	97.66
7	1946-1955	32	2032	1.56	99.22
8	1936-1945	11	2043	0.54	99.76
9	1926-1935	5	2048	0.24	100.00
	Total	**2048**	**2048**	**100.00**	**100.00**

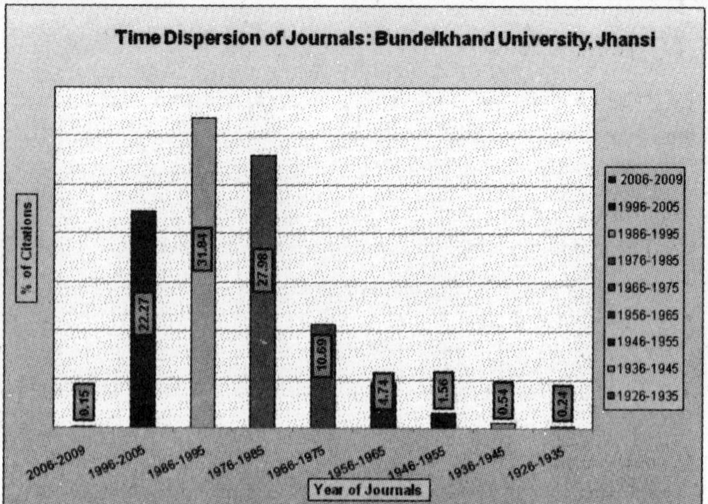

Fig. 13

Time Dispersion of Journals in Jiwaji University, Gwalior

Table-17 and figure-14 displays the age wise distribution of literature in Jiwaji University, Gwalior. As is depicted in the table below the years 1986-1995 shows a higher percentage of use of published materials 1379 (29.56%) than the years 1976-1985 with 1250 (26.80%) and the years 1966-1975 with 860 (18.44%), during 1996-2005 with 499 (10.70%), years 1956-1965 with 396 (8.49%),years 1946-1955 with 173 (3.71%), years 1936-1945 with 78 (1.67%),years 1926-1935 with 15 (0.32%), and 2006-2009 with 15 (0.32%) out of total 4665 citations.

Table 17. Time Dispersion of Journals : Jiwaji University, Gwalior

S. No.	Year of Journals	No. of Citations	Cumulation No. of Citations	% of Citations	Cumulation % of Citations
1	2006-2009	15	15	0.32	0.32
2	1996-2005	499	514	10.70	11.02
3	1986-1995	1379	1893	29.56	40.58
4	1976-1985	1250	3143	26.80	67.37
5	1966-1975	860	4003	18.44	85.81
6	1956-1965	396	4399	8.49	94.30
7	1946-1955	173	4572	3.71	98.01
8	1936-1945	78	4650	1.67	99.68
9	1926-1935	15	4665	0.32	100.00
	Total	**4665**	**4665**	**100.00**	**100.00**

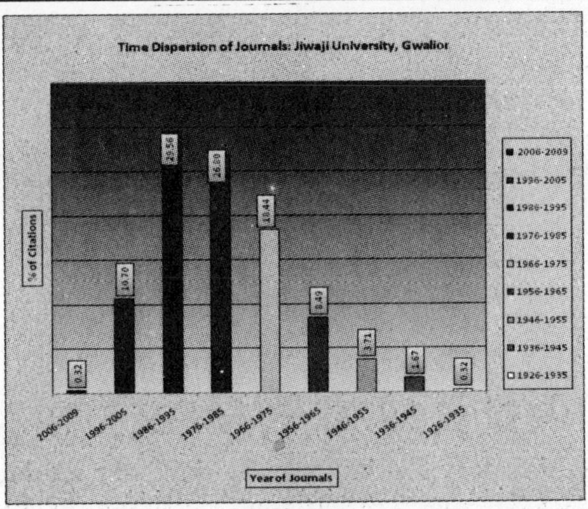

Fig. 14

Time Dispersion of Journals : Dr. Harisingh Gour University, Sagar

Table-18 and figure-15 gives the result of cites journals in Dr. Harisingh Gour University, Sagar. All the 2953 citations to by 28 scholars in their research output are arranged in a decreasing chronological order. In which 1986-1995 is the most productive year's covers 996 (33.73%) citations followed by 1976-1985 covers 618(20.93%) citations, 1996-2005 covered 737 (24.96 %) citations and 1966-1975 covered 354 (11.99 %) citations. Compare to 1956-1965 covered 171 (5.79%) citations followed by 1946-1955 covered 34 (1.15%) citations, 2006-2009 covered 33 (1.12%), 1926-1935 covered 8 (0.27%) citations ,1936-1945 covered 2 (0.07%) citations, are less productive years.

Table 18. Time Dispersion of Journals : Dr. Harisingh Gour University, Sagar

S. No.	Year of Journals	No. of Citations	Cumulation No. of Citations	% of Citations	Cumulation % of Citations
1	2006-2009	33	33	1.12	1.12
2	1996-2005	737	770	24.96	26.08
3	1986-1995	996	1766	33.73	59.80
4	1976-1985	618	2384	20.93	80.73
5	1966-1975	354	2738	11.99	92.72
6	1956-1965	171	2909	5.79	98.51
7	1946-1955	34	2943	1.15	99.66
8	1936-1945	2	2945	0.07	99.73
9	1926-1935	8	2953	0.27	100.00
	Total	**2953**	**2953**	**100.00**	**100.00**

6.7. COUNTRYWISE DISTRIBUTION OF JOURNALS IN LIBRARY & INFORMATION SCIENCE

Geographical analysis of citations provides information about the countries active in a subject field and their relative contribution. Provided the information about the geographical distribution of citations of journals.

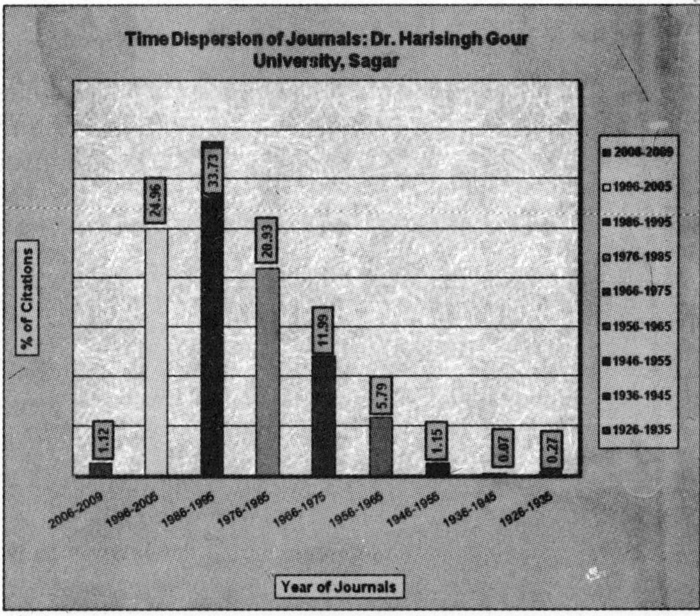

Fig. 15

The data has been arranged in six columns. The first column indicates the serial number, the second one indicates the place/country of publication, and column three lists the number of citations covered by journals. Column four lists the number of cumulation number of citations covered by journals, the fifth column provides % of citation and column sixth provide cumulation % of Citations covered by journals.

Countrywise Dispersion of Journals : Bundelkhand University, Jhansi

Table-19 and figure-16 displays the country wise dispersion of citations in Library & Information Science in BundelkhandUniversity, Jhansi. The table clearly indicates the dispersion of citations according to countries. U.S.A. has scored the maximum number of citations 122 (43.42%) of the total number of journals 281, this is followed by India scored 47 (16.73%), U.K.

scored 46 (16.37%), and Netherlands scored 25 (8.90%), of citations. Canada scored 6 (2.14%), Australia 5 (1.78%), West Germany and Japan scored same rank i.e.4 (1.42%) the rest of the countries like Africa, China, Europe, Jamaica, New Zealand, Pakistan are covered same citations i.e.2 (0.71%) and Brazil, Denmark, France, East Germany,Jordan, Korea, Russia, Slovenia, South Africa, Sweden scored only 1 (0.36%).

Table 19. Countrywise Dispersion of Journals: Bundelkhand University, Jhansi

S. No.	Year of Journals	No. of Citations	Cumulation No. of Citations	% of Citations	Cumulation % of Citations
1	U.S.A.	122	122	43.42	43.42
2	India	47	169	16.73	60.14
3	U.K.	46	215	16.37	76.51
4	Netherlands	25	240	8.90	85.41
5	Canada	6	246	2.14	87.54
6	Australia	5	251	1.78	89.32
7	West Germany	4	255	1.42	90.75
8	Japan	4	259	1.42	92.17
9	Africa	2	261	0.71	92.88
10	China	2	263	0.71	93.59
11	Europe	2	265	0.71	94.31
12	Jamaica	2	267	0.71	95.02
13	New Zealand	2	269	0.71	95.73
14	Pakistan	2	271	0.71	96.44
15	Brazil	1	272	0.36	96.80
16	Denmark(DK)	1	273	0.36	97.15
17	France	1	274	0.36	97.51
18	East Germany	1	275	0.36	97.86
19	Jordan	1	276	0.36	98.22
20	Korea	1	277	0.36	98.58
21	Russia	1	278	0.36	98.93
22	Slovenia	1	279	0.36	99.29
23	South Africa	1	280	0.36	99.64
24	Sweden	1	281	0.36	100.00
	Total	281	281	100.00	100.00

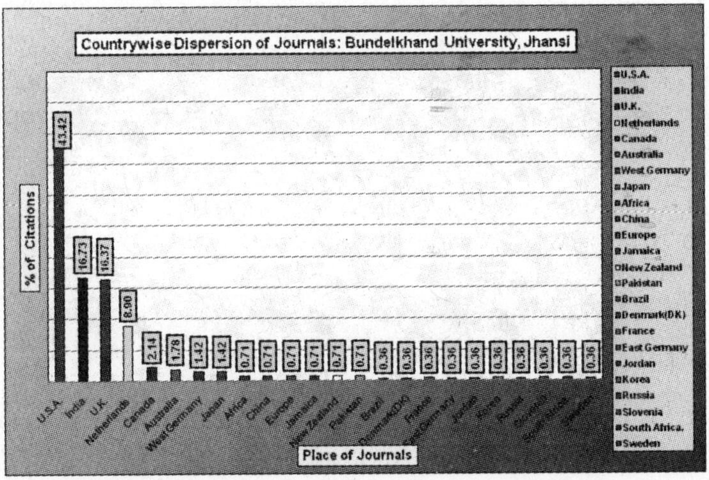

Fig. 16

Countrywise Dispersion of Journals : Jiwaji University, Gwalior

Table-20 and figure-17 shows the geographical distribution of 543ranked journals covering 4665 citations. It is observed from the study that U.S.A. occupied the top position and covered 256 citations (47.15%). India is covered second ranked 105 citations (19.34%) and U.K. is the third position and scored 83 citations (15.29%), followed by Netherlands 31 citations (5.71%), Australia 12 citations (2.21%), Canada 9 citations (1.66%) and Europe obtain 7 citations (1.29 %). West Germany and Japan have obtain equal number of citations 6-6 (1.10 %) followed by Brazil, Pakistan, Russia covered 3-3 citations (0.55%), Malaysia, Nigeria, Singapore, South Africa scored 2-2 citations (0.37%) and rest of countries like Africa, China, Colombia, East Germany, *Egypt*, France, *Iran*, Korea, Newzeland,Slovenia and Taiwan are covered only 1-1 citation (0.18%) and in last position.

Table 20. Countrywise Dispersion of Journals : Jiwaji University, Gwalior

S. No.	Year of Journals	No. of Citations	Cumulation No. of Citations	% of Citations	Cumulation % of Citations
1	U.S.A.	256	256	47.15	47.15
2	India	105	361	19.34	66.48
3	U.K.	83	444	15.29	81.77
4	Netherlands	31	475	5.71	87.48
5	Australia	12	487	2.21	89.69
6	Canada	9	496	1.66	91.34
7	Europe	7	503	1.29	92.63
8	WestGermany	6	509	1.10	93.74
9	Japan	6	515	1.10	94.84
10	Brazil	3	518	0.55	95.40
11	Pakistan	3	521	0.55	95.95
12	Russia	3	524	0.55	96.50
13	Malaysia	2	526	0.37	96.87
14	Nigeria	2	528	0.37	97.24
15	Singapore	2	530	0.37	97.61
16	South Africa	2	532	0.37	97.97
17	Africa	1	533	0.18	98.16
18	China	1	534	0.18	98.34
19	Colombia	1	535	0.18	98.53
20	East Germany	1	536	0.18	98.71
21	Egypt	1	537	0.18	98.90
22	France	1	538	0.18	99.08
23	Iran	1	539	0.18	99.26
24	Korea	1	540	0.18	99.45
25	Newzeland	1	541	0.18	99.63
26	Slovenia	1	542	0.18	99.82
27	Taiwan	1	543	0.18	100.00
	Total	**543**	**543**	**100.00**	**100.00**

Countrywise Dispersion of Journals: Dr. Harisingh Gour University, Sagar

Table-21 and figure-18 shows thatin term of total number and percentages of citations by countries U.S.A. contributes the most number of citations used by researchers of Dr. Harisingh Gour University, Sagar with

114 (44.71%) citations, followed by India with 59 (23.14%) citations, U.K. with 41 (16.08%) citations, Netherlands with 13 (5.10%) citations, Australia with 8 (3.14%) citations, Canada with 5 (1.96%) citations, Nigeria with 4 (1.57%) citations, South African with 3 (1.18%) citations, West Germany with 2 (0.78%) citations. It has to be noted here that Taiwan Africa, France, Japan, Pakistan, South Australia produce same citation i.e. only 1 (0.39%) citations.

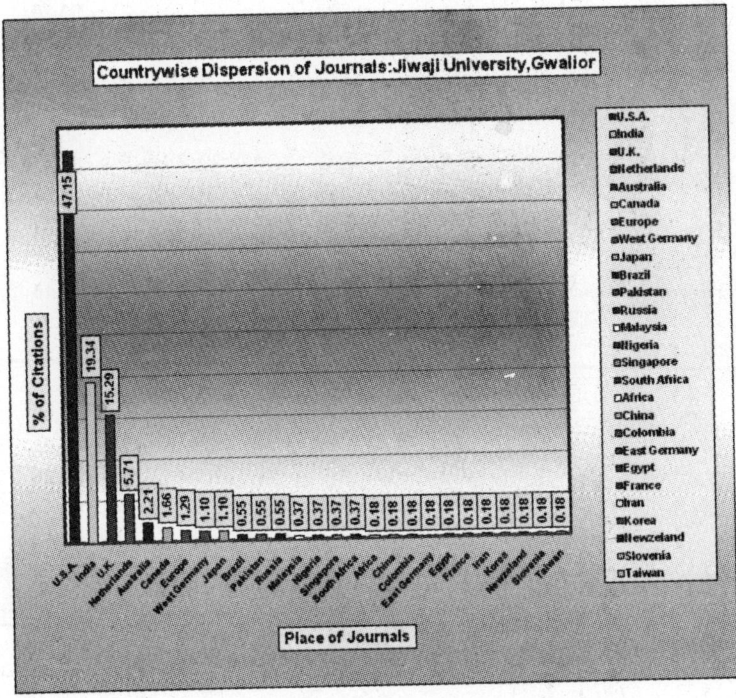

Fig. 17

Table 21. Countrywise Dispersion of Journal: Dr. Harisingh Gour University, Sagar

S. No.	Year of Journals	No. of Citations	Cumulation No. of Citations	% of Citations	Cumulation % of Citations
1	U.S.A.	114	114	44.71	44.71
2	India	59	173	23.14	67.84
3	U.K.	41	214	16.08	83.92
4	Netherlands	13	227	5.10	89.02
5	Australia	8	235	3.14	92.16
6	Canada	5	240	1.96	94.12
7	Nigeria	4	244	1.57	95.69
8	South African	3	247	1.18	96.86
9	West Germany	2	249	0.78	97.65
10	Taiwan	1	250	0.39	98.04
11	Africa	1	251	0.39	98.43
12	France	1	252	0.39	98.82
13	Japan	1	253	0.39	99.22
14	Pakistan	1	254	0.39	99.61
15	South Australia	1	255	0.39	100.00
	Total	**255**	**255**	**100.00**	**100.00**

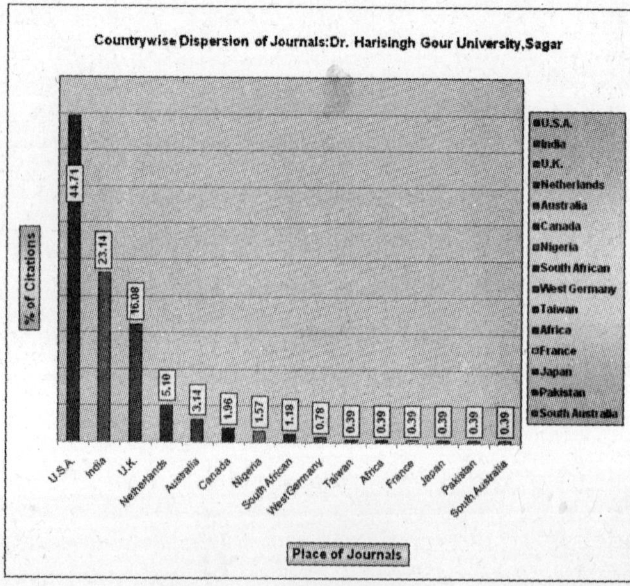

Fig. 18

7

Comparative Study in Selected Universities

7.1. INTRODUCTION

According to Eugene Garfield the qualitative measure is that the Science management applications of the SCI data base began with the simplest measure: Citation rates; underlying their use is the obvious need for some objective measure of contributions made by individual researchers papers, journals, programmes, regions and nations. Because they reflect the number of times individual scientists consider a given document important enough to cite in their own work, citation rates appear to be such a measure. The nature of the quality that citation rates measure is elusive. It has been described variously as signification, impact, utility and effectiveness, but no one has succeeded in defining it in more tangible terms.

7.2. COMPARISON OF AVERAGE CITATIONS PER THESIS

The present comparative studies cover 128 theses, each thesis with an average citation of 220.70. In Bundelkhand University, Jhansi covers the 6198 citations in total number of 35 theses, followed by Jiwaji University,

Gwalior 14767 in total number of 65 theses and Dr. Harisingh Gour University, Sagar covers 7284 citations in total number of 28 theses. The following Table-1 shows average citation per thesis.

Figure-1 shows that Bundelkhand University, Jhansi the average number of citations per thesis is 177.09, followed by Jiwaji University, Gwalior with 227.18, and the Dr. Harisingh Gaur University, Sagar with 260.14 citations respectively.

Table 1 : Comparison of Average Citations per Thesis

S.No.	Name of University	No. of Theses	No. of Citations	Average No. of Citation
1	BundelkhandUniversity, Jhansi	35	6198	177.09
2	JiwajiUniversity, Gwalior	65	14767	227.18
3	Dr. Harisingh Gaur University, Sagar	28	7284	260.14
	Total	**128**	**28249**	**220.70**

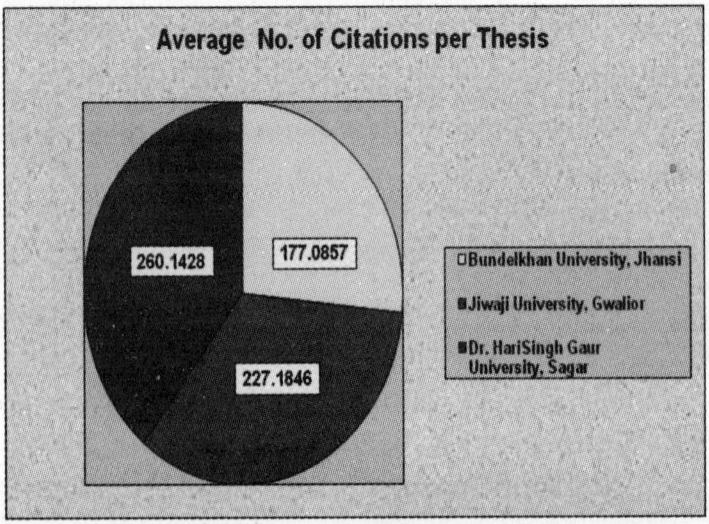

Fig. 1

7.3. COMPARISON OF BIBLIOGRAPHIC FORM DISPERSION

Table-2 and figure-2 shows that, the total number of citations in three universities is of 28,249. In Bundelkhand University, Jhansi covers the 6198 citations followed by Jiwaji University, Gwalior 14767 and Dr. Harisingh Gour University, Sagar covers 7284 citations. Distribution of citations by bibliographic format all 28,249 citations are identified based on ten bibliographic forms.

Where Books/Guides are most used format in Bundelkhand University, Jhansi 41.40% and Jiwaji University, Gwalior 42.52%, the journals cover first place in Dr. Harisingh Gaur University, Sagar 40.54 %.Journals cover 33.04 % space in Bundelkhand University, Jhansi, and 31.59 % space in Jiwaji University, Gwalior and 40.54% in Dr. Harisingh Gaur University, Sagar. These two formats of information resources make up almost 70 % of the total citations.

Other formats of information are like websites 9.44%, and conferences proceedings 6.10%. reports 2.16 % followed by Govt. publications 1.68%, theses 1.16%, case study/survey 0.77%, reference sources 1.74%, letters/lectures 2.50% of space cover in the field of library science research in Bundelkhand University, Jhansi

In Jiwaji University, Gwalior conference proceedings is 5.95%, followed by report 5.21%, web sites 4.04 %, Govt. publications 3.88 %, reference sources 3.61%, thesis 1.79 %, letters/lectures 1.04%, and case studies 0.37%.

In Dr.Harisingh Gaur University,.Sagar It is found that reports are 7.04% and conference proceedings 6.27 %. Reference sources is 5.64% followed by theses 3.03%, case study/survey 2.86%, govt.publications 2.17%,web sites 2.17%, and letters/lectures 0.19%.

Table 2. Comparison of Bibliographic Form Dispersion: Bundelkhand University, Jhansi; Jiwaji University, Gwalior & Dr. Harisingh Gour University, Sagar

S. No.	Bibliographic Form	No. of Citations			% of Citations		
		BU	**JU**	**HSG**	**BU**	**JU**	**HSG**
1	Books/Guides	2566	6279	2191	41.40	42.52	30.07
2	Case Study/Survey	48	55	208	0.77	0.37	2.86
3	Conference Proceedings	378	879	457	6.10	5.95	6.27
4	Govt. Publications	104	573	158	1.68	3.88	2.17
5	Journal Articles	2048	4665	2953	33.04	31.59	40.54
6	Letters/Lectures	155	153	14	2.50	1.04	0.19
7	Reference Sources	108	533	411	1.74	3.61	5.64
8	Reports	134	769	513	2.16	5.21	7.04
9	Theses	72	265	221	1.16	1.79	3.03
10	Web sites	585	596	158	9.44	4.04	2.17
	Total	**6198**	**14767**	**7284**	**100.00**	**100.00**	**100.00**

Notes : BU — Bundelkhand University, Jhansi

JU — Jiwaji University, Gwalior

HSG — Dr. Hari Singh Gour University, Sagar

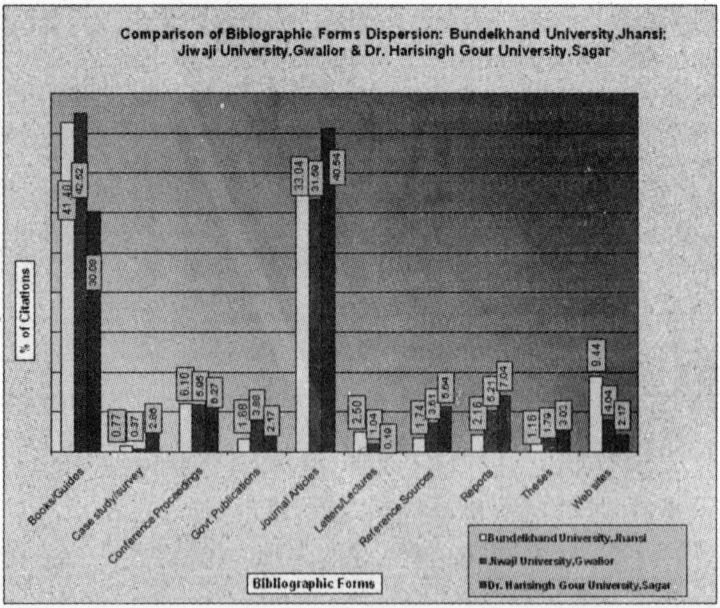

Fig. 2

7.4. COMPARISON OF AUTHORSHIP DISPERSION

The characteristics of subject literature consist of not only the basic publishing patterns but the authors. Authorship has been analyzed to determine the percentage of single and multiple authors. Table-3 and Fig-3 shows that in all three universities viz : Bundelkhand University, Jhansi; Jiwaji University, Gwalior & Dr. Harisingh Gour University, Sagar. The single authorship pattern secures the highest position and second highest position covers the two authorship followed by three authors and more than three authors.

In Bundelkhand University, Jhansi citation of single authorship is 1764 (68.75%), two authors 589 (22.95%) followed by three authors 86 (3.35%), more than three authors 127 (4.95%) in out of 2566 citations.

In Jiwaji University, Gwalior citation of single authorship is 4928 (78.48%), two authors 1066 (16.98%) followed by three authors 100 (1.59%), more than three authors 185 (2.94%) in out of 6279 citations.

And in Dr. Harisingh Gour University, Sagar citation of single authorship is 1703 (77.73%), two authors 409 (18.67%) followed by three authors 25 (1.14%), more than three authors 54 (2.46%) in out of 2191 citations.

Table 3. Comparison of Authorship Dispersion: Bundelkhand University, Jhansi; Jiwaji University, Gwalior & Dr. Harisingh Gour University, Sagar

S. No.	Bibliographic Form	No. of Citations			% of Citations		
		BU	JU	HSG	BU	JU	HSG
1	Single Author	1764	4928	1703	68.75	78.48	77.73
2	TwoAuthors	589	1066	409	22.95	16.98	18.67
3	Three Authors	86	100	25	3.35	1.59	1.14
4	More than ThreeAuthors	127	185	54	4.95	2.94	2.46
	Total	2566	6279	2191	100.00	100.00	100.00

Notes : BU — Bundelkhand University, Jhansi

JU — Jiwaji University, Gwalior; HSG — Dr. Hari Singh Gour University, Sagar

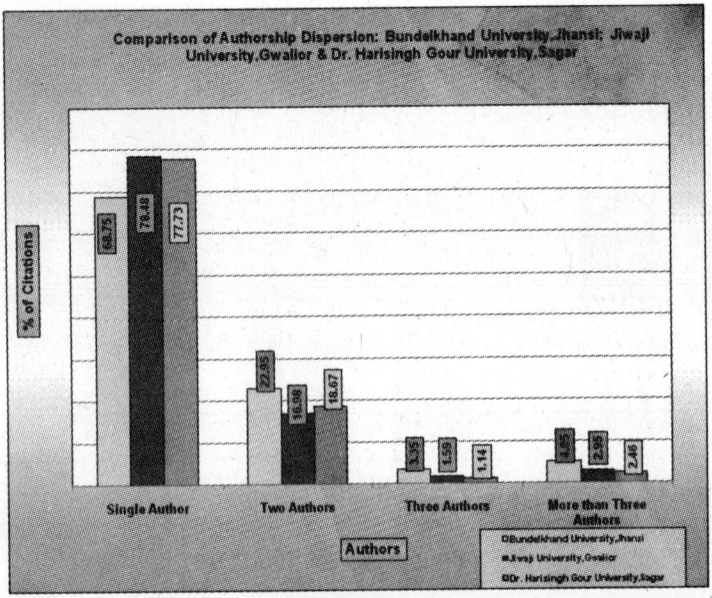

Fig. 3

7.5. COMPARISON OF DEGREE OF COLLABORATION

Table-4 and Fig-4shows that the degree of collaboration in Bundelkhand University, Jhansi is 0.31, Jiwaji University, Gwalior is 0.21 and Dr. Harisingh Gour University, Sagar is 0.22.

Table 4. Comparison of Degree of Authorship Collaboration : Bundelkhand University, Jhansi; Jiwaji University, Gwalior & Dr. Harisingh Gour University, Sagar

S. No.	Name of University	Degree of Authorship Collaboration
1.	Bundelkhand University, Jhansi	0.31
2.	Jiwaji University, Gwalior	0.21
3.	Dr. Harisingh Gaur University, Sagar	0.22

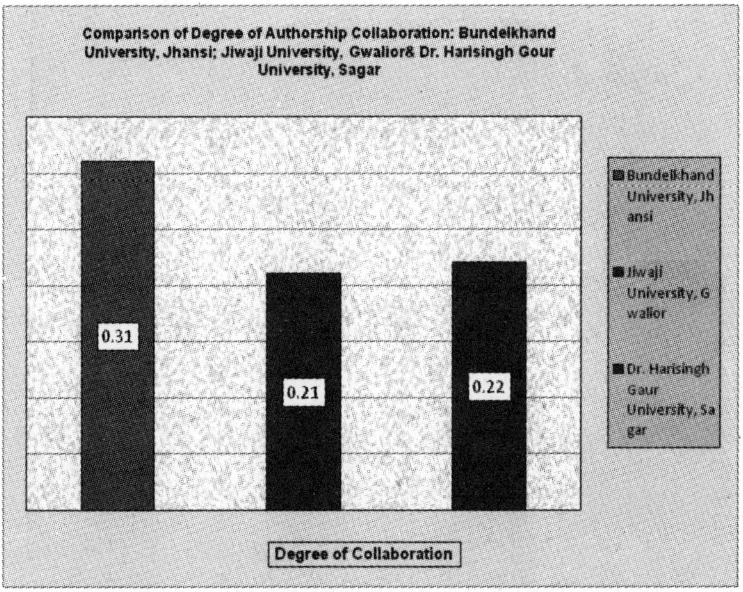

Fig. 4

7.6. COMPARISON OF TIME DISPERSION OF BOOKS

Table-5 and figure-5, shows all the 11036 (2566 + 6279 + 2191) citations to by 128 scholars collect from three universities in their research output are arranged in decreasing chronological order in Table-16. All these citations fall into nine sequences. The oldest 1926-1935 and earliest, and the latest 2006-2009 citations fall into first and last group respectively.

Clearly indicates that in Bundelkhand University, Jhansi 683 (26.62%) citations refer to current literature i.e. for 1986-1995. Citation belonging to this period refers to nascent literature, followed by 616 (24.01%) citations of 1976-1985, with 589 (22.95%) citations of 1996-2005. These sequences have got the largest number of citations. Compare to productive years 1956-1965 with 136 (5.30%) citations, followed by 49 (1.91%) citations in 1946-1955,

24 (0.94%) citations in 1936-1945, and 15 (0.58%) citations in 1926-1935 have got lowest number of citations out of total citations 2566.

Display the age wise distribution of books in Jiwaji University, Gwalior, as is depicted in the table below the years 1986-1995 shows a higher percentage of use of published materials 1729 (27.54%) citations in years 1986-1995, 1672 (26.63%) citations in years 1976-1985, than 1163 (18.52%) citations in years of 1966-1975, followed by 650 (10.35%) citations in years 1996-2005, 589 (9.38%) citations in years 1956-1965, 303 (4.83%) citations in years 1946-1955, 93 (1.48%)citations in years 1936-1945, 51 (0.81%)citations years 1926-1935, out of 6279 citations.

Table 5. Comparison of Time Dispersion of Books: Bundelkhand University, Jhansi; Jiwaji University, Gwalior & Dr. Harisingh Gour University, Sagar

S. No.	Year of Books	No. of Citations			% of Citations		
		BU	JU	HSG	BU	JU	HSG
1	2006-2009	1	29	32	0.04	0.46	1.46
2	1996-2005	589	650	461	22.95	10.35	21.04
3	1986-1995	683	1729	749	26.62	27.54	34.19
4	1976-1985	616	1672	506	24.01	26.63	23.09
5	1966-1975	453	1163	265	17.65	18.52	12.09
6	1956-1965	136	589	122	5.30	9.38	5.57
7	1946-1955	49	303	29	1.91	4.83	1.32
8	1936-1945	24	93	16	0.94	1.48	0.73
9	1926-1935	15	51	11	0.58	0.81	0.50
	Total	**2566**	**6279**	**2191**	**100.00**	**100.00**	**100.00**

Notes : BU — Bundelkhand University, Jhansi; JU — Jiwaji University, Gwalior; HSG — Dr. Hari Singh Gour University, Sagar

Table gives the result of cites documents of books in Dr. Harisingh Gour University, Sagar. All the 2191 citations collect from research output of using pattern of books. In which 1986-1995 is the most productive year's covered 749 (34.19%) citations followed by 1976-1985 covered 506(23.09%) citations, 1996-2005 covered 461 (21.04%) citations and 1966-1975 scored 265 (12.09%) citations. Compare to 1956-1965 covers 122 (5.57%) citations followed by 2006-2009 covered 32(1.46%),1946-1955 covered 29 (1.32%) citations, 1936-1945 scored 16(0.73%) citations, 1926-1935 covered 11 (0.50%) citations have less productive years.

The analysis of chronological distribution of citation can indicate the correctness of the literature being used in research. Table shows the literature that is most significant from the library and information scientist's point of view belongs to the 1986-1995, 1976-1985, and 1996-2005.

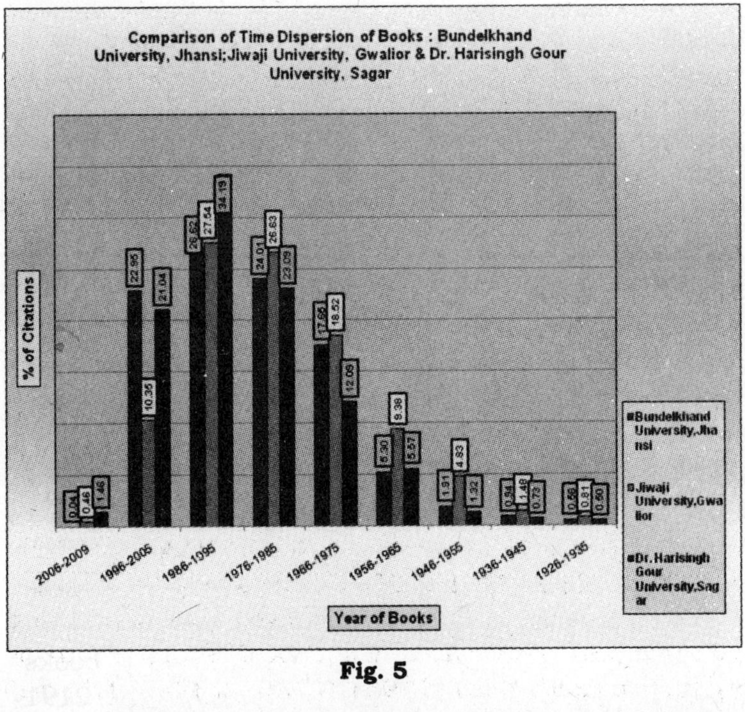

Fig. 5

7.7. COMPARISON OF TIME DISPERSION OF JOURNALS

Table-6 and figure-6 all the 9,666 citations of journals by 128 scholars collect from three universities in their research output are arranged in decreasing chronological order in Table-20. All these citations fall into nine sequences. The oldest 1926-1935 and earliest, and the latest 2006-2009 citations fall into first and last group respectively.

In Bundelkhand University, Jhansi the total number of citations in journals analyzed for determining the age of utility of the publications are 2048. The study covers the time span under the year blocks in decades. The analysis reveals that the 652 (31.84%) citations in years 1986-1995 is the most productive decade followed by 573 (27.98%) citations in years 1976-1985 is at second position, the citations 456 (22.27%) in years 1996-2005, 219(10.69%) citations in the years 1966-1975, 97 (4.74%) citations in the years 1956-1965, 32 (1.56%) citations in the years 1946-1955, 11 (0.54%) citations in the years 1936-1945 and 5 (0.24%) citations in the years 1926-1935 and only 3 (0.15%) citations in year 2006-2009.

The age wise distribution of journals in Jiwaji University, Gwalior. As is depicted in the table below the years 1986-1995 shows a higher percentage of use of published materials years 1986-1995 with 1379 (29.56%), years 1976-1985 with 125 (26.80%), than the years of 1966-1975 with 860 (18.44%), years 1996-2005 with 499 (10.70%), years 1956-1965 with 396 (8.49%), years 1946-1955 with 173 (3.71%), years 1936-1945 with 78 (1.67%), years 1926-1935 with 15 (0.32%), and 2006-2009 with 15 (0.32%) out of 4665 citations.

The result of cites journals in Dr. Harisingh Gour University, Sagar. All the 2953 citations to by 28 scholars in their research output are arranged in a decreasing chronological order. In which 1986-1995 is the most productive year's covered 996 (33.73%) citations followed by 1976-1985 covered 618 (20.93%) citations, 1996-2005 covers 737 (24.96%) citations and 1966-1975 (11.99 %) covered 354 citations. Compare to 1956-1965 covered 171 (5.79%) citations followed by 2006-2009 covered 33

(1.12%),1946-1955 covered 34 (1.15%) citations, 1936-1945 covered 2 (0.07%) citations, 1926-1935 covered 8 (0.27%) citations are less productive years.

The maximum Journal used in Library & Information science is published during the 1995- 1986, 1985-1976 and 2005-1996.

Table 6. Comparison of Time Dispersion of Journals: Bundelkhand University, Jhansi; Jiwaji University, Gwalior & Dr. Harisingh Gour University, Sagar

S. No.	Year of Books	No. of Citations BU	JU	HSG	% of Citations BU	JU	HSG
1	2006-2009	3	15	33	0.15	0.32	1.12
2	1996-2005	456	499	737	22.27	10.70	24.96
3	1986-1995	652	1379	996	31.84	29.56	33.73
4	1976-1985	573	1250	618	27.98	26.80	20.93
5	1966-1975	219	860	354	10.69	18.44	11.99
6	1956-1965	97	396	171	4.74	8.49	5.79
7	1946-1955	32	173	34	1.56	3.71	1.15
8	1936-1945	11	78	2	0.54	1.67	0.07
9	1926-1935	5	15	8	0.24	0.32	0.27
	Total	**2048**	**4665**	**2953**	**100.00**	**100.00**	**100.00**

Notes : BU — Bundelkhand University, Jhansi; JU — Jiwaji University, Gwalior; HSG — Dr. Hari Singh Gour University, Sagar

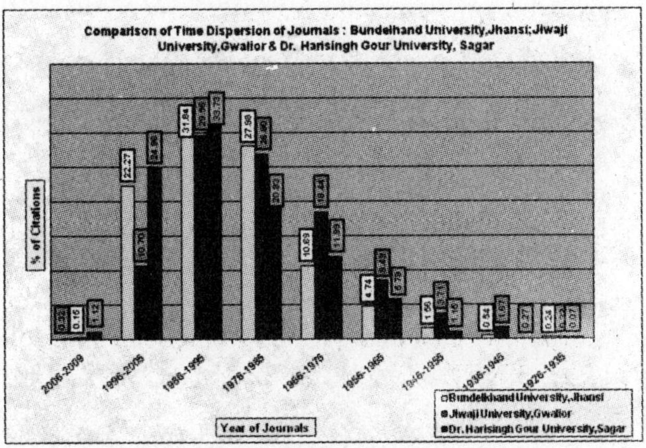

Fig. 6

8
Ranking of Journals

8.1. INTRODUCTION

Journal citations studies have been used as a means to measure the utility of journal in general as well as in specific area of Library & Information Science. Core journals ranking studies are usually made to help in the selection of journals and in assessing the importance of one or more journals in a particular subject field. The criterion for ranking is purely quantitative.

Studies on the information use pattern of research scholars is perhaps one of the effective methods of understanding the information requirements of our research scholars. The phenomenal growth of publications, diversified nature of the user's requirements, inter and multi-disciplinary nature of research, escalating cast of documents juxtaposed with the limited financial resources are forcing librarians to think more and more in terms of quantitative techniques for decision making purposes. The progress of research in science and technology or social science is impeded unless new knowledge generated by research flows freely, quickly and timely among the scientific and technical community.

Major portion of the library budget is spent towards

subscriptions to periodicals. Libraries may never mind to spend enormous for subscriptions of periodicals. But how many readers utilize these periodicals is a question. There is usually a small group of readers who use the periodicals collections. The increase the utility of the periodicals at various levels, the librarian and his staff has made various approaches according to the capacity of the users.

Arranged of the columns in the tables, the first column indicates the running serial number of the entries. The second column provides the name of the ranked journals with their country of origin. The third column shows the lists of actual rank of the journals in order of its importance, which is based on the grand total of citations in the source documents. Naturally, the serial number and the number of the ranking order will change as two or more journals may occupy the same rank and hence the same rank number, but their serial number will differ from one another as each journal has its own separate serial number. The forth column indicates the number of times the journal has been cited in the source documents. Column five provide cumulative number of citations. Percentage of each journals citation is presented in column sixth. Column seven provides the cumulative percentage of citations.

Provides an overall ranking list of journals in the field of Library and Information Science, prepared on the basis of the number of grand total of citations of individual journals counted in the source documents. Ranking list connotes a list of core journals arranged in the descending order of the number of citations. That is the journal with the highest number of citations occupies the highest rank and thus obviously the most important journal in the field of library and information science, and the lease important titles are automatically placed at the bottom of the table.

8.2. RANKING OF JOURNALS: BUNDELKHAND UNIVERSITY, JHANSI

Table-1, Ranking of the journals has been done on the basis of total citations frequency received by each journal. The titles have been arranged in descending order of the number of citations.

There are 281 journals arranged in order of their ranked, from the table it is ascertained that ILA Bulletin (11.96%), Library Science journal occupies the first rank as the most preferred journal having been cited 245 times. Library Herald (11.33%) occupies the second rank getting 232 citations, followed by Journal of Documentation (7.08%) with 145 citations, Annals of Library Science and Documentation (5.66 %) with 116 citations, IASLIC Bulletin (5.27%) with 108, Library Trends (3.81%) with 78 citations, University News (3.42%) with 70 citations, Bulletin of Medical Library Association (3.32%) with 68 citations, Journal of American Society for Information Science and Technology (3.08%) with 63 citations, Library Science with Slant to Documentation (2.88%) with 59 citations, respectively. The first ten journals in the ranking list together account for 57.81% of the total citations. However, table shows that first 50 Journals accounted for nearly 81.35%.

It is interesting to note here that the general science journals namely, Science (0.73%). Nature (0.44%) is occupying 18th and 22th rank in the ranking list respectively. Engineering journals IEEE/ACM Transactions on Networking (0.15%) is occupied the 28th rank and Journal of Theoretical Biology journals has also occupied the 28th (0.15%) same placed 28th rank in the ranked list. Journal of Management is covered (0.10%) with 29th place in the rank list.

Whereas journals like : Botany, Geology, Mathematics and Physics journals have been occupied same placed at Canadian Journal of Botany (0.05%),

Geological Abstract (0.05%), Mathematical Biosciences (0.05%) and Physica A (0.05%) 30th last rank in the ranked list.

Thus, it is noted that a few journals yielded more citations and more journals yielded few citations. A high concentration of citations in a few periodicals is evident. Therefore, core or productive journals can be identified on the basis of the ranked list.

Table 1. Ranking of Journals : Bundelkhand University, Jhansi

S. No.	Name of Journals	Rank No.	No. of Citations	Cumu. No. of Citations	% of Citations	Cumu.% of Citations
1	ILA Bulletin (India)	1	245	245	11.96	11.96
2	Library Herald (India)	2	232	477	11.33	23.29
3	Journal of Documentation (U.K.)	3	145	622	7.08	30.37
4	Annals of Library Science Documentation (India)	4	116	738	5.66	36.04
5	IASLIC Bulletin (India)	5	108	846	5.27	41.31
6	Library Trends (U.S.A.)	6	78	924	3.81	45.12
7	University News (India)	7	70	994	3.42	48.54
8	Bulletin of Medical Library Association (India)	8	68	1062	3.32	51.86
9	Journal of American Society for Information Science and Technology (U.S.A.)	9	63	1125	3.08	54.93
10	Library Science with Slant to Documentation (India)	10	59	1184	2.88	57.81
11	Library Quarterly (U.S.A.)	11	32	1216	1.56	59.38
12	ASLIB Proceeding (U.K.)	12	23	1239	1.12	60.50
13	Journal of Academic Librarianship (U.K.)	12	23	1262	1.12	61.62
14	Journal of Information Science (U.K.)	12	23	1285	1.12	62.74
15	Journal of Library Administration (U.S.A.)	13	22	1307	1.07	63.82
16	DESIDOC Bulletin of Information Technology (India)	14	21	1328	1.03	64.84

S. No.	Name of Journals	Rank No.	No. of Citations	Cumu. No. of Citations	% of Citations	Cumu.% of Citations
17	Indian Journal of Library and Information Society (India)	14	21	1349	1.03	65.87
18	Journal of Librarianship and Information Science (U.K.)	15	20	1369	0.98	66.85
19	Herald of Library Science (India)	16	18	1387	0.88	67.72
20	UNESCO Bulletin for Libraries (U.S.A.)	16	18	1405	0.88	68.60
21	Special Libraries (U.S.A.)	17	16	1421	0.78	69.38
22	CALIBER (India)	18	15	1436	0.73	70.12
23	Science (U.S.A.)	18	15	1451	0.73	70.85
24	College And Research Libraries (U.S.A.)	19	14	1465	0.68	71.53
25	Vidura (India)	19	14	1479	0.68	72.22
26	D-Lib Magazines (U.K.)	20	12	1491	0.59	72.80
27	Journal of Management System (U.S.A.)	21	10	1501	0.49	73.29
28	Journal of World Business (Netherland)	21	10	1511	0.49	73.78
29	Wilson Library Bulletin (U.S.A.)	21	10	1521	0.49	74.27
30	Annual Review of Information Science and Technology (U.S.A.)	22	9	1530	0.44	74.71
31	Journal of Library and Information Science (U.S.A.)	22	9	1539	0.44	75.15
32	Library Journal (U.S.A.)	22	9	1548	0.44	75.59
33	Nature (U.K.)	22	9	1557	0.44	76.03
34	Serial Librarian (U.S.A.)	22	9	1566	0.44	76.46
35	IAALD Quarterly Bulletin (U.K.)	23	8	1574	0.39	76.86
36	Journal of Career Development (U.S.A.)	23	8	1582	0.39	77.25
37	Economic and Political Weekly (India)	24	7	1589	0.34	77.59
38	Information and Control (Netherland)	24	7	1596	0.34	77.93
39	Ariodne (U.K.)	25	6	1602	0.29	78.22
40	DESIDOC Letters (India)	25	6	1608	0.29	78.52
41	Education Library Bulletin (U.K.)	25	6	1614	0.29	78.81

S. No.	Name of Journals	Rank No.	No. of Citations	Cumu. No. of Citations	% of Citations	Cumu.% of Citations
42	Information Resource Management Journals (U.S.A.)	25	6	1620	0.29	79.10
43	International Library Review (U.K.)	25	6	1626	0.29	79.39
44	Journal of American Statistical Association (U.S.A.)	25	6	1632	0.29	79.69
45	Journal of Computer Science and System Biology (U.S.A.)	25	6	1638	0.29	79.98
46	Lucknow Librarian (India)	25	6	1644	0.29	80.27
47	Scientometric (Netherland)	25	6	1650	0.29	80.57
48	The Indian Journal of Technical Education (India)	25	6	1656	0.29	80.86
49	Collection Management (U.S.A.)	26	5	1661	0.24	81.10
50	Drexel Library Quarterly (U.S.A.)	26	5	1666	0.24	81.35
51	Glottometrics (West Germany)	26	5	1671	0.24	81.59
52	Information Processing and Management (U.K.)	26	5	1676	0.24	81.84
53	Information Technology and Libraries (U.S.A.)	26	5	1681	0.24	82.08
54	Library Hi-Tech (U.S.A.)	26	5	1686	0.24	82.32
55	Library Resources and Technical Services (U.S.A.)	26	5	1691	0.24	82.57
56	LIBRI (Germany)	26	5	1696	0.24	82.81
57	LRTS (U.S.A.)	26	5	1701	0.24	83.06
58	NISSAT Newsletter (India)	26	5	1706	0.24	83.30
59	Nucleic Acids Research Management (U.K.)	26	5	1711	0.24	83.54
60	Physical Review E (U.S.A.)	26	5	1716	0.24	83.79
61	Advance in Librarianship (India)	27	4	1720	0.20	83.98
62	ALA Bulletin (U.S.A.)	27	4	1724	0.20	84.18
63	American Society of Information Science (U.S.A.)	27	4	1728	0.20	84.38
64	Canadian Library Journal (Canada)	27	4	1732	0.20	84.57
65	International Journal of Information Studies (Canada)	27	4	1736	0.20	84.77

S. No.	Name of Journals	Rank No.	No. of Citations	Cumu. No. of Citations	% of Citations	Cumu.% of Citations
66	Journal of Library Administration (U.S.A.)	27	4	1752	0.20	85.55
67	Management Information System Quarterly (U.S.A.)	27	4	1740	0.20	84.96
68	News Letter Of NIC (India)	27	4	1744	0.20	85.16
69	SRELS Journal of Information Management (India)	27	4	1748	0.20	85.35
70	Australian Library Journal (Australia)	28	3	1755	0.15	85.69
71	Economic Letters (Netherland)	28	3	1758	0.15	85.84
72	Electronic Library (U.S.A.)	28	3	1761	0.15	85.99
73	European Physical Journal (Europe)	28	3	1764	0.15	86.13
74	IEEE/ACM Transactions On Networking (U.S.A.)	28	3	1767	0.15	86.28
75	Indian Journal of Agricultural Library and Information (India)	28	3	1770	0.15	86.43
76	Indian Management (India)	28	3	1773	0.15	86.57
77	Information Development (U.K.)	28	3	1776	0.15	86.72
78	Information Today and Tomorrow (India)	28	3	1779	0.15	86.87
79	International Journal of Information Management (Netherland)	28	3	1782	0.15	87.01
80	International Library Progress (India)	28	3	1785	0.15	87.16
81	Journal of Theoretical Biology (Netherland)	28	3	1788	0.15	87.30
82	Journal of Applied Psychology (U.S.A.)	28	3	1791	0.15	87.45
83	Journal of Chemical Documentation (U.S.A.)	28	3	1794	0.15	87.60
84	Journal of Higher Education (U.S.A.)	28	3	1797	0.15	87.74
85	Journal of System Engineering (U.S.A.)	28	3	1800	0.15	87.89
86	KELPRO Bulletin (India)	28	3	1803	0.15	88.04
87	Library Focus Group (U.S.A.)	28	3	1806	0.15	88.18
88	Library Progress (International) (India)	28	3	1809	0.15	88.33

S. No.	Name of Journals	Rank No.	No. of Citations	Cumu. No. of Citations	% of Citations	Cumu.% of Citations
89	Program (U.K.)	28	3	1812	0.15	88.48
90	AALD Bulletin (U.K.)	29	2	1814	0.10	88.57
91	Academy of Management Journal (U.S.A.)	29	2	1816	0.10	88.67
92	ALIS bulletin (Canada)	29	2	1818	0.10	88.77
93	American Journal of Psychology (U.S.A.)	29	2	1820	0.10	88.87
94	Archives of Psychology (U.S.A.)	29	2	1822	0.10	88.96
95	Australian College Libraries (Australia)	30	2	1900	0.10	92.77
96	Computer and Information System (U.S.A.)	29	2	1824	0.10	89.06
97	Computer in Libraries (U.S.A.)	29	2	1826	0.10	89.16
98	DESIDOC Annual Report (India)	29	2	1828	0.10	89.26
99	Employment News (India)	29	2	1830	0.10	89.36
100	Fractals(U.S.A.)	29	2	1832	0.10	89.45
101	Indian Journal of Adult Education (India)	29	2	1834	0.10	89.55
102	Information Science (Netherland)	29	2	1836	0.10	89.65
103	Information Storage and Retrieval (U.S.A.)	29	2	1838	0.10	89.75
104	Inter Lending and Document Supply (U.K.)	29	2	1896	0.10	92.58
105	Inter-National Journal of Information and Library Research (U.K.)	29	2	1840	0.10	89.84
106	International Journal of Information Resource Management (U.S.A.)	29	2	1842	0.10	89.94
107	International Journal of Manpower Journal (U.K.)	29	2	1868	0.10	91.21
108	International Library Movement (Australia)	29	2	1844	0.10	90.04
109	International Social Education Journal (U.S.A.)	29	2	1846	0.10	90.14
110	Journal of Adult Education (U.S.A.)	29	2	1848	0.10	90.23
111	Journal of American Institute for Conversation (U.S.A.)	29	2	1850	0.10	90.33

S. No.	Name of Journals	Rank No.	No. of Citations	Cumu. No. of Citations	% of Citations	Cumu.% of Citations
112	Journal of Applied Behavioral Science (U.S.A.)	29	2	1852	0.10	90.43
113	Journal of Infection (Netherland)	29	2	1854	0.10	90.53
114	Journal of Information Technology (U.K.)	29	2	1856	0.10	90.63
115	Journal of Management (U.S.A.)	29	2	1858	0.10	90.72
116	Librarianship (Sweden)	29	2	1860	0.10	90.82
117	Library Administration and Management (U.S.A.)	29	2	1862	0.10	90.92
118	Library Management (U.K.)	29	2	1864	0.10	91.02
119	Library Review (U.K.)	29	2	1898	0.10	92.68
120	Library Science (India)	29	2	1866	0.10	91.11
121	Library World (Japan)	29	2	1874	0.10	91.50
122	Microform Review (U.S.A.)	29	2	1872	0.10	91.41
123	New Fortiers in Educations (India)	29	2	1876	0.10	91.60
124	OEMGHA (U.S.A.)	29	2	1878	0.10	91.70
125	Operating Systems Review (U.S.A.)	29	2	1880	0.10	91.80
126	Physical Review Letters (U.S.A.)	29	2	1882	0.10	91.89
127	Public Library Quarterly (U.S.A.)	29	2	1884	0.10	91.99
128	Reference Librarian (U.S.A.)	29	2	1886	0.10	92.09
129	School Library Media Quarterly (U.S.A.)	29	2	1888	0.10	92.19
130	Science And Technology Libraries (U.S.A.)	29	2	1890	0.10	92.29
131	Technology Review (U.S.A.)	29	2	1892	0.10	92.38
132	The Electronic Library (U.K.)	29	2	1894	0.10	92.48
133	The Use of Microcomputers for Information Management (U.S.A.)	29	2	1870	0.10	91.31
134	Advance in Complex Systems (U.S.A.)	30	1	1902	0.05	92.87
135	African Journal of Library (Africa)	30	1	1903	0.05	92.92
136	AGLIS journal (India)	30	1	1904	0.05	92.97
137	American Association of Law Libraries (U.S.A.)	30	1	1905	0.05	93.02

S. No.	Name of Journals	Rank No.	No. of Citations	Cumu. No. of Citations	% of Citations	Cumu.% of Citations
138	American Documentation (U.S.A.)	30	1	1906	0.05	93.07
139	American Journal of Economics and Sociology (U.S.A.)	30	1	1907	0.05	93.12
140	American Sociological Review (U.S.A.)	30	1	1908	0.05	93.16
141	Annals of American Academy of Political and Social Sciences (U.S.A.)	30	1	1909	0.05	93.21
142	ASLIB Managing Information (U.K.)	30	1	1910	0.05	93.26
143	Australian Academic and Research Libraries (Australia)	30	1	1911	0.05	93.31
144	Behavioral Science (U.S.A.)	30	1	1912	0.05	93.36
145	Biometrics (U.S.A.)	30	1	1913	0.05	93.41
146	Biometrika (U.K.)	30	1	1914	0.05	93.46
147	Biosystems (Netherland)	30	1	1915	0.05	93.51
148	Book Notes (New Zealand)	30	1	1916	0.05	93.55
149	Brain Science (U.S.A.)	30	1	1917	0.05	93.60
150	British Journal of Academic Librarianship (U.K.)	30	1	1918	0.05	93.65
151	British Lending Library Review (U.K.)	30	1	1919	0.05	93.70
152	Bulletin of the Library Association of China (China)	30	1	1920	0.05	93.75
153	Canada Bulletin (Canada)	30	1	1921	0.05	93.80
154	Canadian Journal of Botany (Canada)	30	1	1922	0.05	93.85
155	Cape Librarian (South Africa)	30	1	1923	0.05	93.90
156	Chemical Engineering Progress (U.S.A.)	30	1	1924	0.05	93.95
157	Chemistry in Britain (U.K.)	30	1	1925	0.05	93.99
158	Ciencia Da Informacao (Brazil)	30	1	1926	0.05	94.04
159	Communication in Statistical Theory & Methods (U.S.A.)	30	1	1927	0.05	94.09
160	Computer in Human Services (Netherland)	30	1	1929	0.05	94.19

S. No.	Name of Journals	Rank No.	No. of Citations	Cumu. No. of Citations	% of Citations	Cumu.% of Citations
161	Creole Language Library (U.S.A.)	30	1	1930	0.05	94.24
162	Current Contents (U.S.A.)	30	1	1931	0.05	94.29
163	Current Science (U.S.A.)	30	1	1932	0.05	94.34
164	Data (Denmark(DK))	30	1	1933	0.05	94.38
165	DELNET Newsletter (India)	30	1	1934	0.05	94.43
166	DESIDOC News (India)	30	1	1935	0.05	94.48
167	Ecology Modeling (Netherland)	30	1	1936	0.05	94.53
168	Economic Journal (Netherland)	30	1	1937	0.05	94.58
169	Emergency Librarian (U.S.A.)	30	1	1938	0.05	94.63
170	European Journal of Marketing (Europe)	30	1	1939	0.05	94.68
171	Exploratorium Quarterly (U.S.A.)	30	1	1940	0.05	94.73
172	First Monday (France)	30	1	1941	0.05	94.78
173	Geological Abstract (Netherland)	30	1	1942	0.05	94.82
174	IASLIC Serial Publication (India)	30	1	1943	0.05	94.87
175	IATUL (West Germany)	30	1	1944	0.05	94.92
176	IEEE Infocom (U.S.A.)	30	1	1945	0.05	94.97
177	IFLA Journal (Netherlands)	30	1	1946	0.05	95.02
178	ILA Newsletter (India)	30	1	1947	0.05	95.07
179	India Library Movement (India)	30	1	1948	0.05	95.12
180	Indian Journal of Library Science (India)	30	1	1949	0.05	95.17
181	Indian Journal of Social Work (India)	30	1	1950	0.05	95.21
182	Indian Librarian(India)	30	1	1951	0.05	95.26
183	Industrial and Engineering Chemistry (U.S.A.)	30	1	1952	0.05	95.31
184	INFLIBNET Newsletter (India)	30	1	1953	0.05	95.36
185	Information and Library Manager (U.K.)	30	1	1954	0.05	95.41
186	Information Research (U.K.)	30	1	1955	0.05	95.46
187	Information Services and Use (Netherland)	30	1	1956	0.05	95.51

S. No.	Name of Journals	Rank No.	No. of Citations	Cumu. No. of Citations	% of Citations	Cumu.% of Citations
188	INSPEL(West Germany)	30	1	1957	0.05	95.56
189	International Journal of Sociology (U.S.A.)	30	1	1958	0.05	95.61
190	International Forum Information Documentation (Netherland)	30	1	1959	0.05	95.65
191	International Information and Library Review (Netherland)	30	1	1960	0.05	95.70
192	International Information Communication and Education (India)	30	1	1961	0.05	95.75
193	International Journal of Information Technology (Jordan)	30	1	1962	0.05	95.80
194	International Journal of Librarian, Archivists and Information Specialists (Australia)	30	1	1963	0.05	95.85
195	International Journal of Man-Machine Studies (Netherland)	30	1	1964	0.05	95.90
196	International Journal of Quality & Reliability Management (U.K.)	30	1	1965	0.05	95.95
197	International Library Management (U.K.)	30	1	1967	0.05	96.04
198	International Social Science Journal (U.S.A.)	30	1	1968	0.05	96.09
199	Internet Librarian International(U.K.)	30	1	1966	0.05	96.00
200	Internet Reference Services Quarterly (U.S.A.)	30	1	1969	0.05	96.14
201	Jamaica Library Association Bulletin (Jamaica)	30	1	1970	0.05	96.19
202	Jamaica Association of Bulletin (Jamaica)	30	1	1971	0.05	96.24
203	Joint Academic Network (U.K.)	30	1	1972	0.05	96.29
204	Joint Acquisition List of Africana (Africa)	30	1	1973	0.05	96.34
205	Journal of Physical Society of Japan (Japan)	30	1	1974	0.05	96.39

S. No.	Name of Journals	Rank No.	No. of Citations	Cumu. No. of Citations	% of Citations	Cumu.% of Citations
206	Journal of Political Economy (U.S.A.)	30	1	1975	0.05	96.44
207	Journal of Complexity (Netherland)	30	1	1901	0.05	92.82
208	Journal of Geophysical Research (U.S.A.)	30	1	1976	0.05	96.48
209	Journal of Library Automation (U.S.A.)	30	1	1977	0.05	96.53
210	Journal of Quantitative Linguistics (U.S.A.)	30	1	1978	0.05	96.58
211	Journal of Agricultural Science (Canada)	30	1	1979	0.05	96.63
212	Journal of Chemical and Computer Science (U.S.A.)	30	1	1980	0.05	96.68
213	Journal of Chemical Technology and Biotechnology (U.S.A.)	30	1	1981	0.05	96.73
214	Journal of Computer Chemistry (Japan)	30	1	1928	0.05	94.14
215	Journal of Digital Information (U.S.A.)	30	1	1982	0.05	96.78
216	Journal of Economic Studies (U.K.)	30	1	2009	0.05	98.10
217	Journal of Education Administration (U.K.)	30	1	1983	0.05	96.83
218	Journal of Education for Librarianship (U.S.A.)	30	1	1984	0.05	96.88
219	Journal of Education for Library and Information Science (U.S.A.)	30	1	1985	0.05	96.92
220	Journal of Education Technology System (U.S.A.)	30	1	1986	0.05	96.97
221	Journal of Educational Media and Library Science (U.S.A.)	30	1	1987	0.05	97.02
222	Journal of Electronic Materials (U.S.A.)	30	1	1988	0.05	97.07
223	Journal of Immunology (U.S.A.)	30	1	1989	0.05	97.12
224	Journal of Industrial Relation (U.K.)	30	1	1990	0.05	97.17
225	Journal of Information and Library Science (China)	30	1	1991	0.05	97.22

S. No.	Name of Journals	Rank No.	No. of Citations	Cumu. No. of Citations	% of Citations	Cumu.% of Citations
226	Journal of Information System Management (U.S.A.)	30	1	1992	0.05	97.27
227	Journal of Information Technology for Teacher Education (U.S.A.)	30	1	1993	0.05	97.31
228	Journal of Internet Cataloguing (U.K.)	30	1	1994	0.05	97.36
229	Journal of Korean Physical Society (Korea)	30	1	1995	0.05	97.41
230	Journal of Library History Philosophy and Compative Librarianship (U.S.A.)	30	1	1996	0.05	97.46
231	Journal of Libreratarian Studies (U.S.A.)	30	1	1997	0.05	97.51
232	Journal of Psycholinguistic Research (U.S.A.)	30	1	1998	0.05	97.56
233	Journal of Quantitative Linguistics (U.S.A.)	30	1	1999	0.05	97.61
234	Journal of Regional Science (U.S.A.)	30	1	2000	0.05	97.66
235	Journal of Retailing (Netherland)	30	1	2001	0.05	97.71
236	Journal of Rural Development (India)	30	1	2002	0.05	97.75
237	Knjiznica (Slovenia)	30	1	2003	0.05	97.80
238	Kurukshetra (India)	30	1	2004	0.05	97.85
239	Legal Reference Services Quarterly (U.S.A.)	30	1	2005	0.05	97.90
240	Librarian's Handbook (U.S.A.)	30	1	2006	0.05	97.95
241	Librarian's World (U.K.)	30	1	2007	0.05	98.00
242	Libraries & Culture (U.S.A.)	30	1	2008	0.05	98.05
243	Library and Information Research (U.K.)	30	1	2013	0.05	98.29
244	Library and Information Studies (U.K.)	30	1	2011	0.05	98.19
245	Library Association Record (U.K.)	30	1	2010	0.05	98.14
246	Library Point (U.S.A.)	30	1	2012	0.05	98.24
247	Library Science with Slant to Documentation and Information Studies (U.S.A.)	30	1	2014	0.05	98.34

S. No.	Name of Journals	Rank No.	No. of Citations	Cumu. No. of Citations	% of Citations	Cumu.% of Citations
248	Library Technology Report (U.S.A.)	30	1	2015	0.05	98.39
249	Libraries world (U.K.)	30	1	2016	0.05	98.44
250	Management Science (U.S.A.)	30	1	2017	0.05	98.49
251	Managing Information (U.K.)	30	1	2018	0.05	98.54
252	Mathematical Biosciences (Netherland)	30	1	2019	0.05	98.58
253	NACLIN Delnet (India)	30	1	2020	0.05	98.63
254	Nauchno-Tekhnicheskaya – Informatsiya (Russia)	30	1	2022	0.05	98.73
255	New Library World (U.K.)	30	1	2021	0.05	98.68
256	New Scientist (U.K.)	30	1	2023	0.05	98.78
257	New Zealand Libraries (New Zealand)	30	1	2024	0.05	98.83
258	OECD Observer (U.S.A.)	30	1	2025	0.05	98.88
259	Operation Research (Netherland)	30	1	2026	0.05	98.93
260	Orissa Review (India)	30	1	2027	0.05	98.97
261	Pakistan Library Bulletin (Pakistan)	30	1	2028	0.05	99.02
262	Physica A (Netherland)	30	1	2029	0.05	99.07
263	Physics Today (U.S.A.)	30	1	2030	0.05	99.12
264	Psychological Bulletin (U.S.A.)	30	1	2031	0.05	99.17
265	Public Library Catalog (U.S.A.)	30	1	2032	0.05	99.22
266	Publishers Weekly (U.S.A.)	30	1	2033	0.05	99.27
267	Quarterly Journal of Economics (U.S.A.)	30	1	2034	0.05	99.32
268	Quarterly Journal of Electronic Commerce (U.S.A.)	30	1	2035	0.05	99.37
269	Quest (U.S.A.)	30	1	2036	0.05	99.41
270	Quilt (U.S.A.)	30	1	2037	0.05	99.46
271	Research Libraries (U.S.A.)	30	1	2038	0.05	99.51
272	Serial Review (Netherland)	30	1	2039	0.05	99.56
273	Social Psychology Quarterly (U.S.A.)	30	1	2041	0.05	99.66
274	Social Science Computer Review (U.S.A.)	30	1	2040	0.05	99.61
275	The Annual of Urdu Studies (Pakistan)	30	1	2042	0.05	99.71

S. No.	Name of Journals	Rank No.	No. of Citations	Cumu. No. of Citations	% of Citations	Cumu.% of Citations
276	The Hindu (India)	30	1	2043	0.05	99.76
277	The Leadership Quarterly (Netherland)	30	1	2046	0.05	99.90
278	The Library Quarterly (U.S.A.)	30	1	2044	0.05	99.80
279	The Library World (Japan)	30	1	2045	0.05	99.85
280	Tips and Techniques (U.S.A.)	30	1	2047	0.05	99.95
281	Zeitschriftfur Agrain Formatik (East Germany)	30	1	2048	0.05	100.00
	Total		**2048**	**2048**	**100.00**	**100.00**

8.3. RANKING OF JOURNALS: JIWAJI UNIVERSITY, GWALIOR

Table-2, ranking of the journals in Jiwaji University, Gwalior has been done on the basis of total citation frequency received by each journal. The titles have been arranged in decreasing order of the number of citation. It is found that total numbers of 543 journals titles are published from National and International. It is found that out of 543 journals titles 105 are published from India and 256 from U.S.A.

In the study of 543 journals have been noted that ASLIB Proceeding (6.88%), a Library Science journal occupies the first rank as the most preferred journal having been cited 321 times. Annals of Library science Documentation (5.29%) occupies the second rank getting 247 citations, followed by IASLIC Bulletin (5.19%) with 242 citations, College and Research Libraries (4.33%) with 202 citations, Herald of Library Science (4.05%) with 189 citations, Library Herald (3.62%) with 169 citations, ILA Bulletin (3.60%) with 168 citations, Journal of Documentation (2.04%) with 95 citations, Library Journal (1.95%) with 91 citations, Indian Libraries (1.44%) with 67 citations respectively. The first ten journals in the ranking list together account for 38.39 % of the total citations. However, table shows that first 50 Journals accounted for nearly 63.66 %.

A high concentration of citations in a few periodicals is evident. Therefore, core or productive journals can be identified on the basis of the ranked list.

It is interesting to note here that apart from Library and Information Science journals like: Management, Psychology, Medical, Law, Electronic journals namely, Business Information Review (0.81%), is occupying 17th rank followed by Journal of Applied Psychology (0.69%) is occupying 22th rank in the ranking list respectively. Radio and Electronic Engineer (0.11%) with 45th Communication of the ACM (0.09%) with 46th, IEEE Computer (0.06%) with 47th in the ranked list.

Table 2. Ranking of Journals: Jiwaji University, Gwalior

S. No.	Name of Journals	Rank No.	No. of Citations	Cumu. No. of Citations	% of Citations	Cumu.% of Citations
1	ASLIB Proceeding (U.K.)	1	321	321	6.88	6.88
2	Annals of Library Science Documentation (India)	2	247	568	5.29	12.18
3	IASLIC Bulletin (India)	3	242	810	5.19	17.36
4	College and Research Libraries (U.S.A.)	4	202	1012	4.33	21.69
5	Herald of Library Science (India)	5	189	1201	4.05	25.74
6	Library Herald (India)	6	169	1370	3.62	29.37
7	ILA Bulletin (India)	7	168	1538	3.60	32.97
8	Journal of Documentation (U.K.)	8	95	1633	2.04	35.01
9	Library Journal (U.S.A.)	9	91	1724	1.95	36.96
10	Indian Libraries(India)	10	67	1791	1.44	38.39
11	Journal of American Society for Information Science (U.S.A.)	11	64	1855	1.37	39.76
12	DESIDOC Bulletin of Information Technology (India)	12	61	1916	1.31	41.07
13	Special Library (U.S.A.)	13	59	1975	1.26	42.34

S. No.	Name of Journals	Rank No.	No. of Citations	Cumu. No. of Citations	% of Citations	Cumu.% of Citations
14	Library Quarterly (U.S.A.)	14	50	2025	1.07	43.41
15	Library Science with slant to Documentation (India)	14	50	2075	1.07	44.48
16	Library Trends (U.S.A.)	14	50	2125	1.07	45.55
17	International Library Review (U.K.)	15	42	2167	0.90	46.45
18	University News (India)	16	39	2206	0.84	47.29
19	Business Information Review (U.S.A.)	17	38	2244	0.81	48.10
20	Journal of Higher Education (U.S.A.)	18	37	2281	0.79	48.90
21	International Journal of Library Science (U.S.A.)	19	36	2317	0.77	49.67
22	Journal of Academic Librarianship (Netherlands)	20	34	2351	0.73	50.40
23	Journal of Library and Information Science (India)	21	33	2384	0.71	51.10
24	Journal of Applied Psychology (U.S.A.)	22	32	2416	0.69	51.79
25	Journal of Library Administration (U.S.A.)	23	31	2447	0.66	52.45
26	Library Resources & Technical Services (U.S.A.)	23	31	2478	0.66	53.12
27	Organizational Behavior and Human Performance (Netherlands)	24	27	2505	0.58	53.70
28	Bulletin of Medical Library Association (India)	25	26	2531	0.56	54.26
29	CLIS Observer (India)	25	26	2557	0.56	54.81
30	Annals Review of Information Science and Technology (U.S.A.)	26	25	2582	0.54	55.35
31	Administrative Science Quarterly (U.S.A.)	27	23	2605	0.49	55.84
32	Indian Journal of Psychology (India)	28	22	2627	0.47	56.31
33	NISSAT, Newsletter (India)	28	22	2649	0.47	56.78
34	Harvard Science Review (U.S.A.)	29	21	2670	0.45	57.23
35	Journal of Information science (U.K.)	29	21	2691	0.45	57.68
36	Library Progress (International) (India)	29	21	2712	0.45	58.14

S. No.	Name of Journals	Rank No.	No. of Citations	Cumu. No. of Citations	% of Citations	Cumu.% of Citations
37	Nordinfo Nytt (West Germany)	29	21	2733	0.45	58.59
38	Serial Librarian (U.S.A.)	29	21	2754	0.45	59.04
39	Academy of Management Journal (U.S.A.)	30	20	2774	0.43	59.46
40	D- Lib Magazine (U.K.)	30	20	2794	0.43	59.89
41	LIBRI (West Germany)	30	20	2814	0.43	60.32
42	The Serials Librarian (U.S.A.)	31	19	2833	0.41	60.73
43	Wilson Library Bulletin (U.S.A.)	31	19	2852	0.41	61.14
44	Delhi University Magazine (India)	32	18	2870	0.39	61.52
45	Journal of Librarianship (U.K.)	32	18	2888	0.39	61.91
46	Library Point (U.S.A.)	33	17	2905	0.36	62.27
47	Scientometrics (Netherlands)	33	17	2922	0.36	62.64
48	Indian Journal of Applied Psychology (India)	34	16	2938	0.34	62.98
49	Indian Journal of Industrial Relation (India)	34	16	2954	0.34	63.32
50	Information Technology and Libraries (U.K.)	34	16	2970	0.34	63.67
51	South African Journal of Library & Information Science (South African)	34	16	2986	0.34	64.01
52	IFLA Bulletin (Netherlands)	35	15	3001	0.32	64.33
53	Journal of Contemporary Business (U.S.A.)	35	15	3016	0.32	64.65
54	Journal of the Association for Computing Machinery (U.S.A.)	35	15	3031	0.32	64.97
55	Cataloguing Australia (Australia)	36	14	3045	0.30	65.27
56	Human Relations (U.S.A.)	36	14	3059	0.30	65.57
57	Lucknow librarian (India)	36	14	3073	0.30	65.87
58	Online (U.S.A.)	36	14	3087	0.30	66.17
59	Serial Review (Netherlands)	36	14	3101	0.30	66.47
60	Bulletin of American Society for Information Science (U.S.A.)	37	13	3114	0.28	66.75
61	Library Association Record (U.K.)	37	13	3127	0.28	67.03

S. No.	Name of Journals	Rank No.	No. of Citations	Cumu. No. of Citations	% of Citations	Cumu.% of Citations
62	Resource Sharing and Information Networks (U.S.A.)	37	13	3140	0.28	67.31
63	Science (U.S.A.)	37	13	3153	0.28	67.59
64	Personnel Psychology (U.S.A.)	38	12	3165	0.26	67.85
65	Rojgar Nirman (India)	38	12	3177	0.26	68.10
66	Yojana (India)	38	12	3189	0.26	68.36
67	ALIS bulletin (Canada)	39	11	3200	0.24	68.60
68	American Documentation (U.S.A.)	39	11	3211	0.24	68.83
69	American Libraries (U.S.A.)	39	11	3222	0.24	69.07
70	American Sociological Review (U.S.A.)	39	11	3233	0.24	69.30
71	CALIBER (India)	39	11	3244	0.24	69.54
72	Drexel Library Quarterly (U.S.A.)	39	11	3255	0.24	69.77
73	Indian Journal of Adult Education (India)	39	11	3266	0.24	70.01
74	Indian journal of Social Work (India)	39	11	3277	0.24	70.25
75	International Library Movement (India)	39	11	3288	0.24	70.48
76	Journal of Indian History (India)	39	11	3299	0.24	70.72
77	Knjiznica (Slovenia)	39	11	3310	0.24	70.95
78	Psychological Bulletin (U.S.A.)	39	11	3321	0.24	71.19
79	Indian Management (India)	40	10	3331	0.21	71.40
80	Information Development (U.K.)	40	10	3341	0.21	71.62
81	Journal of Librarianship and Information Science (U.K.)	40	10	3351	0.21	71.83
82	Law Library Journal (U.S.A.)	40	10	3361	0.21	72.05
83	LIBRA (India)	40	10	3371	0.21	72.26
84	Library Acquistion : Practice & Theory (U.S.A.)	40	10	3381	0.21	72.48
85	Library and information Science Research (U.K.)	40	10	3391	0.21	72.69
86	Library Management (U.K.)	40	10	3401	0.21	72.90
87	Online Review (U.K.)	40	10	3411	0.21	73.12

S. No.	Name of Journals	Rank No.	No. of Citations	Cumu. No. of Citations	% of Citations	Cumu.% of Citations
88	Research Libraries (U.S.A.)	40	10	3421	0.21	73.33
89	Serial (U.K.)	40	10	3431	0.21	73.55
90	Supreme Court Cases (India)	40	10	3441	0.21	73.76
91	DELNET Newsletter (India)	41	9	3450	0.19	73.95
92	Economic and Political Weekly (India)	41	9	3459	0.19	74.15
93	Human Factors: The Journal of the Human Factors and Ergonomics Society (U.S.A.)	41	9	3468	0.19	74.34
94	Journal of Librarian's and Information Science (U.S.A.)	41	9	3477	0.19	74.53
95	Journal of the Medical Library Association (U.S.A.)	41	9	3486	0.19	74.73
96	Library Review (U.K.)	41	9	3495	0.19	74.92
97	Library and Information Science Research Electronic Journal (Australia)	41	9	3504	0.19	75.11
98	SIGOIS Bulletin (U.S.A.)	41	9	3513	0.19	75.31
99	Timeless Fellow (India)	41	9	3522	0.19	75.50
100	Against the Grain (U.S.A.)	42	8	3530	0.17	75.67
101	ALA Bulletin (U.S.A.)	42	8	3538	0.17	75.84
102	Annals of Library & Information Studies (India)	42	8	3546	0.17	76.01
103	ASLIB Business Information Times (U.K.)	42	8	3554	0.17	76.18
104	Australian Library Journal (Australia)	42	8	3562	0.17	76.36
105	Cataloguing and Index (U.K.)	42	8	3570	0.17	76.53
106	Cultural Forum (U.K.)	42	8	3578	0.17	76.70
107	Indian Journal of Politics Studies (India)	42	8	3586	0.17	76.87
108	Information and Library Management (U.K.)	42	8	3594	0.17	77.04
109	Information Storage and Retrieval (U.S.A.)	42	8	3602	0.17	77.21
110	Journal of Social Psychology (U.S.A.)	42	8	3610	0.17	77.38
111	Management Decision (U.K.)	42	8	3618	0.17	77.56

S. No.	Name of Journals	Rank No.	No. of Citations	Cumu. No. of Citations	% of Citations	Cumu.% of Citations
112	Public Library Journal (U.S.A.)	42	8	3626	0.17	77.73
113	Quarterly Bulletin of the International Association of Agricultural Librarians and Document lists (Netherlands)	42	8	3634	0.17	77.90
114	UNESCO Bulletin for Libraries (U.S.A.)	42	8	3642	0.17	78.07
115	Academic Management Review (U.S.A.)	43	7	3649	0.15	78.22
116	American Psychologist (U.S.A.)	43	7	3656	0.15	78.37
117	Canadian Journal of Information Science (Canada)	43	7	3663	0.15	78.52
118	Electronic Library (U.K.)	43	7	3670	0.15	78.67
119	IBM journal of Research and Development (U.S.A.)	43	7	3677	0.15	78.82
120	IFLA Journal (Netherlands)	43	7	3684	0.15	78.97
121	Information Processing and Management (U.K.)	43	7	3691	0.15	79.12
122	International Forum on Information and Documentation (Australia)	43	7	3698	0.15	79.27
123	International Information and Library review (Netherlands)	43	7	3705	0.15	79.42
124	Journal of Digital Information (U.S.A.)	43	7	3712	0.15	79.57
125	Journal of Washington Academy of Sciences (U.S.A.)	43	7	3719	0.15	79.72
125	Journal of Washington Academy of Sciences (U.S.A.)	43	7	3719	0.15	79.72
126	Maritime Library Association Bulletin –MLA (Canada)	43	7	3726	0.15	79.87
127	Revista Interamericana de Bibliotecología (Colombia)	43	7	3733	0.15	80.02
128	Rural Society Journal (Australia)	43	7	3740	0.15	80.17
129	Telecommunication Policy (Netherlands)	43	7	3747	0.15	80.32

S. No.	Name of Journals	Rank No.	No. of Citations	Cumu. No. of Citations	% of Citations	Cumu.% of Citations
130	Advance in Librarianship (India)	44	6	3753	0.13	80.45
131	Indian Journal of Information Library and Society (India)	44	6	3759	0.13	80.58
132	Journal of Industrial Economics (U.S.A.)	44	6	3765	0.13	80.71
133	Journal of Vocational Behavior (Netherlands)	44	6	3771	0.13	80.84
134	Library and Information Research (U.K.)	44	6	3777	0.13	80.96
135	P C Quest (India)	44	6	3783	0.13	81.09
136	Pratiyogita Darpan (India)	44	6	3789	0.13	81.22
137	Research Quarterly (U.S.A.)	44	6	3795	0.13	81.35
138	Social Studies of Science (U.S.A.)	44	6	3801	0.13	81.48
139	Vine (U.K.)	44	6	3807	0.13	81.61
140	Annals Review of Psychology (U.S.A.)	45	5	3812	0.11	81.71
141	Asian Journal of University Education(Malaysia)	45	5	3817	0.11	81.82
142	Collection Management (U.S.A.)	45	5	3822	0.11	81.93
143	Education and Computing (Netherlands)	45	5	3827	0.11	82.04
144	Education Libraries (U.S.A.)	45	5	3832	0.11	82.14
145	IAALD Quarterly Bulletin (U.K.)	45	5	3837	0.11	82.25
146	Information Services and Use (Netherlands)	45	5	3842	0.11	82.36
147	Information Technology for Development (U.K.)	45	5	3847	0.11	82.47
148	Journal of Career Development (U.S.A.)	45	5	3852	0.11	82.57
149	Journal of Chemical Documentation (U.S.A.)	45	5	3857	0.11	82.68
150	Journal of Health Physical Education and Recreation (U.S.A.)	45	5	3862	0.11	82.79
151	Journal of Hong Kong Library Association (China)	45	5	3867	0.11	82.89
152	Journal of Internet Services and Applications (U.S.A.)	45	5	3872	0.11	83.00

S. No.	Name of Journals	Rank No.	No. of Citations	Cumu. No. of Citations	% of Citations	Cumu.% of Citations
153	Korea Information Science Society for Information Science (Korea)	45	5	3877	0.11	83.11
154	Learned Publishing (U.K.)	45	5	3882	0.11	83.22
155	Library Administration & Management (U.S.A.)	45	5	3887	0.11	83.32
156	Library Bulletin (U.S.A.)	45	5	3892	0.11	83.43
157	Lok Udyog (India)	45	5	3897	0.11	83.54
158	Louisiana Library Association (U.S.A.)	45	5	3902	0.11	83.64
159	Management Review (U.S.A.)	45	5	3907	0.11	83.75
160	Modern Librarian (Lahore) (Pakistan)	45	5	3912	0.11	83.86
161	Nachrichten Fuer Documentation (Russia)	45	5	3917	0.11	83.97
162	Nauchno-Tekh-Information Services (Russia)	45	5	3922	0.11	84.07
163	Outlook on Research Libraries (Australia)	45	5	3927	0.11	84.18
164	Personnel (U.S.A.)	45	5	3932	0.11	84.29
165	Program (U.K.)	45	5	3937	0.11	84.39
166	Psychological Review (U.S.A.)	45	5	3942	0.11	84.50
167	Pustakalaya Sandesh (India)	45	5	3947	0.11	84.61
168	Quest (U.S.A.)	45	5	3952	0.11	84.72
169	Radio and Electronic Engineer (U.S.A.)	45	5	3957	0.11	84.82
170	Reference Librarian (U.S.A.)	45	5	3962	0.11	84.93
171	Rivernia Library Review (Australia)	45	5	3967	0.11	85.04
172	The Electronic Library (U.K.)	45	5	3972	0.11	85.14
173	Today & Tomorrow (Canada)	45	5	3977	0.11	85.25
174	University Today (India)	45	5	3982	0.11	85.36
175	Acquition Librarian (U.S.A.)	46	4	3986	0.09	85.44
176	American Journal of Sociology (U.S.A.)	46	4	3990	0.09	85.53
177	Assistant Librarian (U.K.)	46	4	3994	0.09	85.62
178	Australian College Libraries (Australia)	46	4	3998	0.09	85.70
179	Bulletin Abgilla (India)	46	4	4002	0.09	85.79
180	Communication of the ACM (U.S.A.)	46	4	4006	0.09	85.87

S. No.	Name of Journals	Rank No.	No. of Citations	Cumu. No. of Citations	% of Citations	Cumu.% of Citations
181	Community & Junior College Libraries (U.S.A.)	46	4	4010	0.09	85.96
182	Current Contents (U.S.A.)	46	4	4014	0.09	86.05
183	Employment News (India)	46	4	4018	0.09	86.13
184	European Journal of Marketing (Europe)	46	4	4022	0.09	86.22
185	Fortune Magazine(U.S.A.)	46	4	4026	0.09	86.30
186	INFLIBNET News Letter (India)	46	4	4030	0.09	86.39
187	International Journal of Information Resource Management (U.S.A.)	46	4	4034	0.09	86.47
188	International Journal of Information Security (U.S.A.)	46	4	4038	0.09	86.56
189	International Librarian (U.S.A.)	46	4	4042	0.09	86.65
190	JOPERD - Journal of Physical Education, Recreation and Dance (U.S.A.)	46	4	4046	0.09	86.73
191	Journal of Comparative Psychology (U.S.A.)	46	4	4050	0.09	86.82
192	Journal of Management Development (U.K.)	46	4	4054	0.09	86.90
193	Legal reference Services Quarterly (U.S.A.)	46	4	4058	0.09	86.99
194	Librarian Journal (U.S.A.)	46	4	4062	0.09	87.07
195	Library Focus Group (U.S.A.)	46	4	4066	0.09	87.16
196	Library Movement and Library Development in India (India)	46	4	4070	0.09	87.25
197	Library Technology Report (U.S.A.)	46	4	4074	0.09	87.33
198	Managing Information (U.K.)	46	4	4078	0.09	87.42
199	Public Library Quarterly (U.S.A.)	46	4	4082	0.09	87.50
200	Public Personnel Management (U.S.A.)	46	4	4086	0.09	87.59
201	Publishers Weekly (U.S.A.)	46	4	4090	0.09	87.67
202	Regional Development Dialog (Japan)	46	4	4094	0.09	87.76
203	Scandianavian Public Library Quarterly (Europe)	46	4	4098	0.09	87.85

S. No.	Name of Journals	Rank No.	No. of Citations	Cumu. No. of Citations	% of Citations	Cumu.% of Citations
204	Science & Technology Libraries (U.S.A.)	46	4	4102	0.09	87.93
205	Scientific and Technical Libraries (U.S.A.)	46	4	4106	0.09	88.02
206	SCONUL News (Society of College, National and University Libraries) (U.K.)	46	4	4110	0.09	88.10
207	SRELS- Journal of Information Management (India)	46	4	4114	0.09	88.19
208	Telematics and Informatics (Netherlands)	46	4	4118	0.09	88.27
209	Trans Inst Electron Information Communication Engineering D-Ii (Japan)	46	4	4122	0.09	88.36
210	Advanced Computer Science and Information Technology (U.S.A.)	47	3	4125	0.06	88.42
211	American Journal of Psychology (U.S.A.)	47	3	4128	0.06	88.49
212	American Review of Information Science & Technology (U.S.A.)	47	3	4131	0.06	88.55
213	American Society for Information Science (U.S.A.)	47	3	4134	0.06	88.62
214	ASIS Bulletin (ASIS & T The American Society for Information Science & Technology) (U.S.A.)	47	3	4137	0.06	88.68
215	Australian Specials Libraries (Australia)	47	3	4140	0.06	88.75
216	Canadian Library Journal (Canada)	47	3	4143	0.06	88.81
217	Cataloguing and Classification Quarterly (U.S.A.)	47	3	4146	0.06	88.87
218	CD Rom Professional (U.S.A.)	47	3	4149	0.06	88.94
219	Community & Junior College Libraries (U.K.)	47	3	4152	0.06	89.00
220	Computer Networks (Netherlands)	47	3	4155	0.06	89.07
221	Database (U.S.A.)	47	3	4158	0.06	89.13
222	Electronic Learning (Canada)	47	3	4161	0.06	89.20

S. No.	Name of Journals	Rank No.	No. of Citations	Cumu. No. of Citations	% of Citations	Cumu.% of Citations
223	IATUL Quarterly (West Germany)	47	3	4164	0.06	89.26
224	IEEE Computer (U.S.A.)	47	3	4167	0.06	89.32
225	IEEE Spectrum (U.S.A.)	47	3	4170	0.06	89.39
226	Indian Dissertation Abstract (India)	47	3	4173	0.06	89.45
227	Indian Journal of Labour Economics (India)	47	3	4176	0.06	89.52
228	Indian Library Association Bulletin (India)	47	3	4179	0.06	89.58
229	Industrial and Engineering Chemistry (India)	47	3	4182	0.06	89.65
230	Industrial India (India)	47	3	4185	0.06	89.71
231	Information Studies (India)	47	3	4188	0.06	89.77
232	Information Systems and E-Business Management Information Systems and E-Business Management (U.S.A.)	47	3	4191	0.06	89.84
233	Inforum (Europe)	47	3	4194	0.06	89.90
234	INSPEC (U.S.A.)	47	3	4197	0.06	89.97
235	International Journal of Information Management (Netherlands)	47	3	4200	0.06	90.03
236	International Journal of Medical Informatics (Netherlands)	47	3	4203	0.06	90.10
237	JASIST (Journal of the American Society for Information Science and Technology (JASIST) (U.S.A.)	47	3	4206	0.06	90.16
238	Journal of Abnormal and Social Psychology (U.S.A.)	47	3	4209	0.06	90.23
239	Journal of Education Librarianship (U.S.A.)	47	3	4212	0.06	90.29
240	Journal of Educational Media and Library Science (U.S.A.)	47	3	4215	0.06	90.35
241	Journal of Marketing (U.S.A.)	47	3	4218	0.06	90.42
242	Journal of Medical Education (Iran)	47	3	4221	0.06	90.48
243	Journal of Personality and Social Psychology (U.S.A.)	47	3	4224	0.06	90.55

S. No.	Name of Journals	Rank No.	No. of Citations	Cumu. No. of Citations	% of Citations	Cumu.% of Citations
244	Journal of Scientific and Industrial Research (U.S.A.)	47	3	4227	0.06	90.61
245	Kurukshetra (India)	47	3	4230	0.06	90.68
246	Library Collection, Acquisition & Technical Services (U.S.A.)	47	3	4233	0.06	90.74
247	Library World (Japan)	47	3	4236	0.06	90.80
248	Long Range Planning (Netherlands)	47	3	4239	0.06	90.87
249	Management in Government (India)	47	3	4242	0.06	90.93
250	Mathematical Biosciences (Netherlands)	47	3	4245	0.06	91.00
251	Media Culture and Society (U.S.A.)	47	3	4248	0.06	91.06
252	Modern Asian Studies (India)	47	3	4251	0.06	91.13
253	Nab India (India)	47	3	4254	0.06	91.19
254	Online Information Review (U.K.)	47	3	4257	0.06	91.25
255	Orissa review (India)	47	3	4260	0.06	91.32
256	Productivity (India)	47	3	4263	0.06	91.38
257	Quarterly Bulletin of International Association of Agricultural Information Specialists (Netherlands)	47	3	4266	0.06	91.45
258	Rilisar Bulletin (India)	47	3	4269	0.06	91.51
259	Singapore Libraries (Singapore)	47	3	4272	0.06	91.58
260	Social Review (Netherlands)	47	3	4275	0.06	91.64
261	Sociological Review (U.S.A.)	47	3	4278	0.06	91.70
262	Training & Management Development Methods (U.K.)	47	3	4281	0.06	91.77
263	AALD Bulletin (U.K.)	48	2	4283	0.04	91.81
264	African Research and Documentation (Africa)	48	2	4285	0.04	91.85
265	Airway (CAA'S House Journal) (U.K.)	48	2	4287	0.04	91.90
266	American Archivist (U.S.A.)	48	2	4289	0.04	91.94
267	American Journal of Community Psychology (U.S.A.)	48	2	4291	0.04	91.98

S. No.	Name of Journals	Rank No.	No. of Citations	Cumu. No. of Citations	% of Citations	Cumu.% of Citations
268	American Political Review (U.S.A.)	48	2	4293	0.04	92.03
269	American Sociologist (U.S.A.)	48	2	4295	0.04	92.07
270	ARL Newsletter (U.S.A.)	48	2	4297	0.04	92.11
271	Balletino De Informazioni (U.S.A.)	48	2	4299	0.04	92.15
272	Bibliotek Forum (West Germany)	48	2	4301	0.04	92.20
273	Bookmark Magazine (U.S.A.)	48	2	4303	0.04	92.24
274	British Journal of Educational Technology (U.K.)	48	2	4305	0.04	92.28
275	Business Communication Review (U.S.A.)	48	2	4307	0.04	92.33
276	Catgolic Library World (U.S.A.)	48	2	4309	0.04	92.37
277	Computer in Libraries (U.S.A.)	48	2	4311	0.04	92.41
278	Current Science (U.S.A.)	48	2	4313	0.04	92.45
279	DESIDOC Journal of Library and Information Technology (India)	48	2	4315	0.04	92.50
280	DESIDOC Letters (India)	48	2	4317	0.04	92.54
281	DF Revy (U.S.A.)	48	2	4319	0.04	92.58
282	Distance Education (U.S.A.)	48	2	4321	0.04	92.63
283	Education for Information (U.S.A.)	48	2	4323	0.04	92.67
284	Education Library Bulletin (U.K.)	48	2	4325	0.04	92.71
285	Engineering (U.K.)	48	2	4327	0.04	92.75
286	Government Publications Reviews (India)	43	2	4329	0.04	92.80
287	Granthalaya (India)	48	2	4331	0.04	92.84
288	History of Science (U.K.)	48	2	4333	0.04	92.88
289	IASLIC Proceeding (India)	48	2	4335	0.04	92.93
290	ICSSR Newsletter (India)	48	2	4337	0.04	92.97
291	IEEE Personal Communication (U.S.A.)	48	2	4339	0.04	93.01
292	IEEE Annals of the History of Computer (U.S.A.)	48	2	4341	0.04	93.05
293	IEEE Multimedia (U.S.A.)	48	2	4343	0.04	93.10

S. No.	Name of Journals	Rank No.	No. of Citations	Cumu. No. of Citations	% of Citations	Cumu.% of Citations
294	Illinois Libraries (U.S.A.)	48	2	4345	0.04	93.14
295	INCAE (U.S.A.)	48	2	4347	0.04	93.18
296	Indian Cooperative review (India)	48	2	4349	0.04	93.23
297	Indian Geographical Journal (India)	48	2	4351	0.04	93.27
298	Indian Journal of Agricultural Library and Information (India)	48	2	4353	0.04	93.31
299	Indian Journal of American studies (India)	48	2	4355	0.04	93.35
300	Indian Journal of Medical Research (India)	48	2	4357	0.04	93.40
301	Indian Library Movement (India)	48	2	4359	0.04	93.44
302	Informatics (East Germany)	48	2	4361	0.04	93.48
303	Informatik - Forschung und Entwicklung (U.S.A.)	48	2	4363	0.04	93.53
304	Information Communication and Society (U.K.)	48	2	4365	0.04	93.57
305	Information Technology and People (U.K.)	48	2	4367	0.04	93.61
306	International Classification (U.S.A.)	48	2	4369	0.04	93.65
307	International Forum Information Documentation (Netherlands)	48	2	4371	0.04	93.70
308	International Information Communication and Education (India)	48	2	4373	0.04	93.74
309	International Journal of Development Planning Literature (India)	48	2	4375	0.04	93.78
310	Journal of Communication Management (U.K.)	48	2	4377	0.04	93.83
311	Journal of Counseling Psychology (U.S.A.)	48	2	4379	0.04	93.87
312	Journal of Data Processing (Brazil)	48	2	4381	0.04	93.91
313	Journal of Education for Library and Information Science (U.S.A.)	48	2	4383	0.04	93.95
314	Journal of Educational Multimedia and Higher Media (U.S.A.)	48	2	4385	0.04	94.00

S. No.	Name of Journals	Rank No.	No. of Citations	Cumu. No. of Citations	% of Citations	Cumu.% of Citations
315	Journal of Educational Research (Pakistan)	48	2	4387	0.04	94.04
316	Journal of Electronic Publishing (U.S.A.)	48	2	4389	0.04	94.08
317	Journal of Experimental Psychology (U.S.A.)	48	2	4391	0.04	94.13
318	Journal of Indian Institute of Mass communication (India)	48	2	4393	0.04	94.17
319	Journal of Indian Library Association (India)	48	2	4395	0.04	94.21
320	Journal of Information Technology (U.K.)	48	2	4397	0.04	94.26
321	Journal of International communication (U.S.A.)	48	2	4399	0.04	94.30
322	Journal of Management (U.S.A.)	48	2	4401	0.04	94.34
323	Journal of Occupational Psychology (U.S.A.)	48	2	4403	0.04	94.38
324	Journal of Rural Development (India)	48	2	4405	0.04	94.43
325	Journal of Scholar Publishing (Canada)	48	2	4407	0.04	94.47
326	Knowledge Organization (West Germany)	48	2	4409	0.04	94.51
327	Library and Information Science Research News (U.K.)	48	2	4411	0.04	94.56
328	Library Hi-Tech (U.S.A.)	48	2	4413	0.04	94.60
329	Library Hi-tech News (U.K.)	48	2	4415	0.04	94.64
330	Library Review (U.K.)	48	2	4417	0.04	94.68
331	Library Science with Slant to Documentation & Information Studies (U.S.A.)	48	2	4419	0.04	94.73
332	Malaysian Journal of Economic Studies (MJES) (Malaysia)	48	2	4421	0.04	94.77
333	Management Information System Quarterly (U.S.A.)	48	2	4423	0.04	94.81
334	Management of Personnel Quarterly (U.S.A.)	48	2	4425	0.04	94.86
335	Medical Marketing and Media (U.S.A.)	48	2	4427	0.04	94.90

S. No.	Name of Journals	Rank No.	No. of Citations	Cumu. No. of Citations	% of Citations	Cumu.% of Citations
336	Minerva (U.S.A.)	48	2	4429	0.04	94.94
337	MIS Quarterly (U.S.A.)	48	2	4431	0.04	94.98
338	Moussaion (U.S.A.)	48	2	4433	0.04	95.03
339	Nature (U.K.)	48	2	4435	0.04	95.07
340	Nauchno-Tekhnicheskaya – Informatsiya (Russia)	48	2	4437	0.04	95.11
341	Newzeland Libraries (Newzeland)	48	2	4439	0.04	95.16
342	Open (U.K.)	48	2	4441	0.04	95.20
343	Personality and Social Psychology Bulletin (U.S.A.)	48	2	4443	0.04	95.24
344	PNLA Quarterly (U.S.A.)	48	2	4445	0.04	95.28
345	Prajana (India)	48	2	4447	0.04	95.33
346	Prashanika (India)	48	2	4449	0.04	95.37
347	Reference & User Services Quarterly (U.S.A.)	48	2	4451	0.04	95.41
348	Reference Service Review (U.K.)	48	2	4453	0.04	95.46
349	Research Policy (Netherlands)	48	2	4455	0.04	95.50
350	Science of the Total Environment (Netherlands)	48	2	4457	0.04	95.54
351	Scientific and American (U.S.A.)	48	2	4459	0.04	95.58
352	SLA News (U.S.A.)	48	2	4461	0.04	95.63
353	Social Forces(U.S.A.)	48	2	4463	0.04	95.67
354	Social Science Quarterly (U.S.A.)	48	2	4465	0.04	95.71
355	Social Science Information (U.S.A.)	48	2	4467	0.04	95.76
356	Social Science Institution Studies (Pakistan)	48	2	4469	0.04	95.80
357	The Asian Journal of Psychological Education (India)	48	2	4471	0.04	95.84
358	The Assignation (U.S.A.)	48	2	4473	0.04	95.88
359	The Information Society (U.K.)	48	2	4475	0.04	95.93
360	Trilogia (U.S.A.)	48	2	4477	0.04	95.97
361	Tudomanyos Es Muszaki Tajekoztatas (U.S.A.)	48	2	4479	0.04	96.01

S. No.	Name of Journals	Rank No.	No. of Citations	Cumu. No. of Citations	% of Citations	Cumu.% of Citations
362	Unabashed Librarian (U.S.A.)	48	2	4481	0.04	96.06
363	UNESCO Journal of Information Science (U.S.A.)	48	2	4483	0.04	96.10
364	World Patent Information (Netherlands)	48	2	4485	0.04	96.14
365	Younge India (India)	48	2	4487	0.04	96.18
366	Administration & Society (U.K.)	49	1	4488	0.02	96.21
367	Advance in Library Administration and Organization (U.K.)	49	1	4489	0.02	96.23
368	Advance Management Journals (U.S.A.)	49	1	4490	0.02	96.25
369	Advances in Information Mining (India)	49	1	4491	0.02	96.27
370	AGLIS Journal (India)	49	1	4492	0.02	96.29
371	Amatrya Sen (India)	49	1	4493	0.02	96.31
372	American educational research journal (U.S.A.)	49	1	4494	0.02	96.33
373	American Journal of Agricultural Economics (U.K.)	49	1	4495	0.02	96.36
374	American Journal of Islamic Social Science (U.S.A.)	49	1	4496	0.02	96.38
375	American Journal of Pharmaceutical Education (U.S.A.)	49	1	4497	0.02	96.40
376	American Library Journal (U.S.A.)	49	1	4498	0.02	96.42
377	American Review (U.S.A.)	49	1	4499	0.02	96.44
378	American scientist (U.S.A.)	49	1	4500	0.02	96.46
379	American Studies International (U.S.A.)	49	1	4501	0.02	96.48
380	Analytical Chemistry (U.S.A.)	49	1	4502	0.02	96.51
381	Annals of American Academy of Political and Social Science (U.S.A.)	49	1	4503	0.02	96.53
382	Annals of Japan Society of Library science (Japan)	49	1	4504	0.02	96.55
383	Antioch Notes (U.K.)	49	1	4505	0.02	96.57

S. No.	Name of Journals	Rank No.	No. of Citations	Cumu. No. of Citations	% of Citations	Cumu.% of Citations
384	Arab Journals for Librarianship and Information Science (Egypt)	49	1	4506	0.02	96.59
385	Archives of Neurology and Psychiatry (U.S.A.)	49	1	4507	0.02	96.61
386	Argus (U.K.)	49	1	4508	0.02	96.63
387	ARIST (U.S.A.)	49	1	4509	0.02	96.66
388	ASIS Proceeding (ASIS & T The American Society for Information Science & Technology) (U.S.A.)	49	1	4510	0.02	96.68
389	AT&T technical Journal (U.S.A.)	49	1	4511	0.02	96.70
390	Behavioral Science (U.S.A.)	49	1	4512	0.02	96.72
391	Bendal Library Journal (Australia)	49	1	4513	0.02	96.74
392	Biblos (Japan)	49	1	4514	0.02	96.76
393	Bioscience (U.S.A.)	49	1	4515	0.02	96.78
394	BLRD Report(British Library Reference Division) (U.K.)	49	1	4516	0.02	96.81
395	Bombay Psychologist (India)	49	1	4517	0.02	96.83
396	British Journal of Psychology (U.K.)	49	1	4518	0.02	96.85
397	British Journal of Social and Clinical Psychology (U.K.)	49	1	4519	0.02	96.87
398	British Journal of Sociology (U.K.)	49	1	4520	0.02	96.89
399	British Journal Medical Association (U.K.)	49	1	4521	0.02	96.91
400	British Journal of Preventive and Social Medicine (U.K.)	49	1	4522	0.02	96.93
401	British Medical Journal (U.K.)	49	1	4523	0.02	96.96
402	Bulletin Des Bibliothèques De France (France)	49	1	4524	0.02	96.98
403	Bulletin Institution Information Science (U.S.A.)	49	1	4525	0.02	97.00
404	Bulletin of American Library Association (U.S.A.)	49	1	4526	0.02	97.02

S. No.	Name of Journals	Rank No.	No. of Citations	Cumu. No. of Citations	% of Citations	Cumu.% of Citations
405	Bulletin of the Medical Library Association (U.S.A.)	49	1	4527	0.02	97.04
406	C& L Application (U.K.)	49	1	4528	0.02	97.06
407	Campus Wide Information System (U.K.)	49	1	4529	0.02	97.08
408	Canadian Library Science & Documentation (Canada)	49	1	4530	0.02	97.11
409	Catgolic Library Review (U.S.A.)	49	1	4531	0.02	97.13
410	Chaturanga (India)	49	1	4532	0.02	97.15
411	Chronicle of Higher Education (U.S.A.)	49	1	4533	0.02	97.17
412	Ciencia Da Informacao (Brazil)	49	1	4534	0.02	97.19
413	Collection Building (U.K.)	49	1	4535	0.02	97.21
414	COMLA Newsletter (COMLA - Commonwealth Library Association (U.K.)	49	1	4536	0.02	97.23
415	Computer (U.S.A.)	49	1	4537	0.02	97.26
416	Computer Journal (U.K.)	49	1	4538	0.02	97.28
417	Computer Methods and Program in Biomedicine (Netherlands)	49	1	4539	0.02	97.30
418	Crus News (U.K.)	49	1	4540	0.02	97.32
419	Culture and Society (U.S.A.)	49	1	4541	0.02	97.34
420	Czechoslovak Journal of Physics (U.S.A.)	49	1	4542	0.02	97.36
421	Economic Week (India)	49	1	4543	0.02	97.38
422	Education Review (U.K.)	49	1	4544	0.02	97.41
423	Educational and Psychotically Measurement (U.S.A.)	49	1	4545	0.02	97.43
424	EJOR (European Journal of Operational Research-Description The European Journal of Operational Research (Netherlands)	49	1	4546	0.02	97.45
425	Electronic & Communication Engineering Journals (U.S.A.)	49	1	4547	0.02	97.47
426	Engineering Management (Journal of Engineering and Technology Management) (Netherlands)	49	1	4548	0.02	97.49

S. No.	Name of Journals	Rank No.	No. of Citations	Cumu. No. of Citations	% of Citations	Cumu.% of Citations
427	European Journal of Information Management (Europe)	49	1	4549	0.02	97.51
428	European Research Libraries Cooperation (Europe)	49	1	4550	0.02	97.53
429	Government Quarterly (India)	49	1	4551	0.02	97.56
430	Harvard Business Review (U.S.A.)	49	1	4552	0.02	97.58
431	Health Libraries Review (U.S.A.)	49	1	4553	0.02	97.60
432	IASSI Quarterly newsletter (Indian Association of Social Science Institutions (India)	49	1	4554	0.02	97.62
433	IBM System Journal (U.S.A.)	49	1	4555	0.02	97.64
434	IEEE Journal of Selected Areas in Communication (U.S.A.)	49	1	4556	0.02	97.66
435	IEEE Micro (U.S.A.)	49	1	4557	0.02	97.68
436	IEEE Parallel & Distributed Technology (U.S.A.)	49	1	4558	0.02	97.71
437	ILA Newsletter (India)	49	1	4559	0.02	97.73
438	ILA Proceeding (India)	49	1	4560	0.02	97.75
439	Indian Architect (India)	49	1	4561	0.02	97.77
440	Indian Journal of Extension Education (India)	49	1	4562	0.02	97.79
441	Indian Journal of Information Library Science (India)	49	1	4563	0.02	97.81
442	Indian Psychological Review (India)	49	1	4564	0.02	97.83
443	Information Management and Technology (U.S.A.)	49	1	4565	0.02	97.86
444	Information Economics and Policy(Netherlands)	49	1	4566	0.02	97.88
445	Information Report and Bibliographies (U.S.A.)	49	1	4567	0.02	97.90
446	INICA (U.S.A.)	49	1	4568	0.02	97.92
447	INTELL Motion (U.S.A.)	49	1	4569	0.02	97.94

S. No.	Name of Journals	Rank No.	No. of Citations	Cumu. No. of Citations	% of Citations	Cumu.% of Citations
448	Intelligent Tutoring Media (U.K.)	49	1	4570	0.02	97.96
449	International Educational Journal (Australia)	49	1	4571	0.02	97.98
450	International Cataloguing and Bibliographic Control (ICBC) (Netherlands)	49	1	4572	0.02	98.01
451	International Journal of Biomedical Computing (Netherlands)	49	1	4573	0.02	98.03
452	International Journal of Computer Engineering and Software Technology (India)	49	1	4574	0.02	98.05
453	International Journal of Health Services (U.S.A.)	49	1	4575	0.02	98.07
454	International Journal of Library and Information Science (Nigeria)	49	1	4576	0.02	98.09
455	International Journal of Manpower (U.K.)	49	1	4577	0.02	98.11
456	International Manpower Journal (U.K.)	49	1	4578	0.02	98.14
457	International Journal of Science Education (U.S.A.)	49	1	4579	0.02	98.16
458	International Research Journal of Library, Information and Archival Studies (IRJLIAS) (Nigeria)	49	1	4580	0.02	98.18
459	International Social Science Journal (U.S.A.)	49	1	4581	0.02	98.20
460	Irish Journal of Business and Administration Research (Europe)	49	1	4582	0.02	98.22
461	JAMA (Journal of the American Medical Association) (U.S.A.)	49	1	4583	0.02	98.24
462	Japanese Studies in the History of Science (Japan)	49	1	4584	0.02	98.26
463	JLIS.it (U.S.A.)	49	1	4585	0.02	98.29
464	John Rylands Library Bulletin (U.K.)	49	1	4586	0.02	98.31
465	Journal of Asian Studies (U.S.A.)	49	1	4587	0.02	98.33

S. No.	Name of Journals	Rank No.	No. of Citations	Cumu. No. of Citations	% of Citations	Cumu.% of Citations
466	Journal of Business Finance & Accounting (U.S.A.)	49	1	4588	0.02	98.35
467	Journal of College Science Teaching (U.S.A.)	49	1	4589	0.02	98.37
468	Journal of Consulting Psychology (U.S.A.)	49	1	4590	0.02	98.39
469	Journal of Consumer Research (U.S.A.)	49	1	4591	0.02	98.41
470	Journal of Education (South Africa)	49	1	4592	0.02	98.44
471	Journal of European Research Libraries(Europe)	49	1	4593	0.02	98.46
472	Journal of Indian Sociology of Agricultural Statistics (India)	49	1	4594	0.02	98.48
473	Journal of Indian Sociology of Soil Science (India)	49	1	4595	0.02	98.50
474	Journal of Information & Knowledge Management (JIKM) (Singapore)	49	1	4596	0.02	98.52
475	Journal of Integrated Pest Management (U.S.A.)	49	1	4597	0.02	98.54
476	Journal of Intellectual Disability Research (U.S.A.)	49	1	4598	0.02	98.56
477	Journal of Library Science (Taiwan)	49	1	4599	0.02	98.59
478	Journal of Management Studies (JMS) (U.S.A.)	49	1	4600	0.02	98.61
479	Journal of National Library (India)	49	1	4601	0.02	98.63
480	Journal of Occupational Behavior (U.S.A.)	49	1	4602	0.02	98.65
481	Journal of Psychological Research (U.S.A.)	49	1	4603	0.02	98.67
482	Journal of Research on Adolescence (U.S.A.)	49	1	4604	0.02	98.69
483	Journal of Social Research (U.S.A.)	49	1	4605	0.02	98.71
484	Journal of System Engineering (U.S.A.)	49	1	4606	0.02	98.74

S. No.	Name of Journals	Rank No.	No. of Citations	Cumu. No. of Citations	% of Citations	Cumu.% of Citations
485	Journal of the Institute of Petroleum (U.S.A.)	49	1	4607	0.02	98.76
486	Liasion (U.K.)	49	1	4608	0.02	98.78
487	Library Juice(U.S.A.)	49	1	4609	0.02	98.80
488	Library Mosaics(U.S.A.)	49	1	4610	0.02	98.82
489	Library Philosophy and Practice (LPP) (U.S.A.)	49	1	4611	0.02	98.84
490	Library Student Journal (U.S.A.)	49	1	4612	0.02	98.86
491	Louisiana Library Association Bulletin (U.S.A.)	49	1	4613	0.02	98.89
492	Management Bulletin (U.S.A.)	49	1	4614	0.02	98.91
493	Management Digest Journal (U.K.)	49	1	4615	0.02	98.93
494	Management Science (U.S.A.)	49	1	4616	0.02	98.95
495	Michigan Bar Journal (U.S.A.)	49	1	4617	0.02	98.97
496	Micro Image (U.S.A.)	49	1	4618	0.02	98.99
497	Microform Review (U.S.A.)	49	1	4619	0.02	99.01
498	MIT Solon Management Review (U.S.A.)	49	1	4620	0.02	99.04
499	National Library (India)	49	1	4621	0.02	99.06
500	New Frontiers in Education (India)	49	1	4622	0.02	99.08
501	New Scientist (U.K.)	49	1	4623	0.02	99.10
502	News Letter of NIC (India)	49	1	4624	0.02	99.12
503	Nucleic Acids Research (U.K.)	49	1	4625	0.02	99.14
504	NYLA Bulletin (U.S.A.)	49	1	4626	0.02	99.16
505	OEMGHA(U.S.A.)	49	1	4627	0.02	99.19
506	Operating Systems Review (U.S.A.)	49	1	4628	0.02	99.21
507	Organizational Behavior and Human Decision Process (Netherlands)	49	1	4629	0.02	99.23
508	Punjab Library Association Bulletin (India)	49	1	4630	0.02	99.25
509	Peabody Journal of Education (U.K.)	49	1	4631	0.02	99.27
510	Perceptual and Motor Skills (U.S.A.)	49	1	4632	0.02	99.29

S. No.	Name of Journals	Rank No.	No. of Citations	Cumu. No. of Citations	% of Citations	Cumu.% of Citations
511	Personnel Administrator (U.S.A.)	49	1	4633	0.02	99.31
512	Personnel and Guidance Journal (U.S.A.)	49	1	4634	0.02	99.34
513	Personnel Management (U.S.A.)	49	1	4635	0.02	99.36
514	Perspectives in Psychological Research (U.S.A.)	49	1	4636	0.02	99.38
515	Popular Science(U.S.A.)	49	1	4637	0.02	99.40
516	Proceeding National Academy of Science (U.S.A.)	49	1	4638	0.02	99.42
517	Proceedings Magazine (U.S.A.)	49	1	4639	0.02	99.44
518	Psychological Report (U.S.A.)	49	1	4640	0.02	99.46
519	Psychological Research (U.S.A.)	49	1	4641	0.02	99.49
520	Public Personnel Review (U.S.A.)	49	1	4642	0.02	99.51
521	Punjab University Management Review (India)	49	1	4643	0.02	99.53
522	Resources for Communication Studies (U.S.A.)	49	1	4644	0.02	99.55
523	Revista De Biblioteconimia De Brasila(Brazil)	49	1	4645	0.02	99.57
524	Revue Fracaise Du Marketing (U.S.A.)	49	1	4646	0.02	99.59
525	School Library Journal (U.S.A.)	49	1	4647	0.02	99.61
526	Science Progress (U.S.A.)	49	1	4648	0.02	99.64
527	Science and Public Policy (U.K.)	49	1	4649	0.02	99.66
528	Science as Cultural (U.S.A.)	49	1	4650	0.02	99.68
529	Scottish Libraries (U.K.)	49	1	4651	0.02	99.70
530	Social Policy (U.S.A.)	49	1	4652	0.02	99.72
531	Social Psychology Quarterly (U.S.A.)	49	1	4653	0.02	99.74
532	Social Welfare (India)	49	1	4654	0.02	99.76
533	Sociology of Education (U.S.A.)	49	1	4655	0.02	99.79

S. No.	Name of Journals	Rank No.	No. of Citations	Cumu. No. of Citations	% of Citations	Cumu.% of Citations
534	Sociology of Work and Occupations (U.S.A.)	49	1	4656	0.02	99.81
535	South Asian Research (U.S.A.)	49	1	4657	0.02	99.83
536	Spring (U.S.A.)	49	1	4658	0.02	99.85
537	Studii Cereatari De Documentare Si Bibliogie (U.S.A.)	49	1	4659	0.02	99.87
538	Technology Review(U.S.A.)	49	1	4660	0.02	99.89
539	Telegraph (Canada)	49	1	4661	0.02	99.91
540	Vikalpa (India)	49	1	4662	0.02	99.94
541	Western Law Review (Australia)	49	1	4663	0.02	99.96
542	Work and Occupation (U.S.A.)	49	1	4664	0.02	99.98
543	ZIID Zeitschrift (West Germany)	49	1	4665	0.02	100.00
	Total		**4665**	**4665**	**100.00**	**100.00**

8.4. RANKING OF JOURNALS: DR. HARISINGH GOUR UNIVERSITY, SAGAR

Table-3 shows that total 255 journals with 2953 citations arranged in order decreasing number of their ranked. Coming to the Indian situation as far periodicals literature is concerned, it is found that out of 255 journals titles 59 are published from India. It can be ascertained that IASLIC Bulletin (11.89%), Library Science journal occupies the first rank as the most preferred journal having been cited 351 times. ILA Bulletin (9.35%) occupies the second rank getting 276citations, followed by University News (6.37%) with 188 citations, Herald of Library Science (5.99%) with 177 citations, Library Herald (5.49%) with 162 citations, Annals of Library Science Studies (3.76 %) with 111 citations, Annals of Library Science Documentation (3.08%) with 91 citations, Journal of Documentation (2.88%) with 85 citations, DESIDOC Bulletin of Information Technology (2.81%) with 83 citations, Library Science with slant to Documentation (2.64%) with78 citations respectively. The first ten journals in the ranking list together account for 54.25% of the total % of citations. However, table shows that first 50 Journals accounted for nearly 84.96% of citations.

Apart from Library & Information Science journals have been occupied Management Information System Quarterly (0.64%) with 24th rank, Action Aid Disability News (0.30%) with 32nd rank, Educational and Psychotically Measurement (0.17%) with 36th rank, International Journal of Medical Information (0.14%) with 37th rank, Journalism Quarterly (0.07%) with 39th rank, Applied artificial intelligence (0.03%) with 40th rank in the rank list.

And on the other hand, IEEE Annals of the History of Computer (0.03%), Scientometric (0.03 %) have also occupied the same place i.e.40th rank in the ranked list.

Thus, it is noted that a few journals yielded more citations and more journals yielded few citations. A high concentration of citations in a few periodicals is evident. Therefore, core or productive journals can be identified on the basis of the ranked list.

Table 3. Ranking of Journals: Dr. Harisingh Gour University, Sagar

S. No.	Name of Journals	Rank No.	No. of Citations	Cumu. No. of Citations	% of Citations	Cumu.% of Citations
1	IASLIC Bulletin (India)	1	351	351	11.89	11.89
2	ILA Bulletin (India)	2	276	627	9.35	21.23
3	University News (India)	3	188	815	6.37	27.60
4	Herald of Library Science (India)	4	177	992	5.99	33.59
5	Library Herald(India)	5	162	1154	5.49	39.08
6	Annals of Library Science Studies (India)	6	111	1265	3.76	42.84
7	Annals of Library science Documentation (India)	7	91	1356	3.08	45.92

S. No.	Name of Journals	Rank No.	No. of Citations	Cumu. No. of Citations	% of Citations	Cumu.% of Citations
8	Journal of Documentation (U.K.)	8	85	1441	2.88	48.80
9	DESIDOC Bulletin of Information Technology (India)	9	83	1524	2.81	51.61
10	Library Science with slant to Documentation (India)	10	78	1602	2.64	54.25
11	Journal of Library and Information Science (India)	11	68	1670	2.30	56.55
12	Indian Librarian (India)	12	64	1734	2.17	58.72
13	Lucknow Librarian (India)	13	61	1795	2.07	60.79
14	College and Research Libraries (U.S.A.)	14	57	1852	1.93	62.72
15	ASLIB Proceeding (U.K.)	15	41	1893	1.39	64.10
16	Library Trends (U.S.A.)	16	40	1933	1.35	65.46
17	Indian Journal of Information Library and Society (India)	17	37	1970	1.25	66.71
18	IAALD Quarterly Bulletin (U.K.)	18	36	2006	1.22	67.93
19	Bulletin of Medical Library Association (India)	19	33	2039	1.12	69.05
20	Library Journal (U.S.A.)	20	31	2070	1.05	70.10
21	Special Library (U.S.A.)	20	31	2101	1.05	71.15
22	Library Collection, Acquisition & Technical Services (U.S.A.)	21	25	2126	0.85	71.99
23	Library Acquisition : Practice & Theory (U.S.A.)	22	24	2150	0.81	72.81
24	NISSAT, Newsletter (India)	22	24	2174	0.81	73.62
25	Electronic Library (U.S.A.)	23	20	2194	0.68	74.30
26	Library Progress (International) (India)	23	20	2214	0.68	74.97
27	Management Information System Quarterly (U.S.A.)	24	19	2233	0.64	75.62
28	Blind Welfare (South Australia)	25	18	2251	0.61	76.23
29	Law Library Journal (U.S.A.)	26	17	2268	0.58	76.80
30	ZIID Zeitschrift (West Germany)	26	17	2285	0.58	77.38

S. No.	Name of Journals	Rank No.	No. of Citations	Cumu. No. of Citations	% of Citations	Cumu.% of Citations
31	Journal of American Society for Information Science (U.S.A.)	27	16	2301	0.54	77.92
32	Library Hi-Tech News (U.K.)	27	16	2317	0.54	78.46
33	Program (U.K.)	27	16	2333	0.54	79.00
34	International Library Review (U.K.)	28	14	2347	0.47	79.48
35	CLIS Newsletter (India)	29	13	2360	0.44	79.92
36	Journal of Library Administration (U.S.A.)	29	13	2373	0.44	80.36
37	Library Quarterly (U.S.A.)	29	13	2386	0.44	80.80
38	Library Technology Report (U.S.A.)	30	12	2398	0.41	81.21
39	CALIBER (India)	31	11	2409	0.37	81.58
40	Information Technology and Libraries (U.K.)	31	11	2420	0.37	81.95
41	Journal of Education Librarianship (U.S.A.)	31	11	2431	0.37	82.32
42	Journal of Library Automation(U.S.A.)	31	11	2442	0.37	82.70
43	Action Aid Disability News (India)	32	9	2451	0.30	83.00
44	ARIST (U.S.A.)	32	9	2460	0.30	83.31
45	ERIC (Educational Resources Information Center) (U.S.A.)	32	9	2469	0.30	83.61
46	Library Philosophy and Practice (U.S.A.)	32	9	2478	0.30	83.91
47	Library Review (U.K.)	32	9	2487	0.30	84.22
48	Library and Information Science Research Electronic Journal (Australia)	33	8	2495	0.27	84.49
49	Collection Management (U.S.A.)	34	7	2502	0.24	84.73
50	Electronic Journal of Academic and Special Librarianship (Canada)	34	7	2509	0.24	84.96
51	Indian Management (India)	34	7	2516	0.24	85.20
52	Journal of Library Science (Taiwan)	34	7	2523	0.24	85.44
53	LIBRA (India)	34	7	2530	0.24	85.68
54	Library and Information Science Research (Netherlands)	34	7	2537	0.24	85.91

S. No.	Name of Journals	Rank No.	No. of Citations	Cumu. No. of Citations	% of Citations	Cumu.% of Citations
55	Library Hi-Tech (U.S.A.)	34	7	2544	0.24	86.15
56	Library Resources & Technical Services (U.S.A.)	34	7	2551	0.24	86.39
57	SRELS- Journal of Information Management (India)	34	7	2558	0.24	86.62
58	BMA Newsletter(British Medical Association (U.K.)	35	6	2564	0.20	86.83
59	Drexel Library Quarterly (U.S.A.)	35	6	2570	0.20	87.03
60	International Classification (U.S.A.)	35	6	2576	0.20	87.23
61	International Library Movement (Australia)	35	6	2582	0.20	87.44
62	Open System Review (U.S.A.)	35	6	2588	0.20	87.64
63	Resource Sharing and Information Networks (U.S.A.)	35	6	2594	0.20	87.84
64	Social Science Institution Studies (Pakistan)	35	6	2600	0.20	88.05
65	UNESCO Bulletin for Libraries (France)	35	6	2606	0.20	88.25
66	University Handbook (India)	35	6	2612	0.20	88.45
67	Australian Library Journal (Australia)	36	5	2617	0.17	88.62
68	Computer in Libraries (U.S.A.)	36	5	2622	0.17	88.79
69	Educational and Psychotically Measurement (U.S.A.)	36	5	2627	0.17	88.96
70	International Journal of Information Resource Management (U.S.A.)	36	5	2632	0.17	89.13
71	Journal of Academic Librarianship (Netherlands)	36	5	2637	0.17	89.30
72	The Serials Librarian (U.S.A.)	36	5	2642	0.17	89.47
73	Wilson Library Bulletin (U.S.A.)	36	5	2647	0.17	89.64
74	American Librarian (U.S.A.)	37	4	2651	0.14	89.77
75	Ariodne (U.K.)	37	4	2655	0.14	89.91
76	IFLA Bulletin (Netherlands)	37	4	2659	0.14	90.04

S. No.	Name of Journals	Rank No.	No. of Citations	Cumu. No. of Citations	% of Citations	Cumu.% of Citations
77	Information Today (U.S.A.)	37	4	2663	0.14	90.18
78	International Journal of Medical Informatics (Netherlands)	37	4	2667	0.14	90.31
79	LRTS (U.S.A.)	37	4	2671	0.14	90.45
80	Online (U.S.A.)	37	4	2675	0.14	90.59
81	Public Library Quarterly (India)	37	4	2679	0.14	90.72
82	Vikalpa (India)	37	4	2683	0.14	90.86
83	African Journal of Library Archives & Information Science (Africa)	38	3	2686	0.10	90.96
84	American Psychologist (U.S.A.)	38	3	2689	0.10	91.06
85	British Journal Medical Association (U.K.)	38	3	2692	0.10	91.16
86	Bulletin of American Society (U.S.A.)	38	3	2695	0.10	91.26
87	Canadian Library Journal (Canada)	38	3	2698	0.10	91.36
88	College Management (U.S.A.)	38	3	2701	0.10	91.47
89	Economic and Political Weekly (India)	38	3	2704	0.10	91.57
90	INCAE (U.S.A.)	38	3	2707	0.10	91.67
91	Indian Bulletin review (India)	38	3	2710	0.10	91.77
92	Indian Journal of Agricultural Library and Information (India)	38	3	2713	0.10	91.87
93	Indian Journal of Information Library Science (India)	38	3	2716	0.10	91.97
94	Information Processing Management (U.K.)	38	3	2719	0.10	92.08
95	Information Development (U.K.)	38	3	2722	0.10	92.18
96	JASIST ((Journal of the American Society for Information Science and Technology) (U.S.A.)	38	3	2725	0.10	92.28
97	JLIS (U.S.A.)	38	3	2728	0.10	92.38
98	Journal of Business Research (Netherlands)	38	3	2731	0.10	92.48

S. No.	Name of Journals	Rank No.	No. of Citations	Cumu. No. of Citations	% of Citations	Cumu.% of Citations
99	Journal of Information Science (U.K.)	38	3	2734	0.10	92.58
100	Journal of Librarianship (U.K.)	38	3	2737	0.10	92.69
101	KELPRO Bulletin (India)	38	3	2740	0.10	92.79
102	Library Focus Group (U.S.A.)	38	3	2743	0.10	92.89
103	Library Management (U.K.)	38	3	2746	0.10	92.99
104	Library Science Documentation & Information Science (India)	38	3	2749	0.10	93.09
105	Nigeria Libraries (Nigeria)	38	3	2752	0.10	93.19
106	School Library Journal (U.S.A.)	38	3	2755	0.10	93.29
107	Serial Librarian (U.S.A.)	38	3	2758	0.10	93.40
108	Acquit ion Librarian (U.S.A.)	39	2	2760	0.07	93.46
109	Alexandria (U.K.)	39	2	2762	0.07	93.53
110	Asian Journal Communication (India)	39	2	2764	0.07	93.60
111	Asian Libraries (India)	39	2	2766	0.07	93.67
112	ASLIB Bulletin (U.K.)	39	2	2768	0.07	93.74
113	Assignation(U.S.A.)	39	2	2770	0.07	93.80
114	Australian Libraries (Australia)	39	2	2772	0.07	93.87
115	California Management Review (U.S.A.)	39	2	2774	0.07	93.94
116	D-Lib (U.K.)	39	2	2776	0.07	94.01
117	DELNET Newsletter (India)	39	2	2778	0.07	94.07
118	Database (U.S.A.)	39	2	2780	0.07	94.14
119	Education for Librarianship (U.S.A.)	39	2	2782	0.07	94.21
120	Education Library Bulletin (U.K.)	39	2	2784	0.07	94.28
121	IATUL Quarterly (West Germany)	39	2	2786	0.07	94.34
122	IMFAMA (South Africa)	39	2	2788	0.07	94.41
123	Indian Archives (India)	39	2	2790	0.07	94.48
124	Indian Library Association Bulletin (India)	39	2	2792	0.07	94.55
125	Information Today & Tomorrow (Canada)	39	2	2794	0.07	94.62
126	Inter Lending Document Supply (U.K.)	39	2	2796	0.07	94.68

S. No.	Name of Journals	Rank No.	No. of Citations	Cumu. No. of Citations	% of Citations	Cumu.% of Citations
127	International Information and Library Review (Netherlands)	39	2	2798	0.07	94.75
128	International Information Communication and Education (India)	39	2	2800	0.07	94.82
129	International Journal of Library Science (U.S.A.)	39	2	2802	0.07	94.89
130	JAMA(Journal of the American Medical Association) (U.S.A.)	39	2	2804	0.07	94.95
131	Journal of Acquisition Librarian (U.S.A.)	39	2	2806	0.07	95.02
132	Journal of Education for Library and Information Science (U.S.A.)	39	2	2808	0.07	95.09
133	Journal of Indian Institute (India)	39	2	2810	0.07	95.16
134	Journal of Intellectual Disability Research (U.S.A.)	39	2	2812	0.07	95.23
135	Journal of the National Human Rights Commission (India)	39	2	2814	0.07	95.29
136	Journalism Quarterly (U.S.A.)	39	2	2816	0.07	95.36
137	Learned Publishing (U.K.)	39	2	2818	0.07	95.43
138	Legal Reference Services Quarterly (U.S.A.)	39	2	2820	0.07	95.50
139	Library and Information Research (U.K.)	39	2	2822	0.07	95.56
140	Library Association Record (U.S.A.)	39	2	2824	0.07	95.63
141	Library Point (U.S.A.)	39	2	2826	0.07	95.70
142	LOGOS (U.S.A.)	39	2	2828	0.07	95.77
143	Nab India (India)	39	2	2830	0.07	95.83
144	New Library World (U.K.)	39	2	2832	0.07	95.90
145	Outlook on Research Libraries (Australia)	39	2	2834	0.07	95.97
146	Rilisar Bulletin (India)	39	2	2836	0.07	96.04
147	Science (U.S.A.)	39	2	2838	0.07	96.11
148	Serial Review (Netherlands)	39	2	2840	0.07	96.17
149	South African Journal of Library & Information Science (South Africa)	39	2	2842	0.07	96.24

S. No.	Name of Journals	Rank No.	No. of Citations	Cumu. No. of Citations	% of Citations	Cumu.% of Citations
150	Success and Ability (India)	39	2	2844	0.07	96.31
151	Technology Review (U.S.A.)	39	2	2846	0.07	96.38
152	Trial (U.K.)	39	2	2848	0.07	96.44
153	Work and Occupation (U.S.A.)	39	2	2850	0.07	96.51
154	World Patent information (Netherlands)	39	2	2852	0.07	96.58
155	ABD (American Board of Dermatology) (U.S.A.)	40	1	2853	0.03	96.61
156	Academic Management Review (U.S.A.)	40	1	2854	0.03	96.65
157	Advance in Librarianship (India)	40	1	2855	0.03	96.68
158	Advance in Library Automation and Networking (U.S.A.)	40	1	2856	0.03	96.72
159	Against the grain (U.S.A.)	40	1	2857	0.03	96.75
160	ALA Bulletin (U.S.A.)	40	1	2858	0.03	96.78
161	American Society for Information Science (U.S.A.)	40	1	2859	0.03	96.82
162	Applied Artificial Intelligence (U.K.)	40	1	2860	0.03	96.85
163	Asia Pacific Book News (India)	40	1	2861	0.03	96.88
164	ASLIB information (U.K.)	40	1	2862	0.03	96.92
165	Audiovisual Librarian (U.K.)	40	1	2863	0.03	96.95
166	Australian Academic and Research Libraries (Australia)	40	1	2864	0.03	96.99
167	Biblos (Japan)	40	1	2865	0.03	97.02
168	Bottom Line (U.K.)	40	1	2866	0.03	97.05
169	Cap Librarian (South Africa)	40	1	2867	0.03	97.09
170	Cataloguing Australia (Australia)	40	1	2868	0.03	97.12
171	Chronicle of Higher Education (U.S.A.)	40	1	2869	0.03	97.16
172	Collection Building (U.K.)	40	1	2870	0.03	97.19
173	Communication of the ACM (U.S.A.)	40	1	2871	0.03	97.22
174	Community & Junior College Libraries (U.K.)	40	1	2872	0.03	97.26

S. No.	Name of Journals	Rank No.	No. of Citations	Cumu. No. of Citations	% of Citations	Cumu.% of Citations
175	Community Eye Health (U.K.)	40	1	2873	0.03	97.29
176	Computer and Law (U.S.A.)	40	1	2874	0.03	97.32
177	Computer Networks (Netherlands)	40	1	2875	0.03	97.36
178	CRUS News(U.S.A.)	40	1	2876	0.03	97.39
179	Current Contents(U.S.A.)	40	1	2877	0.03	97.43
180	Delhi University Magazine (India)	40	1	2878	0.03	97.46
181	Developmental Science (U.S.A.)	40	1	2879	0.03	97.49
182	Education Libraries(U.S.A.)	40	1	2880	0.03	97.53
183	Educational and Information Technologies (U.S.A.)	40	1	2881	0.03	97.56
184	EDUCOM Review (U.S.A.)	40	1	2882	0.03	97.60
185	Electronic Learning (Canada)	40	1	2883	0.03	97.63
186	England (U.K.)	40	1	2884	0.03	97.66
187	Ergonomics (U.K.)	40	1	2885	0.03	97.70
188	Fortune Magazine (U.S.A.)	40	1	2886	0.03	97.73
189	Harvard Library Bulletin (U.S.A.)	40	1	2887	0.03	97.76
190	Health Information and Libraries (U.S.A.)	40	1	2888	0.03	97.80
191	Health Libraries Review (U.S.A.)	40	1	2889	0.03	97.83
192	Human Communication Research (U.S.A.)	40	1	2890	0.03	97.87
193	IBM journal of research and Development (U.S.A.)	40	1	2891	0.03	97.90
194	IEEE annals of the history of Computer (U.S.A.)	40	1	2892	0.03	97.93
195	Illinois (U.S.A.)	40	1	2893	0.03	97.97
196	Indian Journal of History of Medicine (India)	40	1	2894	0.03	98.00
197	Indian Society for Technical Education (India)	40	1	2895	0.03	98.04
198	Indian Society for Technical Education News Letter (India)	40	1	2896	0.03	98.07
199	Information Studies (India)	40	1	2897	0.03	98.10
200	INICA (U.S.A.)	40	1	2898	0.03	98.14
201	INSPEC(U.S.A.)	40	1	2899	0.03	98.17

S. No.	Name of Journals	Rank No.	No. of Citations	Cumu. No. of Citations	% of Citations	Cumu.% of Citations
202	International Journal of Information Library Resources (U.S.A.)	40	1	2900	0.03	98.21
203	International Journal of Information Library & Science (Nigeria)	40	1	2901	0.03	98.24
204	International Journal of Science Education (U.S.A.)	40	1	2902	0.03	98.27
205	International Social Science Journal (U.S.A.)	40	1	2903	0.03	98.31
206	IOWA: Iowa Journal of Communication (U.S.A.)	40	1	2904	0.03	98.34
207	ISTE Newsletter(Indian Society for Technical Education) (India)	40	1	2905	0.03	98.37
208	Journal of Library and Information Science (India)	40	1	2906	0.03	98.41
209	Journal of Association of Computing Machinery (U.S.A.)	40	1	2907	0.03	98.44
210	Journal of Documentation Review (U.K.)	40	1	2908	0.03	98.48
211	Journal of Education and Social Change (India)	40	1	2909	0.03	98.51
212	Journal of Education Planning and Administration (India)	40	1	2910	0.03	98.54
213	Journal of Govt Information (India)	40	1	2911	0.03	98.58
214	Journal of Indian History (India)	40	1	2912	0.03	98.61
215	Journal of Indian Law Institute (India)	40	1	2913	0.03	98.65
216	Journal of Library History (U.S.A.)	40	1	2914	0.03	98.68
217	Journal of Maharashtra Agriculture University (India)	40	1	2915	0.03	98.71
218	Journal of Management Development (UK)	40	1	2916	0.03	98.75
219	Journal of Medical Library Association (U.S.A.)	40	1	2917	0.03	98.78

S. No.	Name of Journals	Rank No.	No. of Citations	Cumu. No. of Citations	% of Citations	Cumu.% of Citations
220	Journal of Science (Emerald) (U.K.)	40	1	2918	0.03	98.81
221	Journal of Youth Services in Libraries(U.S.A.)	40	1	2919	0.03	98.85
222	Journal of Administration (U.K.)	40	1	2920	0.03	98.88
223	Jurimetrics Journal (U.S.A.)	40	1	2921	0.03	98.92
224	Kisan World (India)	40	1	2922	0.03	98.95
225	Law Librarian (U.S.A.)	40	1	2923	0.03	98.98
226	Legal Studies Forum(U.S.A.)	40	1	2924	0.03	99.02
227	Librarian Journal (U.S.A.)	40	1	2925	0.03	99.05
228	Library Administration & Management (U.S.A.)	40	1	2926	0.03	99.09
229	Library Bulletin(U.S.A.)	40	1	2927	0.03	99.12
230	Long Range Planning (Netherlands)	40	1	2928	0.03	99.15
231	Maritime Library Association Bulletin –MLA (Canada)	40	1	2929	0.03	99.19
232	Michigan Bar Journal (U.S.A.)	40	1	2930	0.03	99.22
233	Micro Image117 (U.S.A.)	40	1	2931	0.03	99.25
234	Mousaion (U.S.A.)	40	1	2932	0.03	99.29
235	Nigeria Biblios (Nigeria)	40	1	2933	0.03	99.32
236	Nigeria Library Management (Nigeria)	40	1	2934	0.03	99.36
237	Nurse Education Today (Netherlands)	40	1	2935	0.03	99.39
238	OCLC Newsletter (U.S.A.)	40	1	2936	0.03	99.42
239	Online Information Review (U.K.)	40	1	2937	0.03	99.46
240	Open (U.K.)	40	1	2938	0.03	99.49
241	Operating Systems Review (U.S.A.)	40	1	2939	0.03	99.53
242	Physics Today (U.S.A.)	40	1	2940	0.03	99.56
243	Psychological Monograph (U.S.A.)	40	1	2941	0.03	99.59
244	Psychological Research Bulletin (U.S.A.)	40	1	2942	0.03	99.63
245	Reference Librarian (U.K)	40	1	2943	0.03	99.66
246	Research Libraries (U.S.A.)	40	1	2944	0.03	99.70

S. No.	Name of Journals	Rank No.	No. of Citations	Cumu. No. of Citations	% of Citations	Cumu.% of Citations
247	Research Policy (Netherlands)	40	1	2945	0.03	99.73
248	Research Quarterly (U.S.A.)	40	1	2946	0.03	99.76
249	Rivernia Library Review (Australia)	40	1	2947	0.03	99.80
250	Scientrometric (Netherlands)	40	1	2948	0.03	99.83
251	Social Welfare (U.S.A.)	40	1	2949	0.03	99.86
252	Spring (U.S.A.)	40	1	2950	0.03	99.90
253	The Hindu (India)	40	1	2951	0.03	99.93
254	Trilogia (U.S.A.)	40	1	2952	0.03	99.97
255	University of Illinois Bulletin (U.S.A.)	40	1	2953	0.03	100.00
	Total		**2953**	**2953**	**100.00**	**100.00**

9

Application of Bradford Law

9.1. INTRODUCTION

In order to observe the appropriateness of the distribution of journals using the verbal formulation of Bradford law, the following explanations are made and the results are presented. The first part deals with the verbal formulation of the theory based on data consisting whole journals/periodicals references, arranged by their decreasing frequency of citations while the second part examines the graphical representations based on the same data.

9.2. APPLICATION OF BRADFORD LAW IN BUNDELKHAND UNIVERSITY, JHANSI

To test the verbal formulation of Bradford's law tables are prepared with several details of journal citations. The numbers of cited journals are arranged by decreasing number of citations. The rank, number of journals, number of citations, cumulative citations, and log of cumulative number of journals are given in their respective tables.

Bradford's technique is used to group the journals in to three major zones of productivity and "Bradford's law of scattering", as discussed above, is applied to test the appropriateness of verbal formulation.

The distribution of journals and corresponding number of citations in the three zones along with the value of Bradford multiplier are shown in their respective tables.

9.2.1. Verbal Formulation

For testing the Bradford's law, the 281 journal titles (ranked by their decreasing order of productivity) are divided in to three approximately equal zones (p). Since Bradford assumes that there should be minimum three zones. i.e, when p = 3, then the value of k can be calculated using the formula $K = (e^{\gamma} * y_m)^{1/p}$

Application of Leimkuhler Model:

$$K = (e^{\gamma} * y_m)^{1/p}$$
$$= (1.781 * 245)^{1/3}$$
$$= (436.345)^{1/3} = 7.584$$
$$K = 7.58$$
$$y_0 = A / P$$
$$= 2048 / 3$$
$$y_0 = 682.67$$
$$r_0 = T\,(k\text{-}1) / (k^{\,p\text{-}1})$$
$$= 281(7.58 - 1) / (7.58)^3 - 1)$$
$$= 281(6.58) / (435.51 - 1)$$
$$= 1848.98 / 434.51$$
$$r_0 = 4.25$$
$$a = y_0 / \log k$$
$$= 682.67 / \log 7.58$$
$$= 682.67 / 0.8796$$
$$a = 775.81$$
$$b = k - 1/r_0 = (7.58\text{-}1) / 4.25$$
$$= 6.58 / 4.25$$
$$b = 1.55$$

Hence the law of Leimkuhlar for this data (when p = 3 then k = 7.58, r_0 = 4.25 and

y_0 = 682.67, a = 775.81, b = 1.55.)

Value of R (r) can be calculated using the formula R (r) = a log (1 + br)

a = 775.81, b = 1.55 and r = 1, 2, 3

.... (Cumulative No. of Journals)

R (r) = 775.81 log (1+1.55r)

(Values of R (r)..... showed in Chapter 11, Table-2

9.2.2. Bradford's Zones of Scattering

Table-1 show that, 4 journals covered 738 citations of journals, next 32 journals covered 844 citations of journals and the next 245 journals covered 466 citations of journals in total number of 2048 citations. It means 4 journals in the first zone or nucleus and they are the most productive journals devoted to Library & Information Science in Bundelkhand University. The second zone covered 32 journals and the third zone has represented by 245 journals. Each zone has approximately one third (1/3) of the total citations. Hence the journal distribution as per the Bradford's Law the ratio as 4:32:245.

Table 1. Bradford's Zones of Scattering : Bundelkhand University, Jhansi

Zones/ Groups	**No. of Journals**		**No. of citations**	**Bradford Multiplier**
First Zone	r_0=4.2 5 = 4	4	738	-
Second Zone	r_0 k = 4.25*7.58 =32.24	32	844	7.59
Third Zone	r_0 k² = 4.25 *7.58 *7.58 = 244.51	245	466	7.58
All Zones	281.00	281	2048	15.17/2 = 7.58*

Note : * mean value of Bradford Multiplier

The main purpose of this study is to test the two formulations of Bradford's law, verbal and graphical, to determine which one better fits citation data to the Library & Information Science in Bundelkhand University, Jhansi.

9.2.3. Graphical Representsation

Figure-1 provide a curve which categorically establishes the validity of Bradford's empirical law of Bibliometrics. The curve has been drawn by taking cumulative number of citations on the y-axis or vertical axis and logarithm of cumulative number of journals on the x-axis or horizontal axis respectively. Data for plotting this curve is based on informaton furnished in chapter 11, table-2.

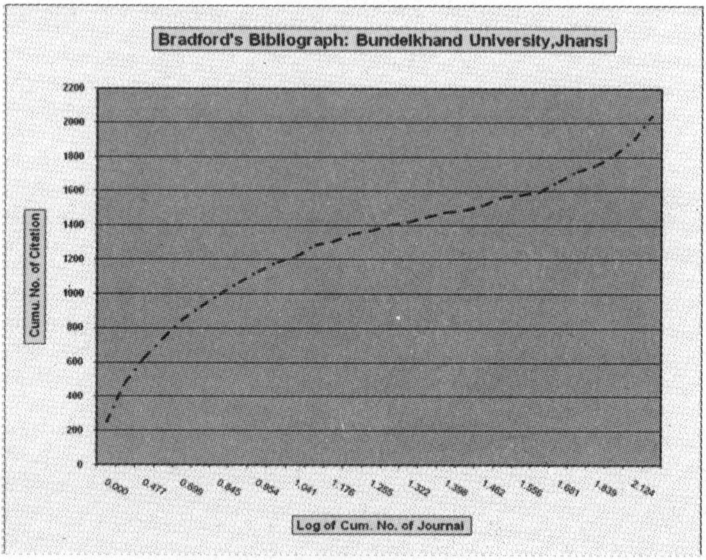

Fig. 1

9.3. APPLICATION OF BRADFORD LAW IN JIWAJI UNIVERSITY, GWALIOR

To test the verbal formulation of Bradford's law tables are prepared with several details of journal citations. The numbers of cited journals are arranged by decreasing number of citations. The rank, number of journals, number of citations, cumulative citations, and log of cumulative number of journals are given in their respective tables.

Bradford's technique is used to group the journals in to three major zones of productivity and "Bradford's law of scattering", as discussed above, is applied to test the appropriateness of verbal formulation. The distribution of journals and corresponding number of citations in the three zones along with the value of Bradford multiplier are shown in their respective tables.

9.3.1. Verbal Formulation

For testing the Bradford's law, the 543 journal titles (ranked by their decreasing order of productivity are divided in to three approximately equal zones (p), since Bradford assumes that there should be minimum three zones. i.e., when p = 3, then the value of k can be calculated using the formula $k = (e^{\gamma} * y_m)^{1/p}$.

Application of Leimkuhler Model

$$k = (e^{\gamma} * y_m)^{1/p} = (1.781 * 321)^{1/3}$$
$$= (571.701)^{1/3} = 8.30$$
$$k = 8.30$$
$$y_0 = A / P = 4665 / 3 = 1555$$
$$r_0 = T (k - 1) / (k^{p-1})$$
$$= 543(8.30 - 1) / (8.30)^3 - 1)$$
$$= 543(7.30) / (571.787 - 1)$$
$$= 3963.9 / 570.787$$
$$r_0 = 6.95$$
$$a = y_0 / \log k = 1555 / \log 8.30$$
$$= 1555 / 0.9190$$
$$a = 1691.95$$
$$b = k\text{-}1/r_0 = (8.30\text{-}1) / 6.95$$
$$= 7.30 / 6.95$$
$$b = 1.05$$

Hence the law of Leimkuhlar for this data (when p = 3. k = 8.30, r_0 = 6.95 and y_0 = 1555)

Value of R(r) can be calculated using the formula R(r) = a log (1 + br)

a = 1691.95, b = 1.05 and r = 1, 2, 3

... (Cumulative No. of Journals)

R (r) = 1691.95 log (1+1.05r)

(Values of R (r)..... showed in chapter 11, table-4)

1.3.2. Bradford's Zones of Scattering

Table-2 shows that, 7 journals covered 1538 citations of journals; next 58 journals covered 1639 citations of journals and the next 478 journals covered 1488 citations of journals in total number of 4665 citations. It means 7 journals in the first zone or nucleus are the most productive journals devoted to Library & Information Science in Jiwaji University, Gwalior. The second zone covered 58 journals and the third zone has represented by 478 journals. Each zone has approximately one third (1/3) of the total citations. Hence the journal distribution as per the Bradford's Law the ratio as 7:58:478.

Table 2. Bradford's Zones of Scattering: Jiwaji University, Gwalior

Zones/ Groups	No. of Journals		No. of citations	Bradford Multiplier
First Zone	r_0 = 6.95 = 7	7	1538	-
Second Zone	r_0 k = 6.95 * 8.30 = 57.64	58	1639	8.29
Third Zone	r_0 k^2 = 6.95 * 8.30 * 8.30 = 478.41	478	1488	8.30
All Zones	543.00	543	4665	16.59/ 2= 8.30*

Note : * mean value of Bradford Multiplier

The main purpose of this study is to test the two formulations of Branford's law, verbal and graphical, to determine which one better fits citation data to the Library & Information Science in Jiwaji University, Gwalior.

9.3.3. Graphical Representsation

Figure-2 provide a curve which categorically

establishes the validity of Bradford's empirical law of Bibliometrics. The curve has been drawn by taking cumulative number of citations on the y-axis or vertical axis and logarithm of cumulative number of journals on the x-axis or horizontal axis respectively. Data for plotting this curve is based on informaton furnished in chapter 11, table-4.

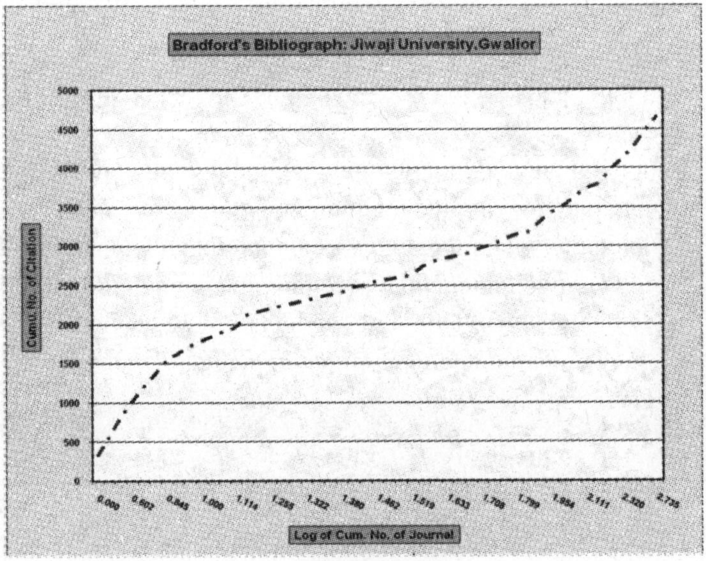

Fig. 2

9.4. APPLICATION OF BRADFORD LAW IN DR. HARISINGH GOUR UNIVERSITY, SAGAR

To test the verbal formulation of Bradford's law tables are prepared with several details of journal citations. The numbers of cited journals are arranged by decreasing number of citations. The rank, number of journals, number of citations, cumulative citations, and log of cumulative number of journals are given in their respective tables.

Bradford's technique is used to group the journals in to three major zones of productivity and "Bradford's law of scattering", as discussed above, is applied to test the appropriateness of verbal formulation. The distribution of journals and corresponding number of citations in the three zones along with the value of Bradford multiplier are shown in their respective tables.

9.4.1. Verbal Formulation

For testing the Bradford's law, the 255 journal titles (ranked by their decreasing order of productivity) are divided in to three approximately equal zones (p), since Bradford assumes that there should be minimum three zones. i.e., when $p = 3$, then the value of k can be calculated using the formula $k = (e^{\gamma} * y_m)^{1/p}$.

Application of Leimkuhler Model

$$k = (e^{\gamma} * y_m)^{1/p} = (1.781 * 351)^{1/3}$$
$$= (625.131)^{1/3} = 8.55$$
$$k = 8.55$$
$$y_0 = A / P = 2953/3 = 984.33$$
$$r_0 = T(k-1) / (k^{p-1}) = 255(8.55-1) / (8.55)^3-1)$$
$$= 255(7.55) / (625.026-1)$$
$$= 1925.25 / 624.026$$
$$r_0 = 3.08$$
$$a = y_0 / \log k = 984.33 / \log 8.55$$
$$= 984.33 / 0.9319 = 1056.16$$
$$a = 1026.16$$
$$b = k - 1/ r_0 = (8.55 - 1) / 3.08$$
$$= 7.55 / 3.08$$
$$b = 2.45$$

Hence the law of Leimkuhlar for this data (when p = 3. $k = 8.55$, $r_0 = 3.08$ and $y_0 = 984.33$.)

Value of R(r) can be calculated using the formula $R(r) = a \log (1+br)$

$a = 1026.16$, $b = 2.45$ and $r = 1, 2, 3$

... (Cumulative No. of Journals) then

$$R(r) = 1026.16 \log (1+2.45r)$$

(Values of R(r)..... showed in chapter 11, table-6.

9.4.2. Bradford's Zones of Scattering

Table-3 shows that, 3 journals covered 815 citations of journals; next 26 journals covered 1453 citations of journals and the next 226 journals covered 685 citations of journals in total number of 2953 citations. It means only 3 journals in the first zone or nucleus and they are the most productive journals devoted to Library & Information Science in Dr. Harisingh Gour University, Sagar. The second zone covered 26 journals and the third zone has represented by 226 journals. Each zone has approximately one third (1/3) of the total citations. Hence the journal distribution as per the Bradford's Law the ratio as 3:26:226.

Table 3. Bradford's Zones of Scattering : Dr. Harisingh Gour University, Sagar

Zones/ Groups	No. of Journals		No. of citations	Bradford Multiplier
First Zone	r_0 =3.08 = 3.08	3	815	-
Second Zone	r_0 k =3.08*8.55=26.33	26	1453	8.56
Third Zone	r_0 k² = 3.08 *8.55*8.55= 225.54	226	685	8.55
All Zones	= 255	255	2953	17.11/ 2= 8.55*5

Note : * mean value of Bradford Multiplier

The main purpose of this study was is to test the two formulations of Branford's law, verbal and graphical, to determine which one better fits citation data to the Library & Information Science in Dr. Harisingh Gour University, Sagar.

9.4.3. Graphical Representsation

Figure-3 provide a curve which categorically establishes the validity of Bradford's empirical law of Bibliometrics. The curve has been drawn by taking cumulative number of citations on the y-axis or vertical axis and logarithm of cumulative number of journals on the x-axis or horizontal axis respectively. Data for plotting this curve is based on informaton furnished in chapter 11, table-6.

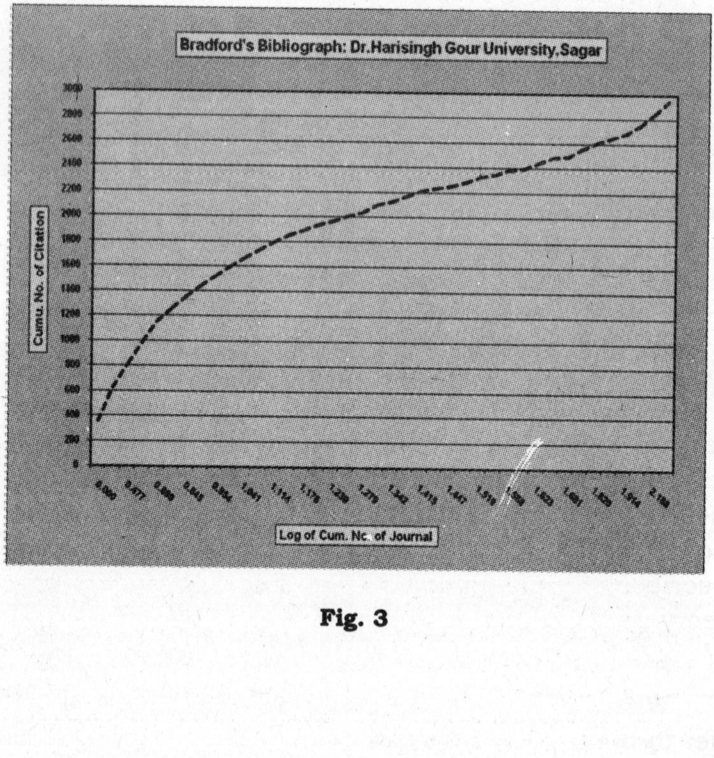

Fig. 3

10
Chi-square Test for Goodness

10.1. INTRODUCTION

The x^2 test (pronounced as chi-square test) is one of the simplest and most widely used non-parametric and most widely used non-parametric test in statistical work. The symbol x^2 is the Greek letter chi. The x2 test was first used by Karl Pearson in the year 1990.The quantity x2 describes the magnitude of the discrepancy between theory and observation. It is define as:

$$x^2 = (O-E)^2 / E$$

Where O refer to the observed frequencies and E refer to the expected frequencies.

Steps : To determine the value of x^2, the steps required are:

I. Calculate the expected frequencies. In general the expected frequency for any call can be calculated from the following equation:

$$E = \frac{RT * CT}{N}$$

E = Expected frequency

RT = the raw total for the row containing the cell

CT = the column total for the column containing the cell

N = the total Number of observations.

II. Take the difference between observed and expected frequencies and obtain the square of these differences, i.e. obtain the value of $(O-E)^2$

III. Divide the values of $(O-E)^2$ obtained in step (ii) by the respective expected frequency and obtain the total $\Sigma[(O-E)^2 /E]$. This gives the value of x^2 which can range from zero to infinity. If x^2 is zero it means that the observed and expected frequencies completely coincide. The greater the discrepancy between the observed and expected frequencies, the greater shall be the value of x^2.

The calculate value of x^2 is compared with the table value of x^2 for given degree of freedom at a certain specified level of significance. If at the stated level (generally 5% level is selected), the calculated value of x^2 is more than the table value of x^2, the difference between theory and observation is considered to be significant ,i.e., it could not have arisen due to fluctuations of simple sampling. If, on the other hand, the calculated value x^2 is less than the table value, the difference between theory and observation is not considered as significant, i.e. it is regarded as due to fluctuations of simple sampling and hence ignored. The computed value of x^2 is a random variable which takes on different values from sample to sample. That is x^2 has a sampling distribution just as do the other test statistics.

It should be noted that the value of x^2 is always positive and its upper limit is infinity. Also since x^2 is derived from observations, it is a statistic and not a parameter (there is no parameter corresponding to it).The x^2 test is, therefore, termed non-parametric. It is one of the great advantages of that test that it involves no assumption about the form of the original distribution from which the observation come.

Degrees of freedom

The use of a chi-square distribution also requires the use of degrees of freedom. Here, in an identical manner as with the t distribution, the sample size determines which distribution to use. If the sample size is n, then there are n -1 degrees of freedom.

10.2. CHI-SQUARE TEST FOR GOODNESS OF CITATION DISTRIBUTION DATA : BUNDELKHAND UNIVERSITY, JHANSI

Calculate the chi square statistic x^2 by completing the following steps:

1. For each observed number in the table subtract the corresponding expected number (O – E).
2. Square the difference $[(O - E)^2]$.
3. Divide the squares obtained for each cell in the table by the expected number for that cell $[(O - E)^2/E]$.
4. Sum all the values for $(O - E)^2 / E$. This is the chi square statistic.

$$x^2 = \sum \frac{(\text{Observed - Expected})^2}{\text{Expected}} \quad \text{OR}$$

The Leimkuhler's equation which is stated below has been used in Chi-Square test for goodness of data and computing the relevant statistics:

$x^2 = (O\text{-}E)^2 / E$

$x^2 = 0.479$ (As computed from Table -2)

$v = n - 1$ (Degree of Freedom d.f.)

Where n = 281

Then $v = 281\text{-}1$

$v = 280$ (d.f.)

If the sample size of n is large (>30), then we can use Fisher's approximation. Using the test statistic is:

$Z = \sqrt{2}\, x^2 - \sqrt{2x} - 1$

So, tabulated $x^2_{0.05}$ for 280 d.f. = 243.176

At 5% or 0.05 alpha level of significance for the table value x^2 is 0.479 much less than critical value for 0.05 probability level or table value of $x^2_{0.05}$ of 280 d.f. 243.176

Therefore calculated x2 < x20.05

0.479 < 243.176

Table 1. Hypothesis Verification: Bundelkhand University, Jhansi

Chi-Square Test Results	
Level of Significance	0.05
Sample Size	281
Degree of Freedom	280
Chi-Square Test Statistic	0.479
Critical Value	243.176
0.479 < 243.176	

Table-2 covered total number of 12 columns and every column calculated by Microsoft spreadsheet. First column is rank number of journals followed by second column number of journals, third column cumulative number of journals, forth column log of cumulative number of journals. Same as fifth column is number of citations and sixth column covered total number of citations. Observed values or cumulative number of citations showed in seventh column, expected values or Leimkuhlar R(r) showed in eighth column. Observed Proportion (O) showed in ninth column, expected proportion (E) showed in tenth column, difference of Observed proportion and expected proportion (O-E) showed in eleventh column. Squared Difference of $(O-E)^2/E$ showed in twelfth column.

The estimated values obtained from Leimkuhler formula, and cumulative number of citations as observed values. Observed and estimated values are shown in Table-2, For the fitness of citation distribution data, Chi-

Table 2. *Chi-Square Test for Goodness of Citation Distribution Data on Bradford's Law: Bundelkhand University, Jhansi*

1	2	3	4	5	6	7	8	9	10	11	12
Rank No.	**No. of Journals**	**Cum. No . of Journal**	**Log**	**No. of Citations**	**Total No. of Citations**	**Cumu.No. of Citations (r) OR Observed**	**Leimkuhlar (E) R(r) OR Expected**	**Observed Proportion (O)**	**Expected Proportion (E)**	**Difference (O-E)**	**Squared Difference $x^2 = \Sigma(O-E)^2)/E$**
1	1	1	0.000	245	245	245	315.398	0.120	0.154	-0.034	0.008
2	1	2	0.301	232	232	477	475.404	0.233	0.232	0.001	0.000
3	1	3	0.477	145	145	622	583.447	0.304	0.285	0.019	0.001
4	1	4	0.602	116	116	738	665.127	0.360	0.325	0.036	0.004
5	1	5	0.699	108	108	846	730.819	0.413	0.357	0.056	0.009
6	1	6	0.778	78	78	924	785.769	0.451	0.384	0.067	0.012
7	1	7	0.845	70	70	994	833.001	0.485	0.407	0.079	0.015
8	1	8	0.903	68	68	1062	874.419	0.519	0.427	0.092	0.020
9	1	9	0.954	63	63	1125	911.298	0.549	0.445	0.104	0.024
10	1	10	1.000	59	59	1184	944.536	0.578	0.461	0.117	0.030
11	1	11	1.041	32	32	1216	974.788	0.594	0.476	0.118	0.029
12	3	14	1.146	23	69	1285	1052.018	0.627	0.514	0.114	0.025
13	1	15	1.176	22	22	1307	1074.273	0.638	0.525	0.114	0.025
14	2	17	1.230	21	42	1349	1114.806	0.659	0.544	0.114	0.024
15	1	18	1.255	20	20	1369	1133.379	0.668	0.553	0.115	0.024
16	2	20	1.301	18	36	1405	1167.710	0.686	0.570	0.116	0.024

1	2	3	4	5	6	7	8	9	10	11	12
Rank No.	No. of Journals	Cum. No . of Journal	Log	No. of Citations	Total No. of Citations	Cumu.No. of Citations (r) OR Observed	Leimkuhlar (E) R(r) OR Expected	Observed Proportion (O)	Expected Proportion (E)	Difference (O-E)	Squared Difference $x^2 = \Sigma(O-E)^2)/E$
17	1	21	1.322	16	16	1421	1183.648	0.694	0.578	0.116	0.023
18	2	23	1.362	15	30	1451	1213.424	0.708	0.592	0.116	0.023
19	2	25	1.398	14	28	1479	1240.782	0.722	0.606	0.116	0.022
20	1	26	1.415	12	12	1491	1253.670	0.728	0.612	0.116	0.022
21	3	29	1.462	10	30	1521	1289.618	0.743	0.630	0.113	0.020
22	5	34	1.531	9	45	1566	1342.131	0.765	0.655	0.109	0.018
23	2	36	1.556	8	16	1582	1361.041	0.772	0.665	0.108	0.018
24	2	38	1.580	7	14	1596	1378.946	0.779	0.673	0.106	0.017
25	10	48	1.681	6	60	1656	1456.483	0.809	0.711	0.097	0.013
26	12	60	1.778	5	60	1716	1530.772	0.838	0.747	0.090	0.011
27	9	69	1.839	4	36	1752	1577.394	0.855	0.770	0.085	0.009
28	20	89	1.949	3	60	1812	1662.451	0.885	0.812	0.073	0.007
29	44	133	2.124	2	88	1900	1796.997	0.928	0.877	0.050	0.003
30	148	281	2.449	1	148	2048	2048.165	1.000	1.000	0.000	0.000
	281	**281**		**1432**	**2048**	**2048**					**0.479**

Square statistical test has carried out on the observed number of journals and articles to see if there is any significant difference in the observed and estimated value (for p = 3). The observed and estimated values obtained from the law of Leimkuhler are very close, and there is a positive fit of the Leimkuhler law in this citation distribution of data. The x^2 value obtained was 0.479 which is found to be less than the 243.176 the table chi-square value at 5% significance level.

10.3. CHI-SQUARE TEST FOR GOODNESS OF CITATION DISTRIBUTION DATA: JIWAJI UNIVERSITY, GWALIOR

The Leimkuhler's equation which is stated below has been used in Chi-Square test for goodness of data and computing the relevant statistics.

$x^2 = (O\text{-}E)^2 / E$

$x^2 = 0.069$ (As computed from Table-4)

$\nu = n - 1$ (Degree of Freedom d.f.)

Where $n = 543$

Then $\nu = 543\text{-}1$

$\nu = 542$ (d.f.)

If the sample size of n is large (>30), then we can use Fisher's approximation. Using the test statistic is: $Z = \sqrt{2}\, x^2 - \sqrt{2x\text{-}1}$

So, tabulated $x^2_{0.05}$ for 542 d.f. = 489.955

At 5 % or 0.05 alpha level of significance for the table value x^2 is 0.479 much less than critical value for 0.05 probability levelor table value $x^2_{0.05}$of 542 d.f. 489.955

Therefore calculated $x^2 < x^2_{0.05}$

$0.069 < 489.955$

Table 3. Hypothesis Verification: Jiwaji University, Gwalior

Chi-Square Test Results	
Level of Significance	0.05
Sample Size	543
Degree of Freedom	542
Chi-Square Test Statistic	0.069
Critical Value	489.955
0.069 < 489.955	

Table-4 shows total number of 12 columns and every column calculated by Microsoft spreadsheet. Column first is rank number of journals followed by column second number of journals, column third cumulative number of journals, and column forth log of cumulative number of journals. Same as column fifth is number of citations and column sixth covered total number of citations. Observed values or cumulative number of citations showed in column seventh, expected values or Leimkuhlar R(r) showed in column eighth. Observed proportion (O) showed in column ninth, expected proportion (E) showed in column tenth, difference of Observed proportion and expected proportion (O-E) showed in column eleventh. Squared Difference of $(O-E)^2/E$ showed in column twelfth.

The estimated values obtained from Leimkuhler formula and cumulative no. of citations as observed values. Observed and estimated values are shown in Table-4, For the fitness of citation distribution data, Chi-Square statistical test has carried out on the observed number of journals and articles to see if there is any significant difference in the observed and estimated value (for p=3). The observed and estimated values obtained from the law of Leimkuhler were very close, and there is a positive fit of the Leimuhler law in this citation distribution data. The x^2 value obtained was 0.069 which is found to be less than the 489.955, the table chi-square value at 5% significance level.

Table 4. Chi-Square Test for Goodness of Citation Distribution Data on Bradford's Law: Jiwaji University, Gwalior

1	2	3	4	5	6	7	8	9	10	11	12
Rank No.	**No. of Journals**	**Cum. No of Journal**	**Log**	**No. of Citations**	**Total No. of Citations**	**Cumu.No. of Citations (r) OR Observed**	**Leimkuhlar (E) R(r) OR Expected**	**Observed Proportion (O)**	**Expected Proportion (E)**	**Difference (O-E)**	**Squared Difference $x^2 = \Sigma(O-E)^2)/E$**
1	1	1	0.000	321	321	321	527.472	0.069	0.113	-0.044	0.017
2	1	2	0.301	247	247	568	831.359	0.122	0.178	-0.056	0.018
3	1	3	0.477	242	242	810	1045.706	0.174	0.224	-0.051	0.011
4	1	4	0.602	202	202	1012	1211.442	0.217	0.260	-0.043	0.007
5	1	5	0.699	189	189	1201	1346.589	0.257	0.289	-0.031	0.003
6	1	6	0.778	169	169	1370	1460.699	0.294	0.313	-0.019	0.001
7	1	7	0.845	168	168	1538	1559.447	0.330	0.334	-0.005	0.000
8	1	8	0.903	95	95	1633	1646.484	0.350	0.353	-0.003	0.000
9	1	9	0.954	91	91	1724	1724.294	0.370	0.370	0.000	0.000
10	1	10	1.000	67	67	1791	1794.648	0.384	0.385	-0.001	0.000
11	1	11	1.041	64	64	1855	1858.850	0.398	0.398	-0.001	0.000
12	1	12	1.079	61	61	1916	1917.891	0.411	0.411	0.000	0.000
13	1	13	1.114	59	59	1975	1972.539	0.423	0.423	0.001	0.000
14	3	16	1.204	50	150	2125	2115.648	0.456	0.454	0.002	0.000
15	1	17	1.230	42	42	2167	2157.763	0.465	0.463	0.002	0.000
16	1	18	1.255	39	39	2206	2197.594	0.473	0.471	0.002	0.000

1	2	3	4	5	6	7	8	9	10	11	12
Rank No.	**No. of Journals**	**Cum. No of Journal**	**Log**	**No. of Citations**	**Total No. of Citations**	**Cumu.No. of Citations (r) OR Observed**	**Leimkuhlar (E) R(r) OR Expected**	**Observed Proportion (O)**	**Expected Proportion (E)**	**Difference (O-E)**	**Squared Difference $x^2 = \Sigma(O-E)^2)/E$**
17	1	19	1.279	38	38	2244	2235.377	0.481	0.479	0.002	0.000
18	1	20	1.301	37	37	2281	2271.312	0.489	0.487	0.002	0.000
19	1	21	1.322	36	36	2317	2305.571	0.497	0.494	0.002	0.000
20	1	22	1.342	34	34	2351	2338.304	0.504	0.501	0.003	0.000
21	1	23	1.362	33	33	2384	2369.640	0.511	0.508	0.003	0.000
22	1	24	1.380	32	32	2416	2399.695	0.518	0.514	0.003	0.000
23	2	26	1.415	31	62	2478	2456.350	0.531	0.527	0.005	0.000
24	1	27	1.431	27	27	2505	2483.120	0.537	0.532	0.005	0.000
25	2	29	1.462	26	52	2557	2533.899	0.548	0.543	0.005	0.000
26	1	30	1.477	25	25	2582	2558.031	0.553	0.548	0.005	0.000
27	1	31	1.491	23	23	2605	2581.395	0.558	0.553	0.005	0.000
28	2	33	1.519	22	44	2649	2626.007	0.568	0.563	0.005	0.000
29	5	38	1.580	21	105	2754	2726.955	0.590	0.585	0.006	0.000
30	3	41	1.613	20	60	2814	2781.474	0.603	0.596	0.007	0.000
31	2	43	1.633	19	38	2852	2815.695	0.611	0.604	0.008	0.000
32	2	45	1.653	18	36	2888	2848.393	0.619	0.611	0.008	0.000
33	2	47	1.672	17	34	2922	2879.698	0.626	0.617	0.009	0.000
34	4	51	1.708	16	64	2986	2938.570	0.640	0.630	0.010	0.000
35	3	54	1.732	15	45	3031	2979.821	0.650	0.639	0.011	0.000

1	2	3	4	5	6	7	8	9	10	11	12
Rank No.	**No. of Journals**	**Cum. No of Journal**	**Log**	**No. of Citations**	**Total No. of Citations**	**Cumu.No. of Citations (r) OR Observed**	**Leimkuhlar (E) R(r) OR Expected**	**Observed Proportion (O)**	**Expected Proportion (E)**	**Difference (O-E)**	**Squared Difference $x^2 = \Sigma(O-E)^2)/E$**
36	5	59	1.771	14	70	3101	3043.811	0.665	0.652	0.012	0.000
37	4	63	1.799	13	52	3153	3091.271	0.676	0.663	0.013	0.000
38	3	66	1.820	12	36	3189	3124.956	0.684	0.670	0.014	0.000
39	12	78	1.892	11	132	3321	3246.098	0.712	0.696	0.016	0.000
40	12	90	1.954	10	120	3441	3350.067	0.738	0.718	0.019	0.001
41	9	99	1.996	9	81	3522	3419.401	0.755	0.733	0.022	0.001
42	15	114	2.057	8	120	3642	3522.145	0.781	0.755	0.026	0.001
43	15	129	2.111	7	105	3747	3612.268	0.803	0.774	0.029	0.001
44	10	139	2.143	6	60	3807	3666.743	0.816	0.786	0.030	0.001
45	35	174	2.241	5	175	3982	3830.759	0.854	0.821	0.032	0.001
46	35	209	2.320	4	140	4122	3964.764	0.884	0.850	0.034	0.001
47	53	262	2.418	3	159	4281	4130.162	0.918	0.885	0.032	0.001
48	103	365	2.562	2	206	4487	4373.037	0.962	0.937	0.024	0.001
49	178	543	2.735	1	178	4665	4664.283	1.000	1.000	0.000	0.000
	543	**543**		**4665**	**4665**	**4665**					**0.069**

10.4. CHI-SQUARE TEST FOR GOODNESS OF DATA DISTRIBUTION : DR. HARISINGH GOUR UNIVERSITY, SAGAR

The Leimkuhler's equation which is stated below has been used in Chi-Square test for goodness of data and computing the relevant statistics:

$x^2 = (O-E)^2 / E$

$x^2 = 0.419$ (As computed from Table-6)

$\nu = n-1$ (Degree of Freedom d.f.)

Where n = 255

Then $\nu = 255-1$

$\nu = 254$ (d.f.)

If the sample size of n is large (>30), then we can use Fisher's approximation. Using the test statistic is: $Z = \sqrt{2x^2} - \sqrt{2x - 1}$

So, tabulated $x^2_{0.05}$ for 254 d.f. = 219.025

At 5 % or 0.05 alpha level of significance for the table value x^2 is 0.479 much less than critical value for 0.05 probability levelor table value $x^2_{0.05}$of 254 d.f. 219.025.

Therefore calculated $x^2 < x^2_{0.05}$

$0.419 < 219.025$

Table 5. Hypothesis Verification
Dr. Harisingh Gour University, Sagar

Chi-Square Test Results	
Level of Significance	0.05
Sample Size	255
Degree of Freedom	254
Chi-Square Test Statistic	0.419
Critical Value	219.025
0.419 < 219.025	

Table-6 shows total number of 12 columns and every column calculated by Microsoft spreadsheet.

Column first is rank number of journals followed by column second number of journals, column third cumulative number of journals, and column forth log of cumulative number of journals. Same as column fifth is number of citations and column sixth covered total number of citations. Observed values or cumulative number of citations showed in column seventh, expected values or Leimkuhlar R(r) showed in column eighth. Observed Proportion (O) showed in column ninth, expected proportion (E) showed in column tenth, difference of Observed proportion and expected proportion (O-E) showed in column eleventh. Squared Difference of (O-E)) ^{2}/E showed in column twelfth.

The estimated values obtained from Leimkuhler formula and cumulative number of citations as observed values. Observed and estimated values are shown in Table-6, For the fitness of citation distribution data, Chi-Square statistical test has carried out on the observed number of journals and articles to see if there is any significant difference in the observed and estimated value (for p=3). The observed and estimated values obtained from the law of Leimkuhler were very close, and there is a positive fit of the Leimkuhler law in this citation distribution data. The x^2 value obtained was 0.419 which is found to be less than the 219.025 the table chi-square value at 5% significance level.

Table 6. Chi-Square Test for Goodness of Citation Distribution Data on Bradford's Law: Dr. Harisingh Gour University, Sagar

1	2	3	4	5	6	7	8	9	10	11	12
Rank No.	**No. of Journals**	**Cum. No of Journal**	**Log**	**No. of Citations**	**Total No. of Citations**	**Cumu.No. of Citations (r) OR Observed**	**Leimkuhlar (E) R(r) OR Expected**	**Observed Proportion (O)**	**Expected Proportion (E)**	**Difference (O-E)**	**Squared Difference $x^2 = \Sigma(O-E)^2)/E$**
1	1	1	0.000	351	351	351	568.023	0.119	0.192	-0.073	0.028
2	1	2	0.301	276	276	627	814.143	0.212	0.276	-0.063	0.015
3	1	3	0.477	188	188	815	973.448	0.276	0.330	-0.054	0.009
4	1	4	0.602	177	177	992	1091.461	0.336	0.370	-0.034	0.003
5	1	5	0.699	162	162	1154	1185.240	0.391	0.401	-0.011	0.000
6	1	6	0.778	111	111	1265	1263.061	0.428	0.428	0.001	0.000
7	1	7	0.845	91	91	1356	1329.575	0.459	0.450	0.009	0.000
8	1	8	0.903	85	85	1441	1387.654	0.488	0.470	0.018	0.001
9	1	9	0.954	83	83	1524	1439.199	0.516	0.487	0.029	0.002
10	1	10	1.000	78	78	1602	1485.531	0.542	0.503	0.039	0.003
11	1	11	1.041	68	68	1670	1527.611	0.566	0.517	0.048	0.004
12	1	12	1.079	64	64	1734	1566.152	0.587	0.530	0.057	0.006
13	1	13	1.114	61	61	1795	1601.704	0.608	0.542	0.065	0.008
14	1	14	1.146	57	57	1852	1634.698	0.627	0.554	0.074	0.010
15	1	15	1.176	41	41	1893	1665.477	0.641	0.564	0.077	0.011

1	2	3	4	5	6	7	8	9	10	11	12
Rank No.	**No. of Journals**	**Cum. No of Journal**	**Log**	**No. of Citations**	**Total No. of Citations**	**Cumu.No. of Citations (r) OR Observed**	**Leimkuhlar (E) R(r) OR Expected**	**Observed Proportion (O)**	**Expected Proportion (E)**	**Difference (O-E)**	**Squared Difference $x^2 = \Sigma(O-E)^2/E$**
16	1	16	1.204	40	40	1933	1694.319	0.655	0.574	0.081	0.011
17	1	17	1.230	37	37	1970	1721.455	0.667	0.583	0.084	0.012
18	1	18	1.255	36	36	2006	1747.075	0.679	0.592	0.088	0.013
19	1	19	1.279	33	33	2039	1771.339	0.690	0.600	0.091	0.014
20	2	21	1.322	31	62	2101	1816.326	0.711	0.615	0.096	0.015
21	1	22	1.342	25	25	2126	1837.267	0.720	0.622	0.098	0.015
22	2	24	1.380	24	48	2174	1876.481	0.736	0.635	0.101	0.016
23	2	26	1.415	20	40	2214	1912.605	0.750	0.648	0.102	0.016
24	1	27	1.431	19	19	2233	1929.653	0.756	0.653	0.103	0.016
25	1	28	1.447	18	18	2251	1946.090	0.762	0.659	0.103	0.016
26	2	30	1.477	17	34	2285	1977.297	0.774	0.670	0.104	0.016
27	3	33	1.519	16	48	2333	2020.454	0.790	0.684	0.106	0.016
28	1	34	1.531	14	14	2347	2033.982	0.795	0.689	0.106	0.016
29	3	37	1.568	13	39	2386	2072.326	0.808	0.702	0.106	0.016
30	1	38	1.580	12	12	2398	2084.426	0.812	0.706	0.106	0.016
31	4	42	1.623	11	44	2442	2129.869	0.827	0.721	0.106	0.015
32	5	47	1.672	9	45	2487	2180.991	0.842	0.739	0.104	0.015
33	1	48	1.681	8	8	2495	2190.565	0.845	0.742	0.103	0.014
34	9	57	1.756	7	63	2558	2268.779	0.866	0.768	0.098	0.012

1	2	3	4	5	6	7	8	9	10	11	12
Rank No.	**No. of Journals**	**Cum. No of Journal**	**Log**	**No. of Citations**	**Total No. of Citations**	**Cumu.No. of Citations (r) OR Observed**	**Leimkuhlar (E) R(r) OR Expected**	**Observed Proportion (O)**	**Expected Proportion (E)**	**Difference (O-E)**	**Squared Difference $x^2 = \Sigma(O-E)^2/E$**
35	9	66	1.820	6	54	2612	2335.579	0.885	0.791	0.094	0.011
36	7	73	1.863	5	35	2647	2381.546	0.896	0.806	0.090	0.010
37	9	82	1.914	4	36	2683	2434.593	0.909	0.824	0.084	0.009
38	25	107	2.029	3	75	2758	2556.122	0.934	0.866	0.068	0.005
39	47	154	2.188	2	94	2852	2722.608	0.966	0.922	0.044	0.002
40	101	255	2.407	1	101	2953	2953.447	1.000	1.000	0.000	0.000
	255	**255**		**2953**	**2953**	**2953**					**0.419**

10.5. REFERENCES

1. Gupta, S. P. (2001). Statistical methods. 13th revised edition, New Delhi: Sultan Chand & Sons. p.p 954-955.
2. http://enviroliteracy.org/pdf/materials/1210.pdf
3. http://uregina.ca/~gingrich/ch10.pdf
4. http://www.phy.ilstu.edu/slh/chi-square.pdf

11
Findings

11.1. INTRODUCTION

Citation study is of great help in formulating a result oriented acquisition policy for the librarians. It is important to know the users and their requirements. Citation analysis as a science is of recent origin and can be relied upon to provide trends and information about research efforts. Citation analysis makes use of bibliographic references, which form an active part of the primary literature and its analysis gives valuable results and serves manifold purposes. It is universally acknowledged that the number of references appended to research papers or theses are a valid indicator of its significance. References provide a club to the kind of material, the quality and age of the materials and how the material is being used.

Research in Science & Technology and Social Science is well established. However, need for research in Library & Information Science has not been fully recognized especially in developing countries like India.

The present study is a citation analysis of doctoral dissertations in the Library & information Science. These have been submitted in the departments of Library & Information Science, in the Universities of Bundelkhand region i.e. Bundelkhand University, Jhansi, Jiwaji University, Gwalior and Dr. Harisingh Gour University, Sagar. The aim of the study is to understand the characteristics of literature cited in the doctoral dissertations submitted by the research scholars in the Library& Information Science.

11.2. AVERAGE CITATIONS PER THESIS

Maximum number of theses submitted in Library & Information Science in universities of Bundelkhand region has been one hundred twenty eight (128). A Total number of citation from 128 theses accounted for 28249 citations.

Each thesis with an average citation of 220.70. In Bundelkhand University, Jhansi covers the 6198 citations in total number of 35 theses, followed by Jiwaji University, Gwalior 14767 in total number of 65 thesesand Dr. Harisingh Gour University, Sagar covers 7284 citations in total number of 28 theses.

An average of the citations studied shows that it is not necessary that the number of these would account for the number of citations as it is clear from the analysis that citations basically depend on the discipline.

11.3. BIBLIOGRAPHIC FORM DISPERSION

The analysis of the bibliographic form dispersion of citations identified from the Ph.D. theses submitted to the Universities of Bundelkhand region has been carried out in BundelkhandUniversity, Jhansi, Jiwaji University, Gwalior and Dr. Harisingh Gour University, Sagar.

Form dispersion analysis identified the use of as many as ten types of source forms in this research. It has been found that books/guides are most used bibliographical form in Bundelkhand University, Jhansi with 2566 (41.40%) and Jiwaji University, Gwalior with 6279 (42.52%), while journals are on top in Dr. Harisingh Gour University, Sagar with 2191 (40.54%).

Journals received the second position in their use and their percentage of use is 2048 (33.04%) in Bundelkhand University, Jhansi, and 4665 (31.59%) in Jiwaji University, Gwalior whereas the books are being ranked on number two in Dr. Harisingh Gour University, Sagar i.e.2953 (30.07 %).These two bibliographical forms of information resources make up almost 70% of the total citations.

Other bibliographical forms of information are like websites 585 (9.44%) fall on third position and conferences proceedings with 378 (6.10%) on fourth position. Letters/Lectures on fifth position with 155 (2.50%), reports with 134 (2.16%) on sixth position followed by govt. publications with 104 (1.68%), on seventh position, theses with 72 (1.16%) on eight positions, case study/survey with 48 (0.77%), on ninth position and reference sources with 108 (1.74%) on tenth position, have been cited in the field of library science research in Bundelkhand University, Jhansi.

The ranking of other bibliographic forms being cited by the researches in Jiwaji University, Gwalior has been found that conference proceedings are 879 (5.95%) on third position, followed by reports 769 (5.21%) on fourth position, web sites 596 (4.04%)on fifth position, govt. publications 573 (3.88%), on sixth position reference sources 533 (3.61%) on seventh position, theses 265 (1.79%) on eight position, letters/lectures 153 (1.04%) on ninth position, and case studies with 55 (0.37%) on position tenth.

Similarly in Dr. Harisingh Gaur University, Sagar it has been found that reports are 513 (7.04%) on third position, conference proceedings with 457 (6.27%) on fourth position. Reference sources are 411 (5.64%) on fifth position followed by theses 221 (3.03%) on sixth position, case study/survey with 208 (2.86%) on seventh position, govt. publications with 158 (2.17%) on eight positions, web sites with 158 (2.17%) on ninth position, and letters/lectures 14 (0.19%) tenth on position.

11.4. AUTHOR DISPERSION

The author wise dispersion of citations in Library & Information Science brings forth the finding that single authorship is a common practice which is supplemented by a good number of two authors also. Thus the maximum used books are of single authorshipwhile the least number is of books written by three authors in the discipline Library & Information Science.

As regards the authorship pattern, preference to the single authorship pattern secures the highest position is noticed in the books being cited in Library & Information Science in all the three universities viz: Bundelkhand University, Jhansi with 1764 (68.75%); Jiwaji University, Gwalior with 4928 (78.48%) & Dr. Harisingh Gour University, Sagar with 1703 (77.73%). Second highest position covers the two authorship in Bundelkhand University, Jhansi with 589 (22.95%); Jiwaji University, Gwalior with 1066 (16.98%) & Dr. Harisingh Gour University, Sagar with 409 (18.67%) followed by more than three authors pattern on third position in Bundelkhand University, Jhansi 127 (4.95%); Jiwaji University, Gwalior 185 (2.94%) & Dr. Harisingh Gour University, Sagar with 54 (2.46%) and fourth position is covered by three authors in Bundelkhand University, Jhansi with 86 (3.35%); Jiwaji University, Gwalior with 100 (1.59%) & Dr. Harisingh Gour University, Sagar with 25 (1.14%) of total citations.

11.5. DEGREE OF AUTHORSHIP COLLABORATION

The degree of collaboration in discipline of Library & Information Science in Bundelkhand University, Jhansi is 0.31, in Jiwaji University, Gwalior is 0.21 and in Dr. Harisingh Gour University, Sagar is 0.22. This reflects the degree of prevalence of single authored publication in this discipline.

11.6. TIME DISPERSION OF BOOKS

The analysis of chronological distribution of citations of books can indicate the currency of the literature being used in research. All the 11036 citations of book document collect from three universities in their research output are arranged in decreasing chronological order. All theses citations fall into nine sequences covered from 1926 to 2009. The latest year is 2006-2009 and the oldest year is 1926-1935.Citations fall into first and last group respectively.

A finding of the analysis of the time dispersion of citations of books in Library & Information Science indicates towards the years 1986-1995 as the most productive year having published maximums literature used by researchers in all three universities covered in study as Bundelkhand University, Jhansi with 683 (26.62%), in Jiwaji University, Gwalior with 1729 (27.54%) and Dr. Harisingh Gour University, Sagar with 749 (34.19%).Next productive years seems to be during 1975-1985 as Bundelkhand University, Jhansi with 616 (24.01%), in Jiwaji University, Gwalior with 1672 (26.63%) and Dr. Harisingh Gour University, Sagar 506 (23.09%). Third productive span is of 1996-2005 in citations of Bundelkhand University, Jhansi with 589 (22.95%) and Dr. Harisingh Gour University, Sagar with 461 (21.04%), but third productive years of Jiwaji University, Gwalior is during 1966-1975 covering 1163 (18.52%) of citations. These sequences have got the largest number of citations.

Study shows the literature that is most significant from the library & information scientist's point of view belongs to the 1986-1995, 1976-1985, and 1996-2005.

Productive year having published literature less used by researchers in Bundelkhand University, Jhansi as 1956-1965 covered 136 (5.30%) of citations, followed by years 1946-1955 covered 49 (1.91%) of citations, years 1936-1945 covered 24 (0.94%) of citations, and years

1926-1935 covered 15 (0.58%) of citations out of total citations.

Productive year having published literature less used by researchers in Jiwaji University, Gwalior as 1996-2005 covered 650 (10.35%) of citations, followed by years 1956-1965 covered 589 (9.38%) of citations, years 1946-1955 covered 303 (4.83%) of citations, and years 1936-1945 covered 93 (1.48%) of citations, during 1926-1935 with 51 (0.81%) out of total citations. 2006-2009 with 29 (0.46%).

Productive year having published literature less used by researchers in Dr. Harisingh Gour University, Sagar as 1966-1975 covered 265 (12.09%) of citations, followed by years 1956-1965 covered 122 (5.57%) of citations, years 2006-2009 covered 32 (1.46%) of citations, and years 1946-1955 covered 29 (1.32%) of citations 1936-1945 with 16 (0.73%), 1926-1935with 11 (0.50%) out of total citations.

11.7. TIME DISPERSION OF JOURNAL ARTICLES

All the 9,666 citations of journals by 128 scholars collect from three universities in their research output are arranged in decreasing chronological order. All these citations fall into nine sequences from 1926-2009 Years 2006-2009 latest citations fall into first and 1926-1935 oldest group respectively.

Citation analysis of the journals used by researchers of Library & Information Science in all three universities covered in present study. The study reveals that literature published during years 1986-1995 is most productive period and covered first position in all three universities. Bundelkhand University, Jhansi with 652 (31.84%) of citations, in Jiwaji University, Gwalior with 1379 (29.56%) of citations and Dr. Harisingh Gour University, Sagar with 996 (33.73%) of citations.

Next productive years seems to be during 1976-

1985 in Bundelkhand University, Jhansi covered 573 (27.98%) of citations followed by time span of 1996-2005 on third position which covered 456 (22.27%) of citations, years 1966-1975 on fourth position and covered 219 (10.69%) of citations, and years 1956-1965 on fifth position which covered 97 (4.74%) of citations, years 1946-1955 on sixth position and covered 32 (1.56%) of citations, years 1936-1945 on seventh position and covered 11(0.54%) of citations, years 1926-1935 on eight position, covered 5 (0.24%) of citations, and years 2006-2009 on last position which covered only 3 (0.15%) out of total citations.

Second productive years seems to be during 1976-1985 in Jiwaji University, Gwalior covered 1250 (26.80%) of citations followed by years 1966-1975 on third position and covered 860 (18.44%) of citations, years 1996-2005 on fourth position and covered 499 (10.70%) of citations, and years 1956-1965 on fifth position and covered 396 (8.49%) of citations , years 1946-1955 on sixth position and covered 173 (3.71%) of citations, years 1936-1945 on seventh position and covered 78 (1.67%) of citations, years 1926-1935 and years 2006-2009 on last eight position and covered same 15 (0.32%) of citations out of total citations

Similarly second productive years seems to be during 1996-2005 in Dr. Harisingh Gour University, Sagar and covered 737(24.96%) of citations followed by years 1976-1985 on third position covered 618 (20.93%) of citations, years 1966-1975 on fourth position and covered 354 (11.99 %) of citations, and years 1956-1965 on fifth position and covered 171 (5.79%) of citations , years 1946-1955 on sixth position and covered 34 (1.15%) of citations ,years 2006-2009 in seventh position and covered 33 (1.12%) of citations, years 1926-1935 on eight position and covered 8 (0.27%) of citations, years 1936-1945 on ninth position and covered 2 (0.07%) of citations out of total citations.

11.8. COUNTRYWISE DISPERSION (JOURNAL ARTICLES)

In journals publications of Library & Information Science in Bundelkhand University, Jhansi. Maximum literature consulted in Bundelkhand University seems to be U.S.A. literature with 122 (43.42%). India with 47 (16.73%) and U.K. with 46 (16.37%) on the second and third position in journals publications in field of Library & Information Science. Netherlands is covered fourth position with 25 (8.90%) in journals publications. Canada is on fifth position with 6 (2.14%), Australia with 5 (1.78%) covered sixth position, West Germany and Japan both of countries covered same position i.e. seventh with 4 (1.42%).The rest of the countries like Africa, China, Europe, Jamaica, New Zealand and Pakistan covered 2 (0.71%) while Brazil, Denmark, France, East Germany, Jordan, Korea, Russia, Slovenia, South Africa, Sweden scored only 1(0.36%).

As regards country wise distribution of 543 ranked journals covering 4665 citations, in Library & Information Science at Jiwaji University, Gwalior, U.S.A.is on top with 256 (47.15%) of citations followed by India on second position with 105 (19.34%) of citations, U.K. is on third position with 83 (15.29%) of citations, followed by Netherlands with 31 (5.71%) of citations, Australia with 12 (2.21%) of citations gets fourth and fifth position, Canada on sixth position with 9 (1.66%) of citations and Europe obtain seventh position with 7 (1.29%) of citations. West Germany and Japan have obtain same position i.e. eight with 6 (1.10%) of citations followed by Brazil, Pakistan, Russia covered with 3 (0.55%) of citations are in ninth position, Malaysia, Nigeria, Singapore, South Africa scored tenth position with 2 (0.37%) and rest of countries like Africa, China, Colombia, East Germany, Egypt, France, Iran, Korea, Newzeland, Slovenia and Taiwan have covered 1 (0.18%)of citation and are on last position.

Country wise distribution of the citations in Library and Information science at Dr. Harisingh Gour University, Sagar. U.S.A. with 144 (44.71%) on first position in journals publications, followed by India on second position with 59 (23.14%) of citations, U.K. on third position with 41(16.08%) of citations, Netherlands on fourth position with 13 (5.10%) of citations, Australia on fifth position with 8 (3.14%) of citations, Canada on sixth position with 5 (1.96%) of citations, Nigeria on seventh position with 4 (1.57%) of citations, South Africa eight on position with 3 (1.18 %) of citations, West Germany on ninth position with 2 (0.78%)of citations. It is to be noted that Taiwan Africa, France, Japan, Pakistan, South Australia covered last tenth position with 1(0.39%) out of total number of citations.

The above study shows that countries : U.S.A., India, U.K., Netherlands, Australia and Canada have got the same order in country wise distribution of journal in case of Bundelkhand University, Jhansi, Jiwaji University, Gwalior and Dr. Harisingh Gour University, Sagar.

11.9. RANKING OF JOURNALS

Ranking of journals using Ph.D. theses as sources data reflects the local needs as the prime criterion. In Library & Information Science, the first ten important journals of the ranking list in Bundelkhand University, Jhansi are ILA Bulletin on first rank with 245(11.96%), Library Herald on second rank with 232 (11.33%), Journal of Documentation on third rank with 145 (7.08%), Annals of Library Science and Documentation on fourth rank with 116(5.66 %), IASLIC Bulletin on fifth rank with 108 (5.27%), Library Trends on sixth rankwith 78(3.81 %), University News on seventh rank with 70 (3.42%), Bulletin of Medical Library Association on eight rank with 68 (3.32 Journal of American Society for Information Science and Technology on ninth rank with 63(3.08%), and Library Science with Slant to Documentation on tenth rank with

59(2.88%), respectively.The first ten journals in the ranking list together account for 57.81% of citations; however, analysis shows that first 50 Journals accounted for nearly 81.35% of citations in total of 281 journals. The first ten journals in ranking list of Bundelkhand University, Jhansi, seven journals belong to India, two from U.S.A. and one from U.K.

In the ranking of the journals in Jiwaji University, Gwalior, it is to be noted ASLIB Proceeding on first rank with 321(6.88%), Annals of Library science Documentation with 247(5.29%) occupy the second rank, followed by IASLIC Bulletin occupy third rank with 242 (5.19%), College and Research Libraries occupy fourth rank with 202(4.33%), Herald of Library Science occupy fifth rank with 189(4.05%), Library Herald occupy sixth rank with 169 (3.62%), ILA Bulletin occupy seventh rank with 168 (3.60%), Journal of Documentation occupy eight rank with 95 (2.04%), Library Journal occupy ninth rank with 91 (1.95%), Indian Libraries occupy tenth rank with 67 (1.44%) respectively. The first ten journals in the ranking list together account for 38.39 % of the total citations. However, study shows that first 50 Journals accounted for nearly 63.66 % out of total citations. The first ten important journals in ranking list of Jiwaji University, Gwalior, six journals belong to India, two from U.S.A. and two from U.K.

Ranking of journals using in Ph.D. theses as source data at Dr. Harisingh Gour University, Sagar is as follows IASLIC Bulletin with 351(11.89%), is a journal which is ranked as the most preferred journal, ILA Bulletin with 276(9.35%) covers the second rank, followed by University News on third rank with 188(6.37%), Herald of Library Science at fourth rank with 177(5.99%), Library Herald got fifth rank with 162(5.49%), Annals of Library Science Studies covers sixth rank with 111(3.76%), Annals of Library Science & Documentation covers seventh rank with 91(3.08%), Journal of Documentation covers eight rank with 85(2.88%), DESIDOC Bulletin of Information Technology covers ninth rank with 83(2.81%), Library Science with a slant to Documentation got tenth rank with 78(2.64%) respectively. Study shows that the first ten journals in the ranking list together account for 54.25% out of total citations. However, first 50 Journals accounted for nearly 84.96% of total citations. The first ten important journals in ranking list of Dr. Harisingh Gour University, Sagar, nine journals belong to India, and only one from U.K.

First 20 core journals identified in each University, 10 are common journals belonged to India in all the three lists of journals; these are the most popular journals in the field of Library & Information Science in India. And therefore it may be concluded that atleast these ten title of journals be procured by all institutions associated with LIS training.

In Bundelkhand University, Jhansi, ILA Bulletin with (11.96%), the most preferred journal has been cited 245 times, however in Jiwaji University, Gwalior, ASLIB Proceeding with (6.88%), as the most preferred journal having been cited 321 times and in Dr. Harisingh Gour University, Sagar, IASLIC Bulletin with (11.89%), as the most preferred journals having been cited 351 times.

11.10. BRADFORD'S LAW

By applying the Bradford's Law, the number of core journals in different branches of Library & Information Science under are determined. The number of core journals in Library & Information science at BundelkhandUniversity, Jhansi is 4 whereas the same for Library & Information science at Jiwaji University, Gwalior is 7 and Dr. Harisingh Gour University, Sagar is 3. Hence the journal distribution as per the Bradford's Law the ratio of three zones in Bundelkhand University, Jhansi as 4:32:245, Jiwaji University, Gwalior 7:58:478 and Dr. Harisingh Gour University, Sagar, 3:26:226.

Hence it is observed that the journal usage pattern in the LIS in Bundelkhand University, Jhansi, Jiwaji University, Gwalior and Dr. Harisingh Gour University, Sagar donot satisfy with Bradford's Law of scattering. This may be due to the heavy concentration of citations in a few journals. The Productivity of journals in LIS shows the concertration of more number of citations in a few journals. It is evidence that the number of journals/ titles in each zone is not increasing geometrically.

The observed value is much less compared to the tabular value in all three cases. This is found that in Bundelkhand University, Jhansi observed value 0.479 much less than the tabular value 243.176, Jiwaji University, Gwalior observed value 0.069 much less than the tabular value 489.955 and the same in Dr. Harisingh Gour University, Sagar observed value 0.419 much less than the tabular value 219.025 respectively.It is proved that application of chi-square test hold good in all cases.

Bradford's law is not only about quatitative issues but also about qualitative issues.The most productive journals on a subject are also the best journals and thus the journals that should be selected by libraires and users.Bradford's law is not claiming that scattering is the same from one subject to another. Bradford's law has been regarded as identical with other bibliographic laws and also with laws in quite different domains.

Library & Information Science has an important role to play in the eduaction process,creation of new knowledge in Library &Information Sciecne, solution to the problems faced by Librarians/documantalists/ information scientists. Fresh impetus to research programmes will enable the profession to achieve greater academic,professional and social respect which it still lacks in India.

As a result, theses are analyzed as the serve the best represantation of the research intrest of LIS researchers at Bundelkhand region.The current collection proved to encompass a large varity of the materials cited by the doctoral students.

Citation studies do provide some guide lines for the librarians and informations scientists in the decision making process in their acquistion policy.The exponential growth of knowledge,ever escalating costs of the documents,limited allocation of budgets are some of the factors that are leading the librarians and information scientists to adopt statistical and mathematical techniques for decision making process.

Citation of document implies use of that document by the citing author but it should be evident to anyone who has written a paper that citation does not necessarily fully and faithfully reflect usage. Often what is cited is only a small percentage of what is read not all that is read found useful is cited. Citation reflects the merit underlying assumption in the use of citation counts as quality indicators is that there is a high positive correlation between the author of citations which a particular document .The use of citation analysis for evaluation, the difficulty is that quality is a complex attributed, and there generally is no single widely accepted non-bibliometric measures. A paper might well have been cited because it happened to be on the citer's desk rather than because it was the ideal paper to cite. Researchers cited do not necessarily represent the most outstanding in a particular field instead anything which enhances a researcher's visibility is likely to increase his citation rate, irrespective of the intrinsic quality of his work. A cited document is related in content to the citing document to the extent that citation indexes can be used to retrieve relevant citing documents. Bibliographic coupling is merely an indication of the existence of the probability (possibly zero) of a relationship in the content of the two documents and similarly two papers co-cited do not guarantee a relationship between their contents.

Inspite of the above fact there is no doubt that these finding shall be much helpful for librarians and information scientists while taking decisions regarding collection development, removing out journals and also in maintaining of need based collection in the libraries.

Knowing which resources doctoral students required should enable collection managers to more adequately serve them.The study would help librarians to determine the material being used at our libraries. Ultimately it is also assumed that it leads to an improved collection for future scholars of Library & Information Science.

Although the study has been carried at a regional level, it would be beneficial to replicate this study at some other universities in the same region and compare the results. The results would be helpful to large and small universities to build up their existing collection in field of Library & Information Science.

Selected Bibliography

1. Balrup, J. (1969).Mechanization of library procedures in the medium sized medial library VII:relevancy of cited articles in citation indexing. *Bulletin of Medical Library Association, 57 (3),* 260-263.
2. Bates, Marcia, J. Bates, & Maack, Mary Niles. (Eds.). (2009). *Encyclopedia of Library and Information Sciences.* (3rd ed.). *California*: Taylor& Francis.DOI: 10.1081/E-ELIS3.ISBN: 0-8493-9712-X; eISBN: 0-8493-9711-1.Retrieved August 28, 2011 from http://www.crcpress.com/product/isbn/9780849397127.
3. Bradford, S.C. (1934). Sources of information on specific subjects. *Engineering, 137 (3550),* 85-86.
4. Bradford, S.C. (1950).*Documentation.*Washington, D C: Washington Affairs Press.
5. Bradford. S. C. (1985). Sources of information on specific subjects. *Journal of Information Science, 10(4),* 176-180.
6. Branin, J. (2009). What we need is a knowledge management perspective. *College &Research Libraries,70(2),* 104-5.
7. Brookes, B.C. (1969).Bradford's law and bibliography of science. *Nature, 232(5223),* 955.
8. Brookes, B.C.(1968). Derivation and application of

Bradford-Zipf distribution. *Journal of Documentation, 24 (4),* 247-65.

9. Burton, R.E.,& Kebler, R.W. (1960). The half-life of some scientific and technical literature. *American Documentation, 11 (1),* 18 –22,

10. Chakraborty, Susmita, & Sarkhel, J. K. (2009, August 23-27). *LIS education in India: an appraisal of the* on world library and information congress: 75th IFLA.Retrieved June 28, 2011 fromhttp://conference.ifla.org/past-wlic/2009/86-chakraborty-en.pdf.**11.** Chandrasekhar, M.,& Ramasesh, C.P. (2009). *Library and information science research in India.*Asia-Pacific Conference on Library & Information Education & Practice, *530-534.* Retrieved August 23, 2011, from http://www.tulips.tsukuba.ac.jp/dspace/bitstream/2241/102596/2/PS_11.pdf

12. Chikate, R.V.,& Patil, S.K. (2008).Citation Analysis of theses in library and information science submitted to university of Pune: a pilot study. *Library Philosophy and Practice.*1-15. Retrieved June 28, 2011 from *http://unllib.unl.edu/LPP/chikate-patil.htm*

13. Clark, C.V. (1976).Obsolescent of the patient literature. *Journal of Documentation, 32 (1),* 32-52.

14. De Solla Price, Derek J.(1976). A general theory of bibliometric and other cumulative advantage process. *Journal of American Society Information Science, 27,* 292-306.

15. Dunlop, L.W. (1952).Services to readers. *Library Trends, 1, 27.*

16. Edge, D. (1977). Why I am not a co-citation list. *Society for Social Studies of Science Newsletter, 1,* 13-19.

17. Gagolewski, M. (2011). Bibliometric impact

assessment with R and the CITAN package. *Journal of Informatics, 5(4), 678-692.* doi: 10.1016/ j.joi.2011.06.006. Retrieved from *www.science direct.com.*

18. Ghai, Daljit. (2001). *Citation analysis of Ph.d. dissertations in library and information science submitted to the Universities of Madhya Pradesh & Punjab.* (Doctoral dissertation. Jiwaji University, Gwalior. 2001).
19. Gross, P.L.K.,& Gross, E.M. (1927).College libraries and chemical education. *Science, 66(*27), 385- 389.
20. Gupta, B. M., & Bhattacharya, Sujit. (2004, January). Abibliometric approach towards mapping the dynamics of science and technology. *DESIDOC Bulletin of Information Technology,24 (1),* 3-8.
21. Gupta, S.C.,& Kapoor, V.K. (2002).*Fundamentals of mathematical statistics.* New Delhi: Sultan Chand & Sons.
22. Hamermesh, D.S. Johnson, G.E.,& Weisbrod, B.A. (1982). Scholorship, citations and salaries: economic rewards in economics. *Southern Economics, 49,* 472-81,
23. Haridashan, Sudarma. (2003).*Citation analysis of doctoral dissertation submitted in social sciences at Bundelkhand University, Jhansi (U.P.).* (Doctoral dissertation. Bundelkhand University, 2003).
24. http://www.bujhansi.
25. http://www.csl.du.ac.in
26. http://www.dis.sci.ntu.edu.sg/cisap/schools/india.htm
27. http://www.dl.acm.org
28. http://www.dspace.vidyanidhi.org.in
29. http://www.elsevier.com/locate/infoproman.
30. http://www.emeraldinsight.com

31. http://www.google.com
32. http://www.gslis.utexas.edu/~palmquis/courses/biblio.html
33. http://www.ifla.Org/Annual-Conference/Ifla75/Index.
34. http://www.ifla.org/IV/ifla70/prog04.htm
35. http://www.indiastudycenter.com/univ/distance-education.asp
36. http://www.inflibnet.ac.in/econ
37. http://www.infolibrarian.com
38. http://www.jiwaji.edu
39. http://www.library.iitb.ac.in
40. http://www.lislinks.com
41. http://www.sagaruniversity.nic.in
42. http://www.sciencedirect.com
43. http://www.scopus.com
44. http://www.ulrichsweb.com
45. http://www.vidyanidhi.org.in
46. Hulme, E.W. (1923). *Statistical bibliography in relation to growth of modern civilization.* London: Grafton.
47. Jones, et. al. (1972). Characteristics of the literature used by the Historians. *Journal of Librarianship, 4,* 137-139.
48. Kannappanavar, B.U. (1991). *Citation Analysis of Doctoral Dissertations in Library and Information Science accepted by the Universities in Karnataka.* (Doctoral Dissertation, Karnatak University. Dharwad, 1991).
49. Kawatra, P.S. (2008). *Textbook of information science.* New Delhi: APH Publishing Corporation.
50. Khanna, J.K. (1987). *Library and Society.* Kurushetra: Research Publication.

51. Kothari, C.R. (2011). *Research methodology: methods and techniques.* New Delhi: New Age International (P) LTD Publishers.

52. Krishnaswamy, K.N., Sivakumar, Appa Iyer, & Mathirajan. (2006).*Management research methodology: integration of principles, methods and techniques.* New Delhi: Pearson.

53. Kumar, Suresh,& Sahai, Ramanath. (2011).*Oxford english-english-hindi dictionary.* New Delhi: Oxford University Press.

54. Martyn, J. (1976). Citation analysis. *Journal of Documentation, 31*,290-297.

55. McCain, K.W. (1986).The paper trails of scholarship: mapping the literature of genetics, *Lib. Quart., 56,* 258-271.

56. Menard, H.W. (1971).*Science: growth and change.* Cambridge: Harvard University Press.

57. More, Philip M.,& Leimkular, Ferdinard F. (1979).Technical note: Exact solution for the Bradford distribution and it use in modeling informational data. *Oper Res. 27 (1),* 187-98.

58. Panneerselvam, R. (2011). *Research Methodology.* New Delhi: PHI Learning Pvt. Ltd.

59. Patel, Jasu,&Krishan Kumar.(2001). *Libraries and librarianship in India.* London: Greenwood Press.

60. Price, D.J.D. (1961). *Science since Babylon.* New Haven: Yale University Press.

61. R.R. Bowker Company. (1999). (45th ed.). *Ulrich's international periodicals directory.* New York: Bowker.

62. Ravichandra Rao, I. K. (1983).*Quantitative methods in Library and Information Science.* New Delhi: Wiley Eastern,p196.

63. Sandison Line, M.B.A. (1975).Obsolescence and

changes in use of literature with time. *J. Docum., 30 (3),* 283-350.

64. Satija, M.P. (1999).Doctoral Research in Library and Information Science in India:Some Observations and Comments. *Libri,* 49, 236–242.Retrieved from www.librijournal.org/pdf/1999-4pp236-242.pdf

65. Shivalingaiah, D., Sheshadri, K. N., &Keralapura, Manjunatha. (2009).*LIS Research in India 1980-2007: An Analysis of Doctoral Dissertations.*Asia-Pacific Conference on Library & Information Education & practice,168.Retrievedfromwww.slis.tsukuba.ac.jp/~atsushi/a-iep/proceedings/Papers/a9.pdf

66. Small, H.G. (1973).Co-citation in the scientific literature: a new measure of the relationship between two documents. *Journal of American Social Information Science, 24(4),* 265-256.

67. Smith.L.C. *(1981).Citation analysi. Library Trends, 30(1), 83-106.*Retrieved 30 June 2011 from citeseerx.ist.psu.edu/viewdoc/download?doi=10.1.1.172...

68. Sudhier, K.G. (2010, December). Bradford's law of Scattering Revisited: A study based on the References in Doctoral theses in the area of Physics. *Collnet Journal of Scientometric and Information Management,* 4(2), 1-15.

69. Sudhier, K.G. (2010, March). Application of Bradford.s Law of Scattering to the Physics Literature: A Study of Doctoral Theses Citations at the Indian Institute of Science. *DESIDOC Journal of Library & Information Technology,* 30(2), 3-14.

70. Van Cott, H.P., & Zavala, A. (1968). Extracting the basic structure of scientific literature. *American Documentation, 19,*247-62.

71. White, Howard D., & Mccain, Katherine W. (1989). Bibliometrics.*Ann. Rev. Information Science*

*technology,24,*119-86.

72. Zafrunnisha, N. (2012).Bradford's zones and productivity of journals in psychology doctoral theses. *Annals of Library and Information Studies (ALIS), 59(1),*39-52.

73. Ziman, J.M. (1968).*Public knowledge: An essay concerning the social dimensions of science.* Cambridge: Cambridge University.

Index

E

F

Q

R

S

T